CRUEL CROSSING

Escaping Hitler Across the Pyrenees

Edward Stourton

Doubleday

LONDON · TORONTO · SYDNEY · AUCKLAND · JOHANNESBURG

TRANSWORLD PUBLISHERS
61–63 Uxbridge Road, London W5 5SA
A Random House Group Company
www.transworldbooks.co.uk

First published in Great Britain
in 2013 by Doubleday
an imprint of Transworld Publishers

A CIP catalogue record for this book
is available from the British Library.

ISBNs 9780857520517 (cased)
9780857520524 (tpb)

Addresses for Random House Group Ltd companies outside the UK
can be found at: www.randomhouse.co.uk
The Random House Group Ltd Reg. No. 954009

The Random House Group Limited supports the Forest Stewardship
Council (FSC®), the leading international forest-certification organization.
Our books carrying the FSC label are printed on FSC®-certified paper.
FSC is the only forest-certification scheme endorsed by the leading
environmental organizations, including Greenpeace. Our paper
procurement policy can be found at
www.randomhouse.co.uk/environment

Typeset in 10.5/17pt Versailles Light by
Falcon Oast Graphic Art Ltd.
Printed and bound in Great Britain by
Clays Ltd., Bungay, Suffolk

2 4 6 8 10 9 7 5 3 1

CRUEL CROSSING

www.**transworldbooks**.co.uk

Contents

Acknowledgements   vi

Maps   viii

Introduction   1

1   Tales of Warriors   17

2   The Lines   45

3   Jeanne, Jews and the Camps   63

4   Ninette's Tale   84

5   Fanny/Joan's Tale 1   96

6   Tales of Children   103

7   Belgians, Bravery and Betrayal   119

8   The Officer and the Legionnaire   147

9   Françoise and the Americans   158

10   Tales of Resistance   178

11   Guides, Smugglers and Spaniards   202

12   Death in the Mountains   217

13   Endings   235

14   Fanny/Joan's Tale 2   261

15   Remembering   269

Postscript   296

Appendix: Itinerary of the 2011 Chemin de la Liberté   303

Source Notes   315

Text and Picture Acknowledgements   329

Index   333

Acknowledgements

My thanks go above all to those who made the time to talk about their experiences. They are the true authors of this book – my role was really to edit their stories and put them into context – and it is dedicated to them.

Publication coincides with the twentieth anniversary of the first commemorative walk along the Chemin de la Liberté, and I have been greatly assisted by several people with long associations with the trek. Scott Goodall has been a moving spirit in the organization behind it for many years, and was immensely generous with the voluminous archive of source material he has collected during that time. He read my manuscript and picked me up on some shocking howlers. Keith Janes, who is also a Chemin veteran, gave me help that extended far beyond providing information about his own father. He has an encyclopaedic knowledge of escape line history and his rigorous attention to detail made him the ideal ally as I tried to negotiate my way through some of the denser and more complex material. And Geoff Cowling, chairman of the Escape Lines Memorial Society, pointed me in the direction of some valuable sources.

The BBC team who made my radio series about the Chemin were very good company throughout and made the project fun. I am especially grateful to Graham Hoyland (who is a proper mountaineer) for doing the cooking – that sounds trivial, but after an eight- or ten-hour slog the ability to rustle up something edible on a tiny gas ring becomes a priceless talent. Phil Pegum and I have made a number of radio series together, and this is the second which has become a book; he is a remarkably gifted radio producer with a great flair for storytelling, and some of the most powerful interviews I have used were conducted by him. BBC producers are taught that they must keep 'the talent' (i.e. the presenter, i.e., in this case, me) happy, and Phil is now a master of managing my moods.

For help checking the broader historical material I turned to Dr Tony Millett, once my foreign editor and today a historian with a particular interest in the Second World War; he gave me especially perceptive advice about the sensitivities of writing about the concentration camps.

Susanna Wadeson, my editor, has been a delight to deal with from start to finish. Her judgement about when to get involved in the writing process was immaculate, and she has greatly improved the text with a minimum of pain (so a good diplomat as well as a very classy editor). All the members of her team at Transworld have been supportive: I owe particular thanks to her assistant, Claire Gatzen – who was ruthless in her pursuit of permission to use quotations from sometimes very obscure texts; my copy-editor, the eagle-eyed Deborah Adams; and Sheila Lee, who tracked down some wonderfully evocative photographs. Phil Lord, the design manager, lavished real care on this book and it shows, especially in his collaboration with the cartographer Tom Coulson – his maps are wonderful, clear and informative. Neil Gower's jacket design is simply inspired – it perfectly captures the feel of the period.

It is no exaggeration to say that this book would never have been written without the inspiration provided by my agent, Vivienne Schuster. It began as her idea – born of her enthusiasm for walking and her friendship with Joan Salter (Chapter Five). I have lots of reasons to be grateful to her, but launching me on this hugely enjoyable project is probably top of that long list.

Finally my thanks to my family – Fiona, Ivo, Eleanor, Tom and Rosy – for staying interested (or at least seeming to) when I prattled on about my latest chapter.

Main escape routes

DENMARK

North Sea

GREAT BRITAIN

NETHERLANDS

Amsterdam
Arnhem

Rotterdam

LONDON

Antwerp

Lille

Brussels

BELGIUM

Atlantic Ocean

PARIS

FRANCE

Tours

Dijon

SWITZERLA

Vichy

Bay of Biscay

Limoges

Lyon

Bordeaux

VICHY FRANCE

San Sebastian

Bayonne

Bilbao

Pyrenees

Toulouse

Avignon

Nice

Marseilles

Perpignan

Esterri d'Aneu

PORTUGAL

MADRID

Barcelona

(route closed after Nov 1942)

SPAIN

Mediterranean Sea

Gibraltar

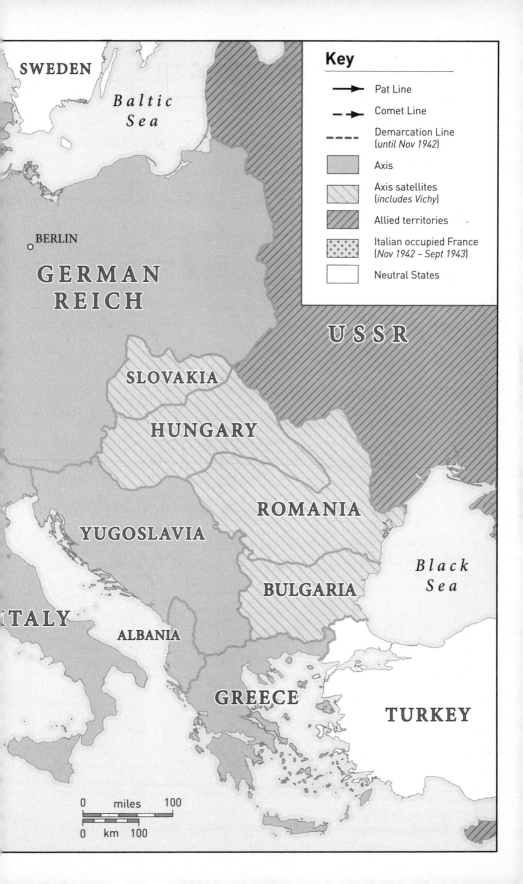

Crossing the Pyrenees

Atlantic
Ocean

Map 1

Laredo

Guernica

Bilbao

San
Sebastian

Bayonne

PYRENEES-
ATLANTIQUES

Pau

Lourdes

Adour

P
y
r
e

Vitoria

Miranda
de Ebro

Logroño

Pamplona

NAVARRA

SPAIN

Jaca

Huesca

Tudela

1 Comet Line

0   miles   5
0   km   5

ATLANTIC
OCEAN

St Jean
de Luz

Ciboure

Hendaye

Urrugne

Irun

FRANCE

San
Sebastian

Montage des
Trois Couronnes

Bidassoa

SPAIN

to Madrid

Agen

Garonne

Montauban

FRANCE

Toulouse

HAUTE-GARONNE

HAUTES-
PYRENEES

Map 2

St Girons

Salat

Montégut-
Plantaurel

ARIEGE

Foix

e   s

Aulus-
les-Bains

Ariège

PYRENEES-
ORIENTALES

ANDORRA

RAGÓN

Sort

3 Pat Line via Perpignan

0   miles   10

0   km   10

Perpignan

Canet

Tech

Céret

Banyuls-
sur-Mer

Figueras

to Barcelona

Map 3

Perpignan

2 Chemin de la Liberté

St Girons

FRANCE

Seix

Refuge des
Estagnous

Col de la Pale
de la Clauere

Borda
Campo

Alos d'Isil

SPAIN

Esterri d'Aneu

to Barcelona

0   miles   5

0   km   5

Girona

CATALUÑA

Sabadell

Barcelona

*Mediterranean
Sea*

0   miles   50

0   km   50

N

'The Secret Hope' by E. H. Shepard, Punch, 13 August 1941

Introduction

ONE AFTERNOON IN OCTOBER 1942, a young man and a young woman could be seen sitting on the back steps of a farmhouse in south-west France, looking up at the Pyrenees as they talked.

Bob Frost was nineteen, and should have been feeling badly shaken by what he had just been through. After baling out of a Wellington bomber over Belgium he had been taken in hand by what was known as the Comet Line, perhaps the most famous of the underground organizations formed to smuggle Allied air-crews out of Nazi-occupied Europe. They had looked after him well, but at one point he had been hauled off a tram and made to lie face down while his pockets were searched, and at the frontier between Belgium and France he'd had a gun thrust in his face by a German soldier who did not like the look of his ill-fitting clothes.

He had been escorted across France in the company of six other Allied evaders, one of whom was an American pilot who had joined the Royal Canadian Air Force as a way of getting into the war. Halfway through the train journey to the south the

American woke up suddenly and spotted a woman standing in the corridor; disorientated by sleep he spoke in English with a broad American accent as he courteously and loudly offered her his seat. She smiled and accepted, and the incident passed, but it was a sharp reminder of how fragile freedom was.

Bob Frost's companion on that afternoon beneath the Pyrenees, the 26-year-old Andrée de Jongh, was one of the most luminous and engaging figures to emerge from the world of underground resistance to the Nazis. Dédée, as she was almost universally known, the daughter of a Belgian schoolmaster, was the leader of the Comet Line, and had been tramping back and forth across the Pyrenees for more than a year, escorting dozens of so-called 'parcels' to safety. She was slightly built, a blue-eyed brunette with a high forehead and strikingly determined features. She cast something of a spell over young men like Bob Frost; far from feeling shaken or frightened, he was calmed by the complete confidence she inspired.

That afternoon Bob Frost asked Dédée de Jongh why she was willing to run the huge risks her work entailed. 'It is simple,' she said. 'It is a job that has to be done to free my country.'

The following day she delivered him successfully to her British contacts in neutral Spain, and he was on his way home. He served out the rest of the war as a gunnery instructor in Shropshire and fell in love with a WAAF, with whom he enjoyed more than half a century of marriage.

Dédée de Jongh's future was rather different. A little over three months after her conversation with Bob Frost she was back in the same farmhouse preparing to take another group across the Pyrenees when the German military police turned up and arrested them all. She was imprisoned, interrogated and tortured by the Gestapo and eventually sent to the Ravensbrück and Mauthausen concentration camps.

Introduction

Bob Frost, well into his eighties now, is overcome with emotion when he remembers her sacrifice; he says he owes 'his whole life' to Andrée de Jongh and her Comet Line. The time he spent on the run between baling out of his Wellington and completing his journey over the Pyrenees was really very brief (it has been said that the Comet Line earned its name because of the speed with which it spirited people to safety), but the experience was so intense that it remained vividly with him; his memory of those days is still astonishingly clear.

That intensity of experience is one of the reasons the Second World War exercises such power over the imagination of my generation. In terms of years it is really not so very far away from our own lives – I was born in 1957, little more than a decade after the war's end – yet in every other way it is so far beyond anything we have known that it seems almost to belong to another dimension. And when you listen to men like Bob Frost describe what they did you realize that it was sometimes – I hesitate to use this word, but I think it is the right one – fun. Escaping across Occupied Europe was a high stakes game, and for the helpers who operated escape lines like Comet it was often deadly. But it was also an adventure, and they were young.

Jean Cassou, a writer, poet and Resistance leader in Toulouse, a critical Resistance hub in the south-west, described the wartime experience: 'For each *résistant* the Resistance was a way of life, a style of living, a life we invented for ourselves. It stays in our memories as a unique period, quite unlike any other experience, something impossible to relate to or explain, almost a dream. We see ourselves there utterly free and naked, an unknown and unknowable version of ourselves, the kind of people no one can ever find again, who existed only in relation to unique and terrible conditions, to things that have since disappeared, to ghosts, or to the dead. If each of us who went through that experience had to define it, we would give it a name that we would not dare give to the ordinary aspects of our lives, and which would surely cause astonishment. We would whisper the word, to ourselves. Some of us would say "adventure". I would call that moment of my life "happiness".'

Of course we can never recreate the 'unique and terrible conditions' of the Second World War – nor would anyone want to – but in 2011 I was commissioned to work on a project which I thought might bring the experience Jean Cassou describes a little closer. It involved walking the Chemin de la Liberté, a commemorative trek across the Pyrenees to remember the escapers, evaders and helpers who made the journey during the Nazi Occupation of France. The project began as a Radio 4 series (perhaps appropriately, given BBC Radio's role in nurturing resistance in Occupied Europe) and became this book because of the richness of the material I found.

The Chemin de la Liberté runs forty miles across the central Pyrenees from the town of St Girons in the Ariège department, and it is walked each July. It has strong links with the Royal British Legion and the Escape Lines Memorial Society, but by no means all those who escaped this way were Allied service personnel; some of the most compelling stories I was told came from Jews fleeing the deportations to the death camps and French refugees who wanted to join the Free French forces in North Africa. In fact I discovered so many different people who tried to cross the Pyrenees for so many different reasons that I came to think of the mountains as a kind of vortex, drawing in all sorts of disparate and dramatic wartime experiences; down-to-earth Londoners like Bob Frost could sometimes find themselves in very diverse and exotic company on this last leg of their journey.

The route – which is laid out in an appendix – is only one of many that were used to cross the Pyrenees in those dark days, but it is among the toughest; it involves climbing some 15,000 feet up and 11,000 feet down, and it takes four days. The 1944 document *Tips for Evaders and Escapers* lays out what today we would call the 'skill set' you need to do it: 'The good escaper,' it says, 'is the man who keeps himself fit, cheerful and comfortable. He is not a "he-man" who boasts about his capacity to endure discomfort. He should be a man with sound common sense and above all a man of great determination.' I am certainly not a 'he-man', I hate discomfort, I am cheerful by nature, I have a reasonable supply of common sense (I hope) and I like to achieve my goals, so I tick most of those boxes. The problem lay in that unassuming little word 'fit'; when I began preparing for the walk I was fifty-three years old, and most of my work involved sitting in studios or at desks. And I liked the good things in life – and, lest that past tense allows for any confusion on this point, I still do.

As soon as the BBC agreed to my proposal for a series of programmes on the Chemin my bosses sent me off – in the best caring traditions of 'Auntie' – to an extreme sports clinic in Harley Street, where I was put through a human version of an MOT. It involved attaching a great number of electrodes to my chest and strapping a strangely fashioned respirator to my mouth, so that I looked like a half-naked Spitfire pilot, or perhaps some ghastly apparition from an S and M film. I was then required to pedal away on an exercise bike until I reached near collapse. A group of technicians monitored the behaviour of my heart and lungs, chatting away calmly as I huffed and puffed to the point where both seemed ready to explode. Once they had inspected their charts and graphs I was given something called an 'exercise prescription' to get me into shape.

Phil Pegum, my producer, is as thin as a whip, and during the weeks leading up to the walk he was often spotted climbing up and down the staircases of the BBC's Manchester offices with a rucksack full of bricks on his back. To help us through the ordeal he recruited an ex-BBC man with a distinguished record of making programmes about climbing; Graham Hoyland is an experienced mountaineer and a veteran of several Everest expeditions, and polished his fitness with a few days' yomping over the Scottish Highlands. I, on the other hand, found it extremely difficult to take my exercise prescription as regularly as I should have done, simply because I was so busy with other projects, many of which involved travelling (BBC budgets do not always stretch to hotels with gyms). There was no doubt about who was the weak link in the chain, and I was duly punished by pain.

The first time I really took in the scale of the Pyrenees was during a French weekend break with my wife, long before this project was conceived. We sat on the terrace of a restaurant called Le Carré de l'Ange in St Lizier, a red-roofed village of winding, narrow streets which, through some long-forgotten accident of history, has two cathedrals (so I suppose it is technically a city twice over rather than a village). The Carré occupies the cellars of the former bishop's palace, and it is one of those French restaurants that immediately tell you – through the starch on the napkins and the glint on the glassware – that you are about to enjoy a treat.

The restaurant says its cooking has been inspired by the 'culinary culture of the Pyrenees' and describes its menu as 'a walk from Catalonia to the Basque country, looking both north and south'. On sunny days this can be enjoyed with the peaks of the Pyrenees shining in the distance. St Lizier sits on a hillside just above St Girons, so the view from the terrace is a view of the Chemin de la Liberté, right up to the towering peak of Mont Valier which stands like a sentinel at the frontier, snow-capped even in high summer. Returning there on the eve of the trek, I wondered why on earth I had decided to turn this wonderful panorama into a sweaty challenge; but I would, I thought, at least be able to enjoy the beauty of the scenery up close.

In that consoling hope I was, it turned out, to be cruelly dis-
appointed. A really tough walk is an absolutely rotten way to enjoy
a landscape; you tend to keep your head down and your eyes on
the boots in front, concentrating on each step as you take it, and
when we stopped for a break I usually found myself flat on my
back staring at the sky. Hugh Dormer was twice dropped into
Occupied France on sabotage missions during the war, and twice
made his way home across the Pyrenees. His *Diaries* include some
of the most vivid writing there is about what it was like – and in
many ways still is – to trek across the mountains. 'The going is so
difficult and varied in the Pyrenees that one can never fall into the
rhythm of walking,' he writes, 'but must concentrate all the time
on the ground at one's feet.' And whenever they stopped, 'I would
throw myself down again on the ground and be instantly asleep,
and wake later cold and shivering in the wind and completely lost
as to where I was or what I was doing there.'

Dormer's account caught my eye partly because I had been
half aware of his exploits since my teenage years; he was an old
boy of my school, and his portrait used to look down at me when
I was working in the library. After his hair-raising missions behind
enemy lines he rejoined his regiment before the D-Day landings
and was killed in Normandy in July 1944. The *Diaries* are a minor
classic, and Dormer acquired a semi-mythic status in school lore
as a kind of ideal of what a Catholic soldier should be.

His journeys across the Pyrenees were of course infinitely
tougher and more dangerous than ours, and he and his party
walked at night to avoid detection, but I do recognize his
description of the Zen-like state the trek sometimes induces: 'As
the hours passed one lost oneself . . . till every action became auto-
matic and the mind soared out from the tired body, either into the
fields of memory or into the realms of imagination, and then one
knew one was asleep. I found myself back again in the peaceful

routine of the Benedictine School and monastery at Ampleforth, or at Oxford, or in the Irish Guards. Sometimes one would walk on like that alone with one's distant thoughts and then suddenly the mind would revert with a start to the dark file of men threading their way through the vineyards in the silence of the starlit sky, and one could not think for a moment what one was doing in such a scene.'

He also witnessed the near collapse of several refugees, including two women who were among his party on his second crossing: 'The women could not have walked along unaided, and even with our help kept on falling down and going over on their ankles,' he records. 'Several times they had implored us to leave them where they fell to the mercies of the Spanish police. It was really terrible to witness their sufferings, which were hard enough for fit men to endure. It was heartbreaking to witness the crucifixion of those two women. It made one, Englishman that one was, realize the price of liberty and how little it is valued in our land.' I never quite got to the point where my limbs refused to respond altogether, but on the afternoon of the third day of the Chemin, on what seemed like a never-ending scramble over scree to reach the relative comfort of the Refuge des Estagnous, I came very close.

The refuge sits in the lee of Mont Valier, over 7,400 feet above sea level and four hours' climb from the nearest village, and it was the scene of one of the more surreal incidents of the trek. It has been there for at least a century but it was recently given a makeover, and now has bunk bedrooms, good kitchens and a bar. After a very good dinner (the food and wine are helicoptered in periodically), I woke at three o'clock in the morning needing a pee with a fierce urgency.

The only power in the refuge comes from a few solar panels, so there are no lights left on at night; when it is cloudy, with no moon and no ambient light, the darkness is uncompromising (and, useless camper that I am, I had of course managed to lose my head torch on the first day). Many of my sleeping companions were former or serving soldiers connected with the Royal British Legion, and I reflected that if I strayed into a neighbouring bunk on my return from the lavatory (always assuming I could find it without opening the wrong door and plunging down the precipice outside) the fighting instincts would kick in, and they would probably kill first and ask questions afterwards.

And then my brain made one of those imaginative leaps that real fear can inspire. I had noticed a tiny pinpoint of light at the on/off switch on the base of my electronic reading device, a Kindle. My mobile phone had long since packed up, but the Kindle battery is remarkably long-lasting, and when I fumbled it out of my rucksack I found it did indeed produce just enough of a glow. I negotiated my way safely to relief and back by Kindle-light.

There were of course some jolly moments too. I noticed that the guides and the old hands were using long, thick staves as supports rather than walking sticks or ski-poles; on a steep descent you can dig your staff into the side of the mountain and punt yourself round it, taking some of the pressure off your knees. So when we reached the town of Seix, where we spent the first night (on the floor of a gym), I bought one. The 'i' in Seix is silent, and you may imagine the amusing jokes my BBC colleagues made about my new pole, which had the town's name proudly emblazoned along one side. One of our guides, an attractive young woman and keen mountaineer, informed us, to our great delight, that she was a member of 'the Seix Outdoors Club'.

Our guides had an unnerving habit of changing their minds about the length of our lunch breaks. Just as you were settling back with a cup of coffee and easing your boots off, one of them would spot a distant cloud somewhere on the horizon; there would be a lot of head-shaking and muttering about the danger of being caught by *orages*, swiftly followed by shouted instructions to get moving again. So it really was only on the overnight stops that we could soak in some of the scenery. The most memorable of them was spent camping outside a shepherd's hut on the second evening of the trek.

There is a tradition of seasonal grazing in this part of the Pyrenees; each spring the villagers in the valleys bring their livestock into the mountains to enjoy the summer pastures, and the odd shepherd is despatched to look after them. It means six months or so living in near-total isolation. Our shepherd was provided with a small amount of power from a solar panel, but that was about it as far as mod cons were concerned. We were told that if we wished to defecate we should walk at least five hundred metres from the camp before doing so, 'but you might want to go further to be on the safe side, since a group from the Parachute Regiment stayed here last week'.

A rumour went round the group that the shepherd – an almost impossibly hairy fellow with two delightful dogs – was a professor of philosophy who had chosen this spartan and lonely life as an aid to contemplation, but when my colleague Graham Hoyland plucked up the courage to ask him, the man himself dismissed this as romantic speculation. 'No, no,' he said, 'my discipline is sociology and I'm only a PhD.'

I hate the whole concept of camping with a passion, and the thought of sharing a tent is beyond hell to me. This is partly because of embarrassment about my snoring (I once drove out a battle-hardened marine captain in the middle of the night in Afghanistan) and partly because the thought of cuddling up heartily with other blokes reminds me uncomfortably of the post-rugby communal shower culture of my schooldays. Since the sky seemed to promise a dry night I decided to risk sleeping in the open, and was rewarded with the most spectacular view of the Milky Way I have ever enjoyed;

the stars seemed to stretch eternally back into the blackness above me. It almost – but not quite – made up for the miseries attendant on sleeping outside (like waking up soaked in dew).

Roger Stanton of the Second World War Escape Lines Memorial Society describes the Chemin as one of the society's 'walking memorials', and at various points along the way there were ceremonies to recall particular events or aspects of the story of the escapers and the *passeurs*, or guides, who helped them. There would usually be a brief speech, a minute's silence, and then someone would play a CD of the 'Song of the Partisans', the unofficial anthem of the Resistance, which was written and composed in London in 1943 and broadcast to France on the BBC. The words of this song – which became so popular that there was a move to make it the national anthem in place of the Marseillaise – are haunting: 'Friend, if you fall another friend will emerge from the shadows to take your place. Tomorrow black blood will be drying in the sunshine on the roads. Sing in the night, for in the night freedom listens to us . . .' But after hearing the same version again and again it began to lose its charm, and, as I walked, I found the tune going round and round in my head in the most irritating way.

For me the walk was made a real memorial not by these formal remembrance ceremonies, but by my fellow walkers.

The English master who introduced me to *The Canterbury Tales* was one of those rare teachers who can change your life; Chaucer's masterpiece remains an intellectual reference point I keep coming back to four decades after his first 'O'-level class on 'The Merchant's Tale'. Walking the Chemin brought home to me what a brilliant conceit lies at the work's heart. Like Chaucer's Wife of Bath, his Knight and his Miller, we walkers were engaged in a kind of pilgrimage, and the group who gathered around the fire outside the home of that sociologist shepherd and toasted the sunset above the clouds at the Refuge des Estagnous had much in common with the pilgrims who met in the Tabard Inn on the way to Canterbury. We were very different people from very different worlds, and without the Chemin we might never have met; but we had been brought together by a common purpose.

Four days is really quite a long time to spend with the same group of people. Whenever we could talk – lack of puff being the main inhibiting factor for me – we did, and, perhaps because the circumstances were so far removed from everyday life, people seemed surprisingly ready to share intimate thoughts and experiences. Almost everyone had some connection with the history we were commemorating, and many of them had the sort of life stories that would have delighted Chaucer.

In 1943 the Gaullist Resistance leader Emmanuel d'Astier de La Vigerie wrote a song called the 'Plaint of the Partisans' (like the 'Song of the Partisans', it was originally sung by Anna Marly, 'the Troubadour of the Resistance', and was later recorded by, among others, Leonard Cohen and Joan Baez):

> The wind blows across the tombs.
> Freedom will come,
> And we shall be forgotten.
> We shall return to the shadows.

He could not have been more wrong; listening to the walkers of the Chemin I came to understand that the memory of what happened in the Pyrenees during the Second World War is not just being kept alive, it is acquiring a new life as it passes down the generations.

I have used my fellow pilgrims as guides back into the world that is explored in this book. Many of those walking the Chemin were fired by a real passion for the past, and listening to them gave me a sense of which parts of this story matter the most. It goes well beyond the history of the Chemin itself; there were dozens of escape routes across the Pyrenees, and they were used by all sorts of different 'escape lines' – as the clandestine organizations which smuggled people out were called.

And as I have researched the subject I have come into contact with more and more people – sometimes in the most surprising circumstances – who have a connection with this relatively little-known chapter of the Second World War. Almost every time I have mentioned what I was doing in public – whether in a newspaper article or while giving a talk at an event – it has prompted someone to get in touch to tell me that they had a father, mother or cousin who was part of the story.

Over the past decade I have developed something of a passion for using journeys as a way of bringing history alive. It began in 2001 with an odyssey around the Mediterranean in the footsteps of St Paul, and since then I have made radio pilgrimages in the footsteps of Mohammed, Moses and Jesus, and negotiated the waters of the Jordan, the Bosphorus and the Nile. Walking the Chemin made me want to know more about the people who made all those cruel crossings to freedom during the war years, and to explore the stories that brought them to the Pyrenees. Those stories in turn led me to try to understand the historical context in which they unfolded and the way they are remembered today.

There is no neat way of telling this piece of history; it is a jumble of individual lives. But the rules of the game in this small corner of south-west Europe kept being changed by the big strategic and political developments of the Second World War, so I have tried to provide some sense of how events in the Pyrenees were influenced by the wider conflict. A trek across the mountains is the most basic form of human activity, requiring very basic human qualities like physical strength and determination. But the conditions under which wartime walkers completed the hike were affected by complex political decisions taken in Moscow, Washington, Berlin and London, and by battles won and lost from Stalingrad to North Africa.

At the pass where we crossed the frontier into Spain – seven and a half thousand feet above sea level – we paused for a moment of silence in remembrance of an RAF evader called Maurice Collins. Collins had needed real grit and determination to get home – he crossed the mountains alone in 1942, 'up to my testicles in snow', as he later so vividly put it in an interview, and spent three months in a Spanish internment camp before the British authorities were able to extract him. Despite this searing experience he became a keen supporter of the Chemin, and when he died in 2006 it was suggested at his funeral that some of his ashes should be scattered here. The ceremony was duly carried out that July.

I have a great affection for this part of France, and it is tempting to think that its attraction to men like Maurice Collins went beyond its connection with their youthful adventures; the Pyrenees, and the central Ariège region in particular, have a distinctive feel, what you might call, to use an almost untranslatable Latin phrase, a *genius loci*, a spirit of the place that makes its association with the idea of escape feel especially appropriate. It is a secretive region, full of deep, unexpected valleys and isolated hamlets that keep their stories to themselves, and it is very easy to disappear there. These days it is full of hippies, many of them quite elderly ones who moved down south on the rebound from the unfulfilled dreams of the heady days of *soixante-huit*. Tony Blair once let slip to me that he used to spend the summers of his hairy teenage years playing in a band in St Martin-d'Oydes, a village some fifteen minutes' drive from St Girons; it seems fitting that the Ariège episode in his endlessly examined life has escaped the attention of his biographers.

Introduction

People have been seeking sanctuary in this region for centuries – millennia, indeed. Not far from the starting point of today's Chemin there is a vast cave called the Grotte du Mas d'Azil. It is five hundred metres long – the river Arize runs through its centre – with an opening fifty metres high and forty-eight wide at the southern end, and it has been providing shelter for human beings for some twenty thousand years. In recorded history it is thought to have served as a sanctuary for early Christians in the third century, Cathar heretics in the thirteenth and Protestants in the seventeenth (Cardinal Richelieu took his revenge by blowing up one of the chambers).

And at the outbreak of world war in 1939 the Pyrenees region as a whole was feeling the impact of one of the most dramatic refugee crises of the twentieth century.

The Spanish Civil War was a source of acute anxiety to the French government, and the fall of Barcelona to General Franco's Fascist forces and their allies in January 1939 precipitated exactly the kind of crisis Paris most feared. A vast exodus of Republican refugees, an 'anthill of human beings', as one observer put it, began to move north towards France. On 28 January fifteen thousand of them walked across the Pyrenean border, and on 5 February the French government was forced to agree that it would accept soldiers of the defeated Republican Army too. Hugh Thomas, in his authoritative history of the Spanish Civil War, estimates that the flood of refugees included 10,000 wounded, 170,000 women and children, 60,000 male civilians and 250,000 soldiers.

Thomas describes the frontier as a 'scene of consummate tragedy', with the long lines of refugees arriving freezing and soaked by Pyrenean rain and snow. An eyewitness recorded 'scenes of utter desolation . . . like pictures of the ravages of a flood or earthquake. It looked as if a giant wave had flung up the broken suitcases, the littered clothes, the swirling heaps of paper. Exhausted refugees flung their possessions from them as they trudged to France.' The French were quite unable to deal with the influx of half a million refugees, and the Retirada, as this moment of mass migration came to be known, was, as we shall see, to have a profound impact on the lives of many of those drawn into the Pyrenean vortex of the war years.

France can be both coy and lazy about her history; there are some episodes she would rather forget, others which have simply disappeared beneath the tide of events. Today you can drive through the French Pyrenees without encountering the remotest clue that they were witness to the greatest movement of people in this part of Europe since the expulsion of Arabs and Jews from Spain in 1492. Part of the purpose of this book is to unlock the secrets of this most secretive region.

1

Tales of Warriors

Peter Janes and Gilberte

KEITH JANES WAS LEAN AND BEARDED and looked frighteningly fit. For a nervous neophyte like me, walking the Chemin for the first time, the intimidating impression was completed by the patina on his gear, which was weathered by long use. He wore his rucksack as comfortably as a cashmere coat and managed his Pyrenean walking pole with practised ease. He was making the trek for the tenth time.

Keith Janes's dedication to the past began with a death and a diary.

Between 26 May and 4 June 1940 more than 300,000 troops – 225,000 of them from the British Expeditionary Force which had been sent to support the French – were evacuated from Dunkirk as the advancing Germans swept through northern France and closed in around them. The armada of pleasure boats and fishing vessels which crossed the Channel to help save them made Dunkirk part of our national myth – by which I do not mean to suggest that the story is not true, simply that the way it has been told has helped form our national memory; the episode became a symbol of British pluck in the face of overwhelming odds. For many French, Dunkirk was an equally powerful symbol of British perfidy.

The story of those who remained in France after Dunkirk is told less often. About 10,000 British soldiers were waiting to be taken home in and around St Valéry-en-Caux, a fishing port on the coast between Dieppe and Le Havre. Here the rescue operation was much less successful; fog in the Channel and German shelling of the beaches made the Royal Navy's task almost impossible. Most of the Allied troops at St Valéry surrendered to General Rommel on 12 June, and one of them was Keith Janes's father, Peter, in civilian life a butcher's assistant from Surrey.

Chance could change everything in those chaotic early days after the fall of France. Peter Janes was trudging along in a column of POWs, heading for Germany and a long stretch in a prison camp, when a French girl darted up to him on the road just outside a village and grabbed his hand. Janes recorded the moment in a diary he had been keeping since he was called up in December 1939. It was two weeks since the surrender, he had become determined to escape, and he had had a premonition that something would happen on Wednesday 24 June.

'A huge crowd of people lined the route for miles, some giving us food, cigarettes and drink, some even soap, towels and razors, some merely to watch us. Then an absolutely mad thing happened. I had just been given a pint of beer by a man, which is mad enough anyway, when a girl grabbed me and hissed *"Toots Sweet, Ally Ally, Toots Sweet"*, and, seizing my arm, gave me a shirt and a pair of miner's trousers. She took me behind a low wall and tried by signs to make me put them on. I took off my overcoat and started taking off my jacket, but she got angry and made me put the clothes on top of them. My mind was in a confused whirl until it came to me that this was Wednesday and the "something" I knew would come that day [had come].'

Janes was shaved, fed on coffee laced with rum, and sent to be looked after by a miner and his family near the village of Calonne-Ricouart. 'It does not seem that I will be able to leave yet for some time,' he recorded in his diary, 'but no doubt something will turn up.' It was the beginning of no less than sixteen months' hiding out in German-occupied France before he was smuggled down to the Pyrenees and freedom.

He never spoke to his son about any of this, and it was only when Keith Janes opened his father's diary after his death in 1998 that he learnt what Peter had been through. 'It was all there,' Keith told me as we stomped up the foothills of the Pyrenees, 'names, addresses, dates, everything.' Armed with the information, the son took off to France with a mission to thank all those who had helped the father. One of the doorbells he rang was answered by a man called Alfred Bodlet; he was the son of the miner who first gave Peter Janes sanctuary, and remembered his parents taking in the stranded British soldier. Keith and Alfred spent a day driving round the Pas de Calais region in search of other families who had looked after Peter.

The discovery of his father's diary gave Keith Janes a new

focus; he has devoted himself to exploring the world of wartime escapers and evaders ever since. His website (www.conscript-heroes.com) is a thing of wonder, jam-packed with information. 'If you want names, places, dates, routes, I probably know it, and if I don't I probably know someone who does,' he told me. There is a section on the site where people can post queries about their own relations, and it is a tribute to our enduring fascination with this piece of the past; all sorts of folk have emailed in asking about fathers' or grandfathers' adventures, and seeking contact with their former comrades and the families in France who helped them.

Keith decided to publish his father's diary as a book (also called, like Keith's website, *Conscript-Heroes*), and it is a completely compelling document, not least because it is so evidently written for private consumption rather than posterity. Indeed it includes a rather alarming challenge: 'You who read this book have no right to, it was never written for publication; in it are things that may shock you but which nevertheless are an integral part of the story. Myself I have never shyed [*sic*] from the truth, that is why I do not hesitate to write it.'

At the time of Peter Janes's escape, the Germans were preparing to push ahead with an invasion of Britain in short order, and the Pas de Calais region was heavily militarized. On 16 July Janes recorded, 'The German troops are moving about a lot now and everyone who comes in seems to have fresh news of troop movements,' and after an outing later the same week he noted, 'Passed several German soldiers on the way home.' His entry for 23 July includes the observation, 'The Germans are very numerous now, so much so that I can't go out at all, they appear to be moving towards the coast for the invasion of England.' The following day he was moved to a new home, where he reported that 'the Germans have about three hundred troops in the same road and they keep passing all day, making it a bit risky to go out'.

Yet one of the most striking features of the diary is the way the German presence (which did, after all, represent a very significant threat indeed to Janes and those helping him) fades into the background of the narrative. Before long the Germans feature more as an irritant than anything else; in early September, for example, Janes records, 'On Thursday I had a full day, first of all I went to have my photo taken for a false passport but there were eight Jerries in the place, so I went for a walk.' Human beings seem able to get used to almost any circumstances, no matter how stressful and unusual they may appear in retrospect, but my sense from the diary is that Peter Janes's apparent insouciance about his clandestine existence among the enemy also reflected the sheer intensity of the experience he found himself living. At times he seems to have been caught up by a sense of exhilaration: 'The day will come again when I can sing "Deep Purple" [a 1930s big-band hit] without fear and when once again we can drink beer and say what we bloody well like. It is a peculiar feeling to walk along and feel that at any moment a bullet will crash through your back, peculiar and not altogether distasteful.'

Janes soon discovered that he was by no means the only British soldier on the run in the region; his French hosts put him in touch with others in similar circumstances, and they established a lively social circle. The amount of 'fraternizing' he reports with the local women is really quite startling. One of his fellow Brits got into trouble for having a flagrant affair with his (married) hostess, and the British fugitives were nearly banned from the location: 'The upshot is that we can go there again,' Janes wrote, 'but *pas de femmes pour couches avec* which of course is *mal heurez* as it includes Gilberte.' Gilberte, an eighteen-year-old farmer's daughter and 'a real beauty in a naturally robust way', features frequently. At about the same time he was fighting off some unwanted attentions, and his casual deployment of a very colloquial French phrase for no-strings sex suggests his language skills were developing impressively; he confided to his diary that there was a 'young married woman . . . [who] badly wants what they call here *un morceau de viande vendu sans ticket* from me and does not hesitate to ask for it'.

There was also work (agricultural jobs like flailing corn and planting potatoes), a good deal of drinking, and straightforward fun, despite the ever-present Germans. When Janes and a group of his friends visited the local swimming pool, 'We knew about half the people there but did not know a couple of Jerries as they had no swastikas on their swimming trunks.'

So why had Janes senior been so reluctant to talk about his experience? He had, after all, an extraordinary story to tell. The so-called escape lines which were established later in the war could spirit British aircrews out of France in a matter of weeks or even days, but Private Janes lived under the Occupation for almost a year and a half. Keith believes that after the war his father simply wanted to 'draw a line under his life in France'. 'It was so different,' he said, and again I encountered that sense of a chasm cutting us off from an unreachable past. Was he a hero? 'Well he was to me, obviously,' Keith says, 'but he would have thought that rubbish.'

While Private Janes was marching in the column of miserable men heading off to POW camp in the summer of 1940, Lieutenant Chandos Sydney Cedric Brudenell-Bruce, Earl of Cardigan and descendant of the man who had led the Charge of the Light Brigade nearly a century earlier, was also heading east. Cardigan had been captured in Flanders at the end of May, and in late June he was being taken from Lille to a prison just over the Belgian border when (Lady Luck waving her wand again) he spotted his chance to make a break for freedom.

He and a group of other officers were being transported in

open lorries, and for most of the way a German NCO and a squad of armed men sat guarding them in the back. But for some reason on the final stretch of the journey they were left unguarded, and the two Germans in the cab of the lorry were their only escorts. When the driver stopped to ask directions Cardigan simply slipped over the tailboard and stood in the road just behind the lorry where neither of the Germans could see him. He waited for the lorry to pull away and dodged off the road.

In the month between the earl's capture and his escape the map of Europe had been completely redrawn.

'In the history of warfare,' wrote the historian Brian Bond, 'few campaigns have been decided so swiftly and conclusively as the German conquest of Western Europe in May and June 1940.' The German offensive began on 10 May with attacks on Luxembourg, the Netherlands and Belgium. Within five days the Allied defences had been so badly breached that Paul Reynaud, the French prime minister, was already talking about defeat. By 20 May the Allied forces in the north had been cut off from the main French forces in the south (precipitating the Dunkirk evacuation). On 8 June the noise of battle could be heard in Paris for the first time, and on the 10th the French government announced that it was leaving the capital. German troops marched unopposed into Paris on 14 June.

Two days later, in a somewhat desperate last throw to keep France in the war, Winston Churchill offered the French government a full union between France and Britain. The idea emerged from a lunch at the Carlton Club that day with General de Gaulle, who spent the last days before the fall of France Channel-hopping between London and the French government. De Gaulle persuaded Churchill that only 'some very dramatic move' would stiffen the resolve of the French government, and his proposal for 'a proclamation of the indissoluble union of the French and British peoples' was endorsed by the British War Cabinet in the course of the afternoon. France's political leadership – like the country as a whole – was in a state of shock, and Reynaud was trying to fight off a strong lobby for capitulation to the Germans within his own government; the British Cabinet believed the initiative would strengthen Paul Reynaud's hand, enabling him to argue that France should continue to fight from her bases in North Africa.

The proposed Declaration of Union stated that 'France and Great Britain shall no longer be two nations, but one Franco-British Union. The constitution of the Union will provide for joint organs of defence, foreign, financial and economic policies. Every citizen of France will enjoy immediately citizenship of Great Britain, every British subject will become a citizen of France.' A draft text for a treaty was scrambled together just in time for the meeting of the French Council of Ministers at 5 p.m., and Churchill read it to Reynaud over the telephone. Encouraged by the response, he boarded a train at Waterloo; a ship was standing by in Southampton to take him to Brittany for a face-to-face meeting with his French counterpart. And what an intriguing and suggestive proposal the idea of union was!

But the way events developed turned it into a footnote. When Reynaud put the proposal to his Council of Ministers (meeting now in Bordeaux), Marshal Pétain, a hugely influential figure, asked why France would want to 'fuse with a corpse'. Paul Reynaud sensed that the mood was running against him and at ten that evening he resigned as prime minister. Pétain, celebrated as the hero of the Battle of Verdun in the First World War then but today more often vilified as the architect of collaboration in the Second, formed a new government. Churchill heard the news aboard the train as he waited to depart for Southampton; he headed home to Downing Street 'with a heavy heart'.

On 22 June France and Germany signed an armistice – the

Germans famously insisting that the ceremony should take place in the railway carriage near Compiègne where Germany had been forced to accept defeat at the end of the First World War (an event described as 'the deepest humiliation of all time' in the German draft of the new Armistice Agreement). The campaign had lasted just six weeks.

Under the terms of the Armistice Marshal Pétain's government – which was to establish its headquarters at the spa town of Vichy – retained theoretical control over most of the territory within France's pre-war borders, but the country was divided between a German Occupied Zone (the Channel and Atlantic coasts, together with most of the north of France, including Paris) and a so-called Free Zone, south of a line running west from the Franco-Swiss border near Geneva and then south from near the city of Tours to the Spanish border. Under a separate agreement Italy occupied a small corner of south-east France.

The new political realities made the Earl of Cardigan's decision easy; as soon as he was free he headed south.

Unlike Private Janes, the earl was anything but reticent about his experiences. He wrote up his diary and published the result under the title *I Walked Alone* as soon as he could (to his irritation, the army censors would not allow him to bring the book out until after the war). He clearly regarded the whole thing as the most tremendous adventure; of his four months on the run he writes, 'while perforce I was a dirty, unkempt alien, adrift in wartime Europe, I lived a life which was sometimes grim, occasionally carefree, but – to me – always vivid with interest'.

The earl's journey is a story of extraordinary good luck and sheer brass neck. At one point he turned the corner of a road to find himself confronted with a bridge guarded by two German sentries. One of them stepped forward and stopped him: 'The man of course wanted to see my papers and said so in quite reasonable

French. I, on the other hand, possessing no such documents, pretended to be baffled by his foreign accent. Germans, however, are persistent, and when this sentry had pronounced the word *papiers* with about half a dozen variations of sound, it seemed futile to continue registering lack of comprehension . . . I had to try new tactics, and so said, in my best imitation of rustic French – "Oh, you mean *papiers*!" (my tone suggesting that this had just dawned on me). "Alas, Monsieur, I would gladly show them to you, but there is a little difficulty. I have lost them." And I continued with a long and confusing explanation of the loss.'

Cardigan found that by stammering he could disguise his lack of fluency in French, and after a lengthy cross-examination the sentries simply let him go; so much for the stereotype of ruthless Teutonic efficiency! The earl had an even narrower escape later on his journey when, as he was walking towards the city of Troyes, a German major stopped his car and offered him a lift. Cardigan felt he had to accept and hastily invented a fictional family of cousins living on a farm nearby to explain the purpose of his journey; squeezed on the back seat next to a large German NCO, he had to keep up the stammering trick throughout the ride.

But no amount of good fortune or courage would have made success possible without the cooperation of the local population. From the moment he jumped off his German lorry Cardigan was helped on his way by ordinary people, first in Belgium and then in France. A man who spotted him making his break for freedom gave him beer, chocolate and a change of clothes – and helped him shave off his moustache so that he looked less like a British officer. Not long after he crossed the border into France (since both this part of France and Belgium were under German occupation there were no guards) he was taken in hand by a villager who instructed him in how to walk like a French peasant, found him a convincingly battered beret and even provided a map.

When he asked for milk and eggs at a farmhouse he was seldom turned away (despite the general shortage of food), and he ate at an endless series of *estimanets,* or village cafés, without anyone betraying him to the authorities. He had some money with him, but often people refused to accept payment. He records that one (very poor) family 'would not be persuaded to accept so much as a *sou*. When pressed, they simply said, "No, we can see that you are a foreigner (alas for my French accent!) and in difficulties. While we have food, you are welcome to share it. These are hard times for everyone, and we just all help as we can."' The words closely echo what Keith Janes told me about the attitude of those who helped his father: ' "It is simply what we did," they said to him. "Here was a man in trouble. It was the right thing to do."'

Cardigan's admiration for the French grows the further he travels. After three weeks on the road he was invited to join a French farming family for breakfast: 'What impressed me here was the perfect manners of everyone concerned. Not a single member of the family expressed the least surprise at finding a tramp of uncertain origin sharing the morning meal. No one cross-questioned me and no one suggested by word or by gesture that I was anything other than a welcome guest. After breakfast, cider was produced (I imagine it to be grown locally) and we all sat around drinking and chatting in perfect harmony until it was time for the men to resume their work . . . I am beginning to think that people like myself – I mean my normal peacetime self – are put to shame by the simple country folk of France.'

Cardigan's encomiums are so enthusiastic they almost make you think Churchill's idea of a union between France and Britain might have worked, and his experience of French generosity is echoed in another (unpublished) diary of the period. Lieutenant J. W. 'Hoppy' Hopkins escaped from a prisoner-of-war column a week or so before the earl, and, with two other officers, he made his way to the Pas de Calais coast in the hope of appropriating a boat to carry them home. Like Cardigan he had decent French, and had no difficulty at all in foraging from those he met on the road. On 22 June he recorded, 'found a farmer, who took us to his orchard in village (no Boche about) and gave us a dinner of soup, fried eggs, bacon, fried potatoes, beer, coffee (oh! boy!) and a wash. Presented us with 3 lbs potatoes, 3 tins bully, 6 packets biscuits; 1 dozen hard boiled eggs, salt, soap, a blanket, a loaf, 1 lb butter. Payment refused! Returned to wood and slept till 18.00. Later a retired Paris dentist living in village brought us tea and brandy and shaving kit.' They rested through the following day: 'Farmer found us a map on very small scale but quite invaluable. Distance to sea about 20 miles. Supper of b & b, h.b. eggs and so to bed. A good day with kind people.' A week later, after receiving another bounty of supplies ('including eggs, jam, meat, sausage, chocolate and also 3 civvy jackets, 3 trousers and 2 caps 1 beret'), Hoppy, who took a dim view of the way the French had conducted themselves in the days before the surrender at St Valéry-en-Caux, delivered the verdict, 'The generosity and kindness of the french [sic] peasant almost makes up for their rotten army.'

There was a strong strand of anti-British prejudice among the officials of the Vichy regime, and pro-Vichy French newspapers pushed the propaganda line that Britain had betrayed France and was responsible for her defeat. Yet only after the British attack on the French fleet in the Algerian port of Mers-el-Kébir did Cardigan experience any serious anti-British feeling from ordinary people. Churchill ordered the destruction of the fleet because he feared its ships would fall into German hands; 1,297 French servicemen were killed when the Royal Navy struck on 3 July 1940.

It happened just as Cardigan was crossing the demarcation line from German-occupied France into the Free Zone. He decided to celebrate with a hearty meal, and announced his identity loudly to the villagers in the first inn he came to. Far from being welcomed he was berated for the way 'Churchill (pronounced Shoor-sheel) has been sinking French ships and killing French sailors'. He had to engage in 'a little pro-British propaganda' before he could enjoy his dinner.

At this period the Free Zone really does seem to have been relatively free. On his arrival in Lyons Cardigan strode into the American consulate (the British having been forced to shut up shop by the Vichy government in reprisal for the attack at Mers-el-Kébir) and secured a loan. Although he could not admit to being an escaped British officer to his landlady, he seems to have been able to live something very close to a normal life. He rebuilt his strength with copious quantities of heavy *cuisine lyonnaise* ('waitresses in restaurants sometimes stare at me in astonishment') and amused himself by going to the movies (a Donald Duck film made him laugh for the first time since his escape). He also made the acquaintance of a rich Belgian couple who wined and dined him in the style to which he was no doubt accustomed in civilian life, and sent him onwards on his journey with a healthy injection of further funds.

He completed the last leg – from Marseilles to the Pyrenees – on a bicycle, and was determined to carry it over the mountains into Spain. He had to invent a wholly unconvincing story about being a businessman on a cycling holiday to get past a suspicious gendarme and somehow managed to drag the bike through the bushes and over the frontier. It was pure *Boy's Own* derring-do.

The blithe spirit that breathes through Cardigan's account of his journey may reflect the influence of a popular book called *The Escaping Club*, written by a First World War veteran called A. J. Evans. M. R. D. Foot, the pre-eminent academic historian of the escapers' world, told me in an interview shortly before his death that 'all the officer class would have read it at their prep schools'. (Professor Foot, who was himself dropped into Occupied France as a young intelligence officer, spoke with an accent that immediately took one back to the black and white world of the 1940s, and he barked this view at me in a way that immediately made me sit up straight in my chair.)

Evans was a spotter plane pilot in the Royal Flying Corps, and he was helping to direct artillery against German positions along the Somme in 1916 when, during an early morning reconnaissance, the engine of his 'splendid machine' died, and he was forced to crash-land behind German lines. He was immediately captured, and after making a thorough nuisance of himself by trying to escape whenever he saw a chance, he was sent to Fort 9, a prison camp reserved for officers who today we would call members of the awkward squad; they were 'mauvais sujets from the German point of view, and [included] all those prisoners of war who had made attempts to escape from other camps'.

The inmates of Fort 9 sound like a criminal fraternity; 'some of the most ingenious people I have come across', Evans wrote. 'Men who could make keys which would unlock any door; men who could temper and jag the edge of an old table-knife so that it would cut iron bars; expert photographers (very useful for copying maps); engineering experts who would be called upon to give advice on any tunnel that was being dug; men who spoke German perfectly; men who shammed insanity perfectly . . .' One officer had tried to escape from a previous camp by painting his face green in the hope that he would look like a water lily while swimming across the moat in daylight 'under the sentry's nose'.

The atmosphere was that of an anarchic British boarding school of the *Tom Brown's Schooldays* variety, and the inmates spent much of their time behaving like members of a rowdy Oxbridge dining club. 'Some of the French had sworn an oath to drive the Commandant off his head,' Evans records. 'He was pretty far gone. Some of the Englishmen, chiefly Oliphant, Medlicott, and Buckley, with these Frenchmen, used to get an enormous amount of amusement by baiting the old fool.' They would barge into the camp commander's office to complain about this or that aspect of the camp regime (often the food: 'It is impossible for anyone but a Bavarian to eat it without wine!' was a favourite rallying cry), and refuse to leave until they had driven him into a fury. The daily roll call was a near riot, with British, French and Russian officers mingling and talking and generally making it as difficult as possible for the guards to count them.

Evans had agreed a code system with his mother before leaving for France, and sent her a long list of items he needed to effect an escape. Two luminous compasses duly arrived – one concealed in a bottle of prunes, one in a jar of anchovy paste – and several sets of large maps (each set 'consisted of six sheets, each a foot square') arrived baked into the middle of cakes. He and another officer jumped off a train while being moved to a new camp and walked to Switzerland. 'I believe we've done it, old man,' he declared as they crossed the border after eighteen days on the run.

Evans's expertise and renown made him a natural candidate for membership of a new organization which was set up in the early days of the Second World War to encourage escapes.

There was a long military tradition that capture meant disgrace, so until the final days of the First World War no one had given much thought to the plight of prisoners of war or to how they might be helped to escape. In 1917 a new section of the War Office intelligence directorate called MI IA was established with the purpose of treating POWs as a valuable source of intelligence. MI IA was closed down with the coming of peace, and revived in 1939 under the new title MI9. The man chosen to run it was

Major (later Brigadier) Norman Crockatt, a 45-year-old infantry officer – much decorated and badly wounded in France during the First World War – who returned to uniform after a spell as a stock-broker during the inter-war years.

Crockatt set up shop in Room 424 of the Metropole Hotel in Northumberland Avenue, which runs from Trafalgar Square down to the Thames. He laid out his objectives for this modest new cousin of MI6 and MI5 like this:

A To facilitate escapes of British prisoners of war, thereby getting back service personnel and containing additional enemy manpower on guard duties.

B To facilitate the return to the United Kingdom of those who succeeded in evading capture in enemy-occupied territory.

C To collect and distribute information.

D To assist in the denial of information to the enemy.

E To maintain the morale of British prisoners of war in enemy prison camps.

Objective A very definitely included the idea of making life as difficult as possible for the Germans in the way A. J. Evans and his friends had done so successfully. 'It has been decided that all those who are captured should try to escape, even if captured again,' said Crockatt. 'The more they do this, the more upheaval they can cause to their German captors.'

Crockatt had a penchant for officers with what M. R. D. Foot called 'sparkle'. Johnny Evans of *The Escaping Club* was duly recruited. When Airey Neave, the future Conservative politician (and victim of the Irish terrorist organization the INLA) made it to Switzerland after escaping from Colditz in 1942, Crockatt had him brought home in double-quick time so that his expertise could be put at MI9's service too. The most singular, troublesome and, in many ways, brilliant of his recruits was a man called Christopher Clayton Hutton, or Clutty.

Clayton Hutton was so desperate to get back into uniform at the beginning of the Second World War that he sent off seventeen telegrams to different departments in the War Office in the course of a week, and he claimed a particular aptitude for intelligence work on the basis of 'a varied and colourful life, during which I had acquired a grounding in and intimate knowledge of journalism in all its multifarious aspects, of advertising and publicity, and of the motion picture industry in both Great Britain and America'. He was called in for interview at MI9 – without of course being told who or what they were – and found that twelve of his seventeen missives had been forwarded there. He clinched his appointment by telling the story of how, as a young man, he had tried to outwit the great Harry Houdini by challenging him to escape from a box which would be built on the stage in front of the audience (and thus could not be tampered with). Houdini won (he bribed the carpenter) but Clutty got the job at MI9 on the strength of this effort; he was to be O/C gadgets.

His first step was to send a telegram to the headmaster of Rugby, Norman Crockatt's old school, informing him that he would be calling on him 'TOMORROW SIXTEEN HUNDRED HOURS TO DISCUSS PROJECT VITAL TO THE NATIONAL INTEREST'. He then tipped up at the British Museum, where he persuaded the chief librarian to send two assistants around second-hand bookshops and publishers to buy copies of absolutely everything written about escaping during the First World War. With his haul piled into the boot of his car he headed straight off up the A5 to the Midlands, where he was duly received by the headmaster of Rugby, Percy Lyon, who was apparently quite unfazed by this surprising eruption of Military Intelligence into his world. Could the sixth form précis the contents of the books in double-quick time? Of course they could.

Four days later Clutty had a crisply condensed document containing everything there was to know on the subject of escapes. 'My roving eye,' he recalled in his autobiography, 'fell on a list of desirable escape aids – dyes, wire, needles, copying paper, saws, and a dozen other items, some of which I should never have dreamed of – and I knew right away that as technical officer to the Escape Department I was in for a very busy time indeed.'

Clayton Hutton had a true inventor's mind, and was always looking for unlikely but promising connections. He commissioned an engineering firm off the Old Kent Road to design the smallest compass they could, and when they presented him with a brass cylinder a quarter of an inch in diameter he was immediately struck by 'a wonderful idea': such cylinders could be hidden in the back of uniform buttons, or in forage-cap badges. Chatting to a friend whose father was a brain specialist, he quickly saw the potential of the flexible Gigli saws then used by surgeons to open up skulls: they could be concealed inside bootlaces. In Clutty's eyes a fountain pen became a weapon for firing darts at German soldiers, and a bicycle pump became a torch for members of the French Resistance to use as a landing flare.

And he seems to have had very little difficulty in coming up with public money for all this. He boasted that 'In the course of a single afternoon, in the course of 1941, the Treasury gave me a credit of £150,000' – a huge sum by the standards of the day. When he turned up at the Wills Tobacco Company in the hope of buying twenty thousand empty cigarette tins he could use as containers for his 'escape kits', he found that there were none available (because of wartime shortages of material), so he simply bought twenty thousand that had already been filled with cigarettes – confident that he could recoup some of the outlay by feeding the million fags he had acquired into the military welfare system.

Dunkirk had a huge impact on the work of MI9, and in his autobiography Clayton Hutton recalls the moment the gravity of what was happening in France was brought home to him. He and Johnny Evans dropped into the office of a newly arrived colleague and found him moving little Union flags around a map of Europe, fixing them into 'an alarmingly small semi-circle with its two arms touching the French coast'. He told them, 'It's all over, boys . . . The whole of the BEF is boxed in round Dunkirk. If we don't get them out, there'll be more prisoners than even you can cope with, Clutty.' Our man was on his way to discuss compasses and food packs with his boss, Norman Crockatt, but he immediately abandoned the mission and instead 'I picked up the telephone, listened impatiently to the usual switchboard buzzing, and then asked for the Air Ministry.' The war was about to take a new direction; with much of the British Army soon to be bottled up at home, MI9's main clients would be the RAF.

The Battle of Britain, fought by the RAF's Fighter Command, is probably the best-remembered battle of the air war, but it was comparatively brief; the German air campaign against Britain began in early July 1940, and two and a half months later, on 17 September, Hitler accepted that it had failed and postponed his invasion plans indefinitely. The air war then became the principal means by which Britain could fight back in the European theatre – which turned the spotlight on Bomber Command.

Bomber Command's war was a much longer haul. On the very first day of hostilities, 3 September 1939, six Hampdens were despatched from Lincolnshire to bomb German warships (they failed). The last strategic raid over Europe (against an oil refinery in Norway) took place more than five years later, on the night of 25/26 April 1945. Between those two dates 364,500 operational sorties were flown and over a million tons of bombs were dropped.

The air campaign is thought to have killed between 300,000 and 600,000 Germans. For the crews the risks were enormous. Of the 125,000 aircrew who flew missions 55,573 were killed and a further 8,403 were wounded; a Bomber Command flyer had a worse chance of survival than an infantry officer on the Western Front in the First World War, and according to Martin Francis's book *The Flyer*, 'At one point in 1942 RAF bomber crews had no more than 10 per cent chance of surviving a full tour of operations.' It has been calculated that if you took a sample of a hundred airmen, their likely fates were as follows: 55 would be killed, 3 injured, 12 taken prisoner after being shot down, 27 would survive and 2 would be shot down and evade capture. MI9's job was to ensure those two evaders were given the best chance possible, and to smuggle escape aids into the camps where those twelve POWs were held.

Clayton Hutton's 'escape boxes' were especially popular with aircrews. Each the size of a large cigarette tin – the Wills supply was soon exhausted, and the design was modified as time went on – they contained malted milk tablets, boiled sweets, plain chocolate, matches, Benzedrine tablets for energy, halazone for purifying water, a rubber bottle which could hold a pint, a razor, a needle and thread and a fishing hook and line. According to M. R. D. Foot, not many fish were caught but the lines often served successfully as makeshift braces. By the autumn of 1940 every airman was provided with a kit before going on operations. The inclusion of Benzedrine may partly have explained the popularity of the boxes; the drug was sometimes used by flyers as a form of self-medication against the stress caused by the extra-ordinary dangers they faced on missions.

Clayton Hutton's other invaluable contribution to the men of Bomber Command was the silk map. Silk was an obvious material for escapers' maps because it was light, did not rustle, and could be tightly folded. The difficulty lay in devising a printing technique which would reproduce images on the material of sufficient clarity to be useful. Clayton Hutton spent hours with a printer friend experimenting and eventually came up with the idea of adding pectin – which helps jam to set – to the dyes. The results were startlingly clear, and have stood the test of time. M. R. D. Foot showed me the map which was sewn into his uniform when he was dropped behind German lines in 1944: the colours were still vibrant, and it remained a truly beautiful artefact. It was about a yard square when laid out flat, but, as Professor Foot put it, 'a flamboyant officer could use it as a pocket handkerchief' when it was folded or crumpled.

As well as providing equipment, MI9 gave escape training. Norman Crockatt was determined to ram home the message that escape was a duty, not merely an option, and sent his lecturers on missionary journeys throughout the armed services to preach the Crockatt gospel. The importance of attempting to get away features right at the top of a list of bullet points in some notes drawn up for an RAF lecture in 1942: 'It is everybody's duty to evade capture or to escape and to rejoin their units,' they state firmly. The notes also include a stern admonition to take Clutty's gadgets seriously – 'They should not be considered toys for they have proved their worth again and again' – together with some suggestions about possible routes home and a warning against giving in too easily. 'Now when one looks at the map of Europe and the countries occupied by the enemy one might be forgiven for thinking "What the Hell? We haven't a chance." That is wrong, for although difficult, the task is not impossible, as has been proved by so many.'

The *Tips for Evaders and Escapers* which I quoted in the introduction is stuffed full of practical advice. Some of it is startlingly obvious – 'Remember the dawn is in the East and sunset in the West' – and some of it intriguing – 'Churches on the Continent are not necessarily aligned East and West', and 'Moss does not grow only on the northern side of tree trunks, as commonly supposed'. The section on eating includes instructions on how to kill a hedgehog – 'Turn them on their backs, tickle the body lightly with a stick or the fingers. It will then poke out its head and neck which can be severed by the stroke of a knife. Skin and cook as in subpara (v)' – and on how to deal with the 'real delicacy' of snails, and it suggests that dogs and cats 'providing so much meat, are worth some trouble in capture by friendly advances'. 'It is possible that your bowels will not move regularly if you are living on strict Escape Box rations,' the document warns. 'Do not let this alarm you.'

But no amount of escape training or clever gadgets could prepare aircrews for the experience of being shot down.

The rear-gunner Bob Frost was something of a veteran when it happened to him – he'd flown twenty-two operations in his Wellington before the raid on the German city of Essen in September 1942 during which the port engine was knocked out by flak. They dropped their bomb load and staggered homewards, but over Belgium the starboard engine conked out too and the crew were forced to bale out. Bob Frost said the only parachute training he had had was 'simply this: jump, count to three and pull the cord. That was all.' He was due to begin a week's leave the following day, and remembered being enraged that he would be missing it as he floated down through a 'cold and damp' cloud before 'the ground came up and hit me – a large Belgian field'. The rest of the crew also baled out successfully, but they came down scattered over an area of twenty-five miles – when soldiers and sailors got into trouble they were usually in a group, but most downed airmen who tried to evade capture began the journey on their own. Bob Frost recalls being dazed by shock for a while; he said being shot down was like being in a 'really horrific car crash'.

George Duffee, by contrast, was on his very first operation when it happened to him. Fresh from his pilot training in the summer of 1943, he took the train from King's Cross to Selby in Yorkshire, and his commanding officer greeted him with the news that he was 'in luck': there was to be a raid that night, so would he like to go along as an observer? On the way back from Germany their Halifax bomber was 'coned' by searchlights, easy prey for a German fighter. Duffee was standing next to the pilot; 'all I could see was twenty millimetre cannon hitting the starboard engine'. They were flying at eighteen thousand feet.

His memory of what happened next was, by his own account, hazy. He remembers handing a parachute pack to the pilot and putting on his own, and he remembers being thrown into the nose of the plane as it went into a spin. The starboard wing was ripped off as the plane fell. The centrifugal forces made it very difficult to move, but somehow he found himself sitting on the edge of the escape hatch. 'It is perfectly true what people say,' he told me. 'All your life goes before you when you think you are going to die – in my case in about twenty seconds.' But somehow he was thrown clear, and pulled his ripcord at fifteen hundred feet, perilously close to the ground. Last of all he remembered the quietness of his short descent by parachute, a sharp contrast to the screaming din of the dying bomber.

There were many cases of crew members being knocked out when their aircraft was hit, falling thousands of feet while unconscious and coming to just in time to pull the ripcord. One airman recalled being jammed into the nose of his bomber by the force of the dive as the plane screamed towards the earth; he was beating the perspex cone with his fist in frustration when a hole suddenly opened up and he fell out, parachuting safely down. There were a few instances of truly miraculous experiences in the moments after baling out. One man fell for nearly two miles without a parachute before hitting another member of his crew who had just pulled his ripcord – he grabbed on to his saviour's legs and they both survived. Even more extraordinary was the case of the sergeant air-gunner who fell eighteen thousand feet without a parachute before landing in a snowdrift on a hillside and lived to tell the tale.

Everyone who baled out experienced the trauma of sudden and total dislocation. 'In the space of a few hours,' wrote the journalist and RAF pilot Aidan Crawley, 'they had been transferred from the comfort of an Air Force station to the middle of enemy territory.' In most cases all this took place in darkness; Bomber Command's practice was to raid by night.

There was seldom much leisure to digest the raw emotions generated by these experiences. Aircrews were taught to hide their parachutes immediately, and then put as much distance as they could between themselves and their aircraft. If they came down on German soil they had to move sharpish; bomber crews were, not unnaturally, less than popular among the German population, and they ran a real risk of being lynched.

Those who came down in German-occupied territory – in the Netherlands, Belgium or France – would very soon be faced with the dilemma involved in approaching someone for help. This was of course a dangerous business – for both parties. M. R. D. Foot, who attended MI9 lectures when he was briefing commandos for raids behind enemy lines, remembered that the lecturers were 'very firm on the frightful difficulties that faced evaders and escapers at this stage'. When you approached someone for assistance, he explained, 'you were asking them to put their lives on the line. Because if the Germans caught them they would be shot, and so would everyone in their family – their wives and children as well as themselves.'

The MI9 advice was to look for a church and throw yourself on the mercy of the parish priest – according to Professor Foot there were no recorded cases of priests in France turning people in to the occupying Germans. A memorandum circulated among all officers in the summer of 1940 advised that 'Village priests are likely to be helpful. Care should be taken in approaching them and one should avoid being seen talking to them.' Failing a man of the cloth, the lecturers advised that the poorest people were most likely to offer help, partly because they would probably not have a stake in the status quo; so at a station, for example, it was judged safer to seek help from a porter than the stationmaster. But there was a limit to how much useful guidance the lecturers could give about what to do at this stage; as Bob Frost so eloquently put it, 'They couldn't really say, "Go and see Madame Fifi Le Bonbon and she'll see you right."' Choosing whom to talk to and when was a lonely decision.

Sometimes airmen might stumble on clues to help them. In Belgium, once he had hidden his parachute, Bob Frost began walking south-west, heading for the Pyrenees and Spain (roughly six hundred miles away), and in the first village he came to he spotted graffiti of the Cross of Lorraine and the Morse code for victory – both symbols of the Resistance. The paint was still wet, and he concluded that there was a reasonable chance of a warm reception. Even though it was the small hours of the morning he plucked up the courage to knock on the door of a house, hoping it would be answered by 'a very old lady' from whom he would be able to escape if his confidence turned out to be misplaced. In fact his knock was answered by 'a burly young man' who turned out to be the local butcher. There followed a pantomime of sign language while Frost tried to explain who he was and what he needed (the butcher spoke only Flemish) and in the course of it the village busybody appeared on the pretext that she wanted to buy meat (at five o'clock in the morning). In due course a member of the local Resistance arrived and took Frost in – he heard later that the Resistance had also called on the nosy neighbour and warned her to keep quiet about what she had seen.

The RAF was an elite service in the sense that it could afford to be selective in its recruiting policy, but it was socially egalitarian; so not many of those who were shot down had the sort of language skills that helped Lord Cardigan and Hoppy on their ways – indeed, many of the young men who spent the war years bombing Continental Europe had never visited it at ground level. Stan Hope, a flight sergeant in a Photographic Reconnaissance Unit, was an exception: his mother had lived in Belgium and he had spent some time there before the war, so he spoke a little French. It gave him a huge advantage.

He was on a mission to Austria when one engine gave out over Salzburg; the pilot turned for home, but the second engine packed up somewhere near Brussels. The Mosquito was 'flying straight and level' when the two of them baled out; Stan Hope enjoyed the parachute drop and had a gentle landing. It was December (in 1942), and before leaving the aircraft he had time to radio a 'Merry Christmas' message back to base.

Hope decided to head for Brussels – with no definite plan in mind of what he would do when he got there. He was wearing a pair of Clutty-designed escapers' flying boots, which were made so that the upper sections could be removed, turning them into a pair of ordinary walking shoes. He also had a sweater knitted by his mother, so he was able to look reasonably inconspicuous.

Confident in his basic French, he adopted a strategy of talking to pretty much everyone he met.

At the first farm he reached he found a woman milking her cows; she gave him some milk to drink, so he knew she would not turn him in. At another farmhouse he picked up some sandwiches, which he ate sitting on a railway embankment while watching a trainload of German soldiers roll by. He spent his first night on the run in the outside lavatory of a cottage.

The owners of the cottage were too frightened to help him, but the following morning a man called Alex gave him an old coat, a scarf and a beret, and directed him to the nearest station (Stan gave Alex some of his RAF escaping kit, including his compass, by way of thanks, and sixty-five years later Alex returned them when the two men were reunited). Using his escapers' money Stan bought a ticket to Brussels, where he spent a day looking for familiar faces and places, getting lost on the buses and sitting in cafés drinking Belgian beer. Fearing a curfew he finally appealed to a waitress for help, and a young man called Maurice turned up with the offer of a bed. By this stage Stan had admitted that he was a British airman to at least a dozen people, and had only been completely rebuffed twice – by the cottagers and a shopkeeper.

Once evaders had found a sympathetic host they were usually treated with extraordinary generosity. Stan Hope stayed with Maurice, his mother and stepfather in their Brussels apartment for a full month. Maurice enjoyed teasing the Germans, and liked to walk past German patrols chatting to Stan in animated French. Stan would go out to the shops to help Maurice's mother with the shopping and joined family outings to the cinema. At a football match he nearly gave himself away by shouting 'Corner!' in his excitement at the game. He remembers a 'wonderful Christmas dinner' – there were five courses and it ended at four in the morning.

'I had a good time in Brussels,' Stan Hope told me. 'You couldn't go creeping about like a criminal because that would give you away – you just had to be as normal as possible. I used to look at the Germans and say to myself, "If only they knew!" I used to enjoy it and so did Maurice – he used to rub his hands.' Stan Hope called Maurice – in a phrase that has clearly shifted its connotation over the decades – 'a real stunner', and the memory of their friendship brought a smile to his lips.

Both Stan Hope and Bob Frost denied being frightened while they were on the run. Admitting to fear was taboo in the wartime RAF; being declared LMF – Lacking Moral Fibre – was the worst form of disgrace (and only 0.4 per cent of aircrew were formally charged with LMF in the course of the entire war). The photographer Cecil Beaton spent long periods with aircrews taking pictures for the Ministry of Information, and his 1942 book *Winged Squadrons* includes some sensitive and perceptive passages about the way they coped with fear. 'There is an un-written law that it is letting down the side to display emotion,' he wrote, 'but the feeling is still there, controlled and smothered by a self-preservation instinct. The realization of their proximity to danger is never far removed from the minds of these men, in spite of their easy grace of heart.'

Not long after his memorably indulgent Christmas dinner Stan Hope received a visitor, a young woman who spoke perfect English. She asked him a number of questions – about, among other things, the Football League – which were clearly designed to establish his bona fides. She left, apparently satisfied, promising that someone would be back in touch 'in a few days'. Stan Hope had been taken into the care of the Comet Line.

2

The Lines

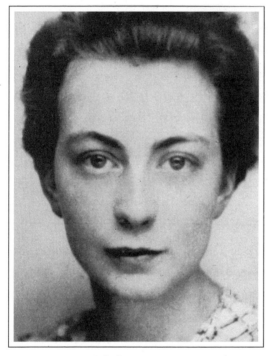

Dédée de Jongh

I‍F THE PHRASE 'ESCAPE LINE' suggests some kind of officially sanctioned or supported organization, it is misleading. As the war went on, MI9 was able to make contact with some of the underground groups working to get people out of Occupied Europe, but most of the lines began spontaneously; they were acts of defiance by people who had been deprived of more conventional means of fighting against Nazi domination. 'There was,' wrote M. R. D. Foot, 'tremendous readiness to help the Allied cause in that originally small but uncommonly tough segment of the newly conquered populations which refused to accept the fact of defeat.'

The number of women who played prominent roles is striking. In his account of the lines M. R. D. Foot contrasted the exclusively male world of prisoner-of-war camps with the often overwhelmingly female world in which those who had evaded capture existed. 'Evaders,' he wrote, 'often found that they had to trust themselves entirely to women; and without the courage and devotion of its couriers and safe-house keepers, nearly all of them women, no escape line could keep going at all.' Most of the helpers were heart-stoppingly young, some no more than teenagers, and the lines were usually organized around a small number of charismatic and exceptional individuals.

The first of the lines emerged from the chaos that followed the fall of France. Millions of people had been displaced in the exodus from Paris and northern France ahead of the German advance in May and June 1940, and as they tried to find their way home after the Armistice the French roads became 'an evader's paradise' where it was easy to get lost in the crowds. British soldiers left behind after the Dunkirk evacuation who had managed to evade capture altogether or, like Peter Janes and the Earl of Cardigan, to escape after surrendering, made their way south, converging on the port city of Marseilles on the Mediterranean coast.

In the early days the attitude of the Vichy authorities towards British servicemen was, as Lord Cardigan discovered in Lyons, somewhat ambiguous. The terms of the Armistice stated that 'Germany must be offered full security for the continuation of the war with England into which she has been forced,' and on 14 July the Vichy government duly ordered the internment of all British servicemen in the Fort St Jean at Marseilles. This intimidating complex of medieval and seventeenth-century buildings stands at the entrance to the port's harbour. British escapers and evaders arriving in 1940 were greeted with a less than cheerful message above the gate: 'You have asked for death and we shall give it to you.' It was a legacy of the fort's service as barracks for the French Foreign Legion.

But the conditions of their internment were in fact easy-going; the men were reasonably well fed, and were allowed out into the city at night as long as they promised to return. In a letter home to his mother Captain Berenger Bradford, an upper-class (and determinedly persistent) escaper in the Cardigan mould, makes internment in the Fort St Jean sound like life at a smart boarding school. 'There are quite a lot of British people collected in Marseilles from all over France and Italy,' he wrote. 'I met an Ionidas whose nephews I knew at Eton, and I am going to tea with them tomorrow . . . We are quartered in a French Foreign Legion Barracks here, and are well treated and have plenty of liberty. There are five of us in a small, dark, dirty room with no furniture except beds, so that writing is not easy. We have black coffee at 7.00 am, lunch at 11.30 am & supper at 5.00 pm – lunch and supper usually consist of stew and we always want something else in the town before going to bed.'

A group of officers and NCOs in Fort St Jean very soon began organizing escapes, and in September 1940 they were joined by the man who could perhaps claim to have been the first leader of a fully organized escape line. Ian Garrow, a captain in the Highland Light Infantry, had managed to evade capture after the disaster at St Valéry-en-Caux, and led a party of men through German lines and across the demarcation line into 'Free' France. He was interned by the French authorities, escaped, was re-arrested and sent to Marseilles. Keith Janes, who has researched his wartime activities in some depth, writes that 'everyone seems to agree that Ian Garrow was a man who inspired confidence and great loyalty among those who worked for him', and quotes the judgement of Nancy Wake (a Garrow lieutenant who earned the nickname 'White Mouse' for her escaping skills and later became a famously ruthless SOE officer) who 'described Garrow as very tall, clean shaven and good looking – a Scot of great charm'. However, Captain Bradford, who was in the Black Watch, a grander regiment than Garrow's, wrote about him rather snootily in a letter home while the two officers were being taken south: 'My companion in captivity is a chap, Garrow, I have met before for a few days at Bélâbre and, unfortunately, do not like very much. However we are both trying hard to get on together. He is a rough sort of chap and was brought up in South Africa.' If there was a little snobbery at play here it seems to have disappeared before too long; in a later letter Bradford reports the two of them enjoying nights at the cinema together in Marseilles.

By early 1941 most of the officers who had been involved in arranging escapes from Marseilles had left for England themselves, but Ian Garrow stayed on. He was greatly helped in his efforts by a somewhat unlikely collaborator in the shape of an enterprising Scottish clergyman called Donald Caskie. The Reverend Caskie was the Church of Scotland minister in Paris when war broke out, and fled the capital not long before it fell. Arriving in Marseilles, he managed to persuade the French police to allow him to take charge of the old British Seamen's Mission on the Rue Forbin in the Vieux Port, where he was permitted to provide assistance to British civilians caught up by the war – all sorts of people were swilling about in the city after the fall of France.

The French authorities warned him that he would himself be interned if he was caught helping servicemen, but he immediately began doing exactly that. In *The Tartan Pimpernel*, his autobiography, he describes frequent raids on the mission by the

Vichy security services. 'The Secret Police knew that the Seamen's Mission was becoming a clearing house for British soldiers in flight out of France,' he wrote. 'As yet, they could not prove it . . . Apart from the regular raids, suspicious-looking men hovered about the building throughout the day. By peeping from a window with heavy curtains, I often saw them keeping an eye on the Seamen's Mission from across the street. Fortunately soldiers coming up the Rue Forbin were warned to move in quickly and stealthily under cover of darkness. But we had narrow escapes, some comic, some eerie, all nerve-racking. Our task was to transform the men quickly and efficiently into civilians, and then despatch them out of France.'

Garrow and Caskie were able to draw on a network of supporters from the local population – notable among them were a Liverpool-born doctor, George Rodocanachie, an Anglophile couple called Nouveau with an apartment overlooking the Vieux Port and Nancy Wake, who was married to a rich French industrialist. Between them they set about organizing escorts to bring escapers down from the German Occupied Zone, and a system of guides to take them over the Pyrenees. Money arrived via letters from the MI9 officer stationed in Lisbon. The going rates for guides taking so-called 'parcels' across the Pyrenees have been put at forty pounds a head for officers and twenty pounds a head for other ranks.

The final piece of this unusual jigsaw fell into place with the arrival of the man who would give his name – or to be more accurate, his alias – to their line. Albert-Marie Guérisse was a doctor serving with a Belgian cavalry regiment when war broke out, and escaped to Britain after the fall of Belgium. He volunteered for special operations and was sent to serve on a French merchant ship which was being used to drop off and collect British agents from the French Mediterranean coast. On his first mission, in April 1941, he was stranded on a beach near Perpignan. He had been given the formal rank of a lieutenant commander in the Royal Navy, but when he was arrested he used his cover story: he gave his name as Patrick Albert O'Leary, claiming to be an evading Canadian airman.

The French had tightened up their internment system by this time and Guérisse soon distinguished himself by his enthusiasm for organizing escapes from St Hippolyte-du-Fort, where he was held. He eventually escaped himself and made contact with Ian Garrow, who recruited him to work on the line – which, in time (and for reasons we shall come to later), would become known as 'the Pat O'Leary Line', or simply 'the Pat Line'. In 1941 the team were going great guns, and by the time Peter Janes was smuggled south in September of that year they had, as Keith Janes puts it, developed 'a well-practised routine'.

In his diary Peter Janes describes the way his group (Janes himself, two other British soldiers, three fighter pilots and a Polish cadet) were given false identities (Janes discovered that he was supposed to be a clergyman, 'which of course I did not in the least resemble') and taken on a train from the Pas de Calais area down to Paris. From the Gare du Nord they took the Métro, 'every one of us jammed in between German soldiers, but we were about used to them by now, and took no notice of them'. They were put up in a hotel 'that was in reality nothing but a brothel'. Janes notes that after dinner one of the pilots, a Czech, took a prostitute to bed, 'but found that he could not do anything with her and asked for his money back' – which on the face of it seems a bit mean and, given the difficulty they would all have faced had she decided to create trouble, risky.

From Paris the group were escorted south to Tours, and they crossed the demarcation line into the Free Zone on foot at night. They travelled to Toulouse by train and then immediately took another to Marseilles, where they spent a night. They left for the Pyrenees at 5 a.m. the following day.

Peter Janes had grown up in Surrey, and had never seen a mountain before. He was greatly struck by the beauty of the Pyrenees, but mountain walking did not agree with him at all. Here is his description of the night his group crossed the border.

'Towards eleven o'clock I was taken ill with violent cramp in my stomach, in addition I found a lot of difficulty in breathing. All at once I collapsed, getting weaker and weaker because each time I had to be sick before my breath would come again. Then it started to rain, and in ten minutes we were soaked to the skin, it simply poured down with the wind driving great gusts into our faces which stung like so much rice. Towards midnight I felt that I was finished, my breath simply would not come, but kept staggering on as best I could. In all we crossed five mountains and my condition was alright in the lower parts, it was on the high parts that it was worse. None of the others were ill but they told me afterwards they were glad of the rest afforded by my halts. At ten to one we crossed into Spain . . .' It is a passage anyone aspiring to walk the Chemin today would do well to read!

The Pat O'Leary Line was at least run by men with some military and organizational experience, and that made it easier to establish links with MI9, which in time provided significant support, both financially and in terms of fielding escapers and looking after them once they reached Spain.

The Comet Line, by contrast, began as a largely amateur affair, and emerged from the activities of a small group of Belgian friends and families in Brussels. Many of those who worked on the line and survived remained close after the war, and they kept the flame of memory burning in a way the survivors of most of the lines did not. The Comet story has been much written about and, sometimes, romanticized. But then it is an almost impossibly romantic story.

Andrée de Jongh (whom we met in the introduction) was at the heart of it from the earliest days. Dédée, as she was known to her friends, was the younger daughter of the headmaster of a primary school in a Brussels suburb. The household was idealistic but – unusually for the period – atheist. Frédéric de Jongh inspired his children with the story of Edith Cavell, the British nurse who stayed in Brussels to look after wounded soldiers during the German occupation of Belgium in the First World War, and helped some two hundred British troops to escape to the Netherlands (she was arrested by the Germans on treason charges and shot in 1915). The young Dédée dreamed of working in a leper colony in Africa, and trained as a nurse in the evenings while studying at art college. When the Nazis invaded Belgium in May 1940 Dédée gave up her job as a commercial artist and responded to the government's appeal for trained nurses.

She was sent to work in a hospital in Bruges. Some of her patients were wounded British soldiers, and according to Gilbert Renault (a French Resistance hero who operated under the code name 'Rémy', and wrote an early history of the Comet Line under the same alias) this was where the idea of facilitating escapes first came to her. Dédée soon made contact with other members of 'that small but uncommonly tough segment' of the Belgian population which refused to accept defeat, in particular with two young cousins called Henri de Blicquy and Arnold Deppe. Airey Neave, who was responsible for a passionate (and sometimes imaginative) biography of Dédée de Jongh, wrote that they set up a network called 'DDD', after the first letters of their surnames.

It cannot have lasted very long. According to Rémy, de Blicquy was arrested by the Germans just a few days after he had introduced Dédée to his cousin Arnold. But Dédée and Arnold

Deppe continued to debate what they could do to frustrate the occupiers, and concluded that an escape line for British service-men was the best option. Before the war Arnold Deppe had worked in St Jean-de-Luz, just north of the Pyrenees on the French Atlantic coast, so he made a trip south in the hope that he could use friends and contacts to put a system in place for taking escapers over the border into Spain.

Through the nascent resistance movement he was put in touch with a redoubtable Belgian woman called Elvire de Greef. She had worked for a Brussels newspaper before the war, and when Belgium fell to the Nazis she and her businessman husband tried to escape to Britain with their children. They failed to secure a place on one of the ships leaving Bordeaux in the last days of the Battle of France, and instead settled in a rented villa by the sea near Bayonne, just south of St Jean-de-Luz.

The family first came into contact with the resistance move-ment when they tried to secure false papers for a British subject who had worked for Fernand de Greef's company. Their circum-stances meant they were particularly well placed to help an escape line. Like all of the Atlantic Coast, the area around Bayonne was part of the German Occupied Zone, and Fernand de Greef got a job as an interpreter in the local German military headquarters. It was to provide good cover for the family's clandestine activities, and allowed him easy access to blank passes and identity cards.

Andrée de Jongh made her first journey south in the summer of 1941, with Arnold Deppe as her guide. They were escorting a group of Belgians who were wanted by the Gestapo, and a mysterious middle-aged Englishwoman, 'Miss Richards', who was trying to get home. Airey Neave, in his biography of Dédée (called *Little Cyclone*, the nickname Frédéric de Jongh used for his wilful daughter), gave an account of the journey which could easily have been written by P. G. Wodehouse.

Miss Richards apparently came dressed for a country house weekend and was most indignant when the plans went awry and the party was forced to swim across the river Somme in darkness. She was a non-swimmer, and had to be pushed across by Dédée, wedged into a rubber tyre. She agreed to part with her suitcase, but several tweed skirts had to be ferried across the river too, and Miss Richards refused to take off her panama hat or her enormous white bloomers, which stood out as a 'ghostly patch of brightness' in the dark. Dédée de Jongh pushed her tyre from behind and was treated to a close-up of Miss Richards's 'vast posterior'. Her charge was punished for her obstinacy when a bicycle passed along the towpath and she was forced to slide into the freezing water, bloomers and all, to conceal herself.

Dédée de Jongh spent an hour and a half swimming back and forth across the Somme that night – six of the Belgian men were also non-swimmers – and her extraordinary powers of physical endurance became part of her legend.

Her next journey to the Pyrenees provided a sobering reminder that she was involved in something much more serious and dangerous than a Wodehouse jape. She and Arnold Deppe took different routes: Dédée took a train to Paris with Private Jim Cromar of the Gordon Highlanders and two Belgian officers, while Arnold set off for Lille with a separate party. He never made the rendezvous they had agreed in the French capital; he and his party were arrested at the station in Lille.

With the other two 'Ds' in German custody, the 25-year-old Dédée de Jongh became the leader of the DDD network – such as it was. When she crossed the Pyrenees with Cromar and her two Belgian charges she did not as yet know that Arnold Deppe had been lost. She made her way to the British consulate in Bilbao, and, having introduced herself and explained what she was up to, asked for money to pay her guides. Her first encounter with

British officialdom is one of the great set-piece moments of escaping history.

Airey Neave has left an account of the interview which, even though it may be a little imaginative in its detail (Neave was still trying to escape from Colditz at the time the meeting took place), reflects the awe Dédée de Jongh inspired in so many men. Dédée was after quite large sums, and the sceptical, pipe-smoking British diplomat she met was by no means convinced of her bona fides. He asked, 'How long did your journey take?' and she responded, 'I have told you, about a week.' The interview continued:

'There was an incredulous tone in his voice:

'"How did you get across the Pyrenees?"

'The girl's blue eyes shone with triumph.

'"I have friends near Bayonne who were able to get a Basque guide. He brought us through without any difficulty. It was a good trip."

'Her hands clutched the side of the leather armchair and, leaning forward eagerly, she continued:

'"There are many British soldiers and airmen hidden in Brussels, most of them survivors from Dunkirk. I can bring them through to you here if you will let me . . ."

'The Consul did not betray his unbelief.

'"How old are you?" he shot at her.

'"I am twenty-five."

'The Consul noticed her bare arms. They were slim and delicate. Her face, without make-up, was intelligent. Her mouth and nose were not beautiful, but determined and arresting. There was an eagerness and power about her that impressed him.

'"But you – you are a young girl. You are not going to cross the Pyrenees again?"

'"But yes. I am as strong as a man. Girls attract less attention in the frontier zone than men . . ."'

In the months that followed, plenty of British servicemen had the opportunity to confirm the accuracy of that self-assessment; it was Dédée's practice to bring up the rear of the parties she escorted across the mountains, encouraging stragglers and, with her apparently tireless strength, shaming them into pressing forward when the spirit was weak. 'Crossing the Pyrenees is an arduous and tricky business,' wrote the vice-consul in Bilbao. 'The Postmistress with her own haversack on her shoulders literally drives the men through this eight hour struggle. They all speak wonderfully of her endurance.' Dédée objected to the code name 'Postmistress', and at her request it was changed to 'Postman'. Stan Hope remembers her as someone you instinctively obeyed: 'If she said do it, you did it,' he says, 'she was that sort of person.' He also suggested that all her 'parcels' were 'a little bit in love with her'.

It took some time before MI9 was persuaded that she was genuine – like Our Man in Bilbao they were sceptical that a young woman of such delicate appearance could be responsible for running such a complex and risky enterprise. But once London sanctioned the cash for guides the returns proved to be spectacular.

The key members of the team who made the enterprise work were, like Dédée herself, highly motivated, brave and individualistic – in some cases to the point of eccentricity. Frédéric de Jongh was fifty-eight when his daughter embarked on this dangerous path, with thick spectacles and a scholarly air. Despite a visit from the Gestapo while Dédée was away on her second run to the Pyrenees he volunteered to help as the leader of the Brussels end of the operation. He took 'Paul' as his *nom de guerre* and, in schoolmasterly fashion, referred to his charges as *'mes enfants'*.

Elvire de Greef became established as an equally critical figure at the other end of the line near the border with Spain. She was a skilled and energetic trader on the black market, where she bought supplies to bolster the strength of the steady stream of British airmen who passed through her villa on the way to the Pyrenees. Escaping was very much a family business: the two children, Freddy and Janine, were recruited to act as couriers, guides and lookouts. Elvire de Greef rejoiced in the mysterious but oddly appropriate code name 'Tante Go'; it derived from the pass-word at the family villa, '*Gogo est mort*', a reference to the passing of a much-loved pet dog.

Parties of escapers often began the last leg of the journey by bicycle; from Bayonne they were led – often by the de Greef children – to a farmhouse near Urrugne, in the foothills of the mountains. Here they were committed to the charge of Florentino Goicoechea, a Basque smuggler who had become Dédée de Jongh's favoured mountain guide.

Like Dédée, Florentino made a powerful impression on every-one who met him. He was illiterate, but had an unsurpassed knowledge of the mountain terrain. He was also immensely strong. Bob Frost, who crossed the Pyrenees with Florentino as his guide in the winter of 1942, fell into a deep culvert on the way; he remembers Florentino coming back to fetch him and hoicking him out 'like a drowned rat'. Rémy recorded an incident in which Florentino carried a fat and exhausted Dutchman on his back across the river Bidassoa in full flood.

Airey Neave, who met him after the war, evoked his command-ing presence: 'Florentino has a face of true grandeur. His features are at once fine and rugged, like a majestic animal. Standing in his garden on a fine summer's day among the bright flowers and butter-flies of the region, he has an august beauty. His nose and mouth have the calm strength of one who communes with Nature. His hands are mighty. There is about his clothes a kind of nonchalance, and he wears his big flat *berét* balanced on his head.'

Florentino had what was politely termed 'a reverence for

brandy'. Bob Frost recalls that from time to time he would call a halt to their march and 'rummage about in a bush', producing a bottle which was passed around for everyone to take a sustaining nip and then replaced for the next time. Florentino was, according to Rémy, completely drunk when he first met Dédée, and kept falling down and demanding kisses as he led her over the mountains in the middle of the night. 'Florentino fell over several times as they made their descent,' Rémy wrote, 'and each time Andrée fell on top of him. Each time, Florentino caught her in his arms and said "*Pequeño baso*" (Just a little kiss). Andrée did not need to understand Spanish to understand what he was suggesting, and protested "No, No".' Dédée seems to have been more amused than disturbed by this first encounter; she declared Florentino the best possible guide 'if only he would drink a little less'. Their partnership was formidably successful; in total the Comet Line brought 289 Allied military personnel across the Pyrenees into Spain.

Fielding escapers and evaders when they reached Spain was an extremely sensitive process because of the delicate and critical nature of the relationship between Britain and Spain in the early stages of the war. Franco's regime was widely regarded as a natural Nazi ally – both because of its ideology and because of the help Franco's Nationalist forces had received from Germany and Fascist Italy during the Spanish Civil War. The consequences of Spain joining the war on the German side would have been disastrous for Britain. Gibraltar would almost certainly have fallen to a joint German-Spanish assault, closing down the Mediterranean and denying Britain the supplies which were shipped up the Suez Canal from India and the colonies.

'All we wanted was the neutrality of Spain,' Churchill wrote later, and at the beginning of June 1940 he sent the former Cabinet minister Sir Samuel Hoare to serve as ambassador to Spain with a mission to (in the words of the foreign secretary, Lord Halifax) go 'to Madrid to do there what you can to improve our relations with Spain'. Hoare found a country where German influence was so all-pervading that Spain was, as he later put it, 'morally occupied', even though it was not occupied in a military sense. 'I had the Gestapo living in the next house looking over the wall between me and them,' he said in a speech to the House of Lords towards the end of the war, 'watching every one of my movements. I had the Gestapo constantly trying to suborn my domestic staff. I saw the Gestapo taking photographs when a mob was stirred up for the purpose of breaking the windows of the British embassy.'

In these difficult circumstances the need to deal with escapers and evaders represented an unwanted claim on the ambassador's attention. The month after his arrival, MI9 despatched an agent called Donald Darling – code-named 'Sunday' – to Spain to establish links with the underground groups operating in France. Sir Samuel took a dim view of this; the discovery of a British intelligence officer operating on Spanish soil would have been less than conducive to good diplomatic relations, and Sir Samuel instructed Sunday to operate from Lisbon instead.

Things became a little easier for MI9 as the risk of a German–Spanish alliance receded. On 23 October 1940 Hitler and Franco met in the French town of Hendaye, just north of the Pyrenean border, to discuss terms. Fortunately for Britain, Franco pushed his luck too far. El Caudillo, as he was known, delivered a lengthy lecture on the parlous state of the Spanish economy and then demanded Gibraltar, French Morocco and part of Algeria in return for supporting Germany. The German side was happy to offer Gibraltar but did not want to damage its relationship with Marshal Pétain's Vichy regime by agreeing to carve up France's colonies, and the summit ended inconclusively. Franco had insisted on interrupting negotiations so that he could take his customary post-prandial siesta, and Hitler famously declared that he would rather have several teeth pulled than sit through another meeting with the Spanish leader.

By 1941 Sir Samuel had become more relaxed about the idea of his embassy being used for questionable purposes. One of his attachés, Sir Michael Creswell – MI9 code name 'Monday' – undertook the task of ferrying British escapers and evaders across the country. Sometimes this meant driving them in his own car – and concealing them in the boot when they crossed the frontier at Gibraltar – and sometimes he was able to put together a coach party of so-called 'students' and send them into British territory more openly.

The danger of Spain being drawn into the war on the German side remained real, and the Spanish attitude to the steady flow of escapers across the border was, to put it at its mildest, ambiguous. In the earliest days some escapers and evaders were simply turned back. Captain Andrew Bradford of the Black Watch fell into the hands of the Spanish Guardia Civil after an arduous night-time crossing of the Pyrenees in August 1940. 'They took us to their post and explained with signs and odd words that we must go back over the frontier,' he wrote. '"Franco's orders" was the most used phrase.' Bradford seems to have had an amazingly cheerful disposition, and even in these crushingly disappointing circumstances he persuaded one of his captors to send a brief letter to his parents describing his trek and remarking on the beauty of the mountains ('We came across some lovely flowers – little rhodos, iris, gentians, violets'). The next morning he and his companion were marched up to the top of the mountains and forced to walk back into France 'while the guards waited with their rifles'.

The Earl of Cardigan was also picked up just after crossing the border with his bicycle, but like many other early escapers he was incarcerated in the notorious Miranda de Ebro camp rather than being sent back. He was there for several weeks before the embassy was able to negotiate his release. Delays in springing British servicemen from Spanish custody were sometimes the result of good old-fashioned bureaucratic obstructiveness (the release of a prisoner had to be approved by the Ministry of Foreign Affairs, the Ministry for the Army, the Police Department and the Inspectorate of Concentration Camps), but they could also reflect arguments over the nice but important legal distinction between an escaper and an evader. Under international law 'escapers' (men like Cardigan and Janes who had been, however briefly, in enemy custody) could claim a right of free passage. 'Evaders' (men like Bob Frost and Stan Hope, who had never been caught in the first place) could be treated as illegal immigrants, and had to invent convincing escape stories to prove their status as former prisoners of war.

As the war progressed the escape lines became better at using guides who could deliver British servicemen directly to the British authorities in Spain (the Comet Line, for example, passed most of their 'parcels' to the British consulate in San Sebastian), and the Spanish – seeing which way the tide of the conflict was flowing – became less hostile to those who arrived over the mountains. From late 1942 many aircrew were interned in hotels in the spa town of Alhama de Aragón.

Bob Frost was one of the lucky ones. While his journey south included some frightening moments, it was achieved without serious mishap. Dédée and Florentino delivered him safely into British hands and when he reached Madrid he was treated to a 'silver service' meal in the embassy coaching stables, in the company of a large number of Polish aircrew in celebratory mood. Before long he was sitting in a coach driving through the Gibraltar crossing, well washed, well fed and with a new set of clothes pro-vided by the Madrid embassy. He should have been relieved, but remembers feeling oddly deflated to be back on British sovereign soil. The greatest adventure of his life was over.

In interviews men like Bob Frost repeatedly returned to the contrast between their own, relatively brief experience of the clandestine life and the long haul of those who ran the lines. The excitement of a few weeks on the run was one thing – the constant fear of discovery, with all the consequences that would bring, continuing for months at a time, was quite another.

Andrée Dumon was just seventeen years old when Frédéric de Jongh spotted her as a suitable candidate for the Comet Line (she was pushing rude cartoons of Hitler through people's letter-boxes in Brussels), and seven decades afterwards she can still remember the terror of her earliest missions as an escort. On one occasion a German soldier checked her papers on the train. He looked at her, looked at the papers, and then looked at her again, clearly not satisfied. He then checked the papers of the group of British airmen she was looking after, and passed them all without a second glance. Then he asked for her papers again, studying them for what seemed an eternity. Not a word was spoken, and she feared the worst. Finally he returned the papers and moved on.

But in the fullness of time Andrée Dumon would discover just how bad the worst could be.

3

Jeanne, Jews and the Camps

Jeanne Rogalle and her parents

THE DAY BEFORE SETTING OFF on the Chemin de la Liberté I made a brief pilgrimage to meet another woman who acquitted herself honourably as a teenager during the Second World War. Jeanne Rogalle lives in Aulus-les-Bains, a twenty-minute drive into the Pyrenees from St Girons. She is something of a local celebrity because she played a minor but highly creditable role in an episode of which France as a whole came to be deeply ashamed.

A 1942 photograph of the nineteen-year-old Jeanne Agouau (as she then was) shows a skinny figure dressed in rough working clothes, a beret and clogs. She looks physically resilient and her unsmiling gaze at the camera suggests a certain mental toughness; when I met her nearly seventy years later she had of course slowed up a little in body, but her mind remained as sharp as a steel trap. Her daughter had kindly driven down from Toulouse to help with the interview, but to me Mme Rogalle seemed able to manage very well on her own.

Set in a bowl in the mountains beside a fast-running stream, Aulus developed as a spa resort in the nineteenth century; rather intriguingly its waters had a reputation for helping what were called 'invalids of love', or, to put it less euphemistically, those suffering from syphilis. It is a little faded today, and its once-bright colours have that 'knocked back' quality so favoured by smart London interior designers, but it still has a certain Belle Epoque charm. And it remains a popular if unsophisticated holiday destination, offering some gentle skiing at the nearby Guzet Neige resort in the winter and walks to the magnificent Cascade d'Ars waterfall in the summer.

In March 1942 the Vichy regime filled the town's hotels with families of foreign Jews. The decision to turn a spa town into an internment centre was symptomatic of the ambiguous Vichy attitude towards Jews at this stage. Vichy's *préfets* – the senior civil servants who run the administrative departments into which France is divided – had been given some discretion about how they could deal with foreign Jews, and one of the options was to assemble them in a *résidence forcée*. Aulus was not a camp, and the Jews were not quite prisoners; on the other hand they were not quite free either, and the isolated mountain location made the resort a difficult place to leave.

Jeanne remembered a mixed reaction to the new arrivals

among the Aulusiens. Some resented them – fearing, she said, that they would prove an added strain on Aulus' resources, already stretched by wartime – some appeared indifferent, and some actively welcomed them. Her own family belonged to the last group; her mother sold milk from their cows to Jewish families and gave vegetables from their garden to anyone who asked for help. Jeanne said they pitied the 'mental anguish' of the Jews they met, and the Agouau family were anyway not naturally well disposed towards the collaborationist Vichy regime and its German friends; Jeanne's father, Jean-Pierre, had fought in the Great War and her brother was languishing in a German POW camp after being captured at Dunkirk.

Most Jews in Aulus seem to have accepted their situation, but a few did try to get away. The Rogalle family, who would become Jeanne's in-laws after the war, hid a group of would-be escapers in their cow barn above the town and were planning to escort them over the mountains. On 25 August 1942, the day before their planned departure for Spain, one of the party asked if she could return to the hotel where she had been staying to collect some clothes. Jean-Baptiste Rogalle, Jeanne's future husband, escorted the woman down from the mountainside, arranging to rendezvous on the bridge across the river Garbet the following morning. She never made it; by the worst imaginable luck she was caught up in one of the most notorious round-ups of Jews ordered by the Vichy regime.

Serge Klarsfeld, a French historian whose father died in Auschwitz and who has devoted his life to researching France's role in the Holocaust, regards the round-ups of the summer of 1942 as 'Vichy's shame', because 'Jews were delivered to the Germans from a part of France where there were no Germans': the Jews rounded up by Vichy were, indeed, the only Jews to die in the Holocaust who were first detained in an area which had no

German military presence. Another historian of Vichy, Michael Curtis, has called the decisions leading up to the round-ups 'Vichy's Rubicon', the moment when the regime chose to step on to the wrong side of history.

Their genesis was a meeting in May 1942 between René Bousquet, the head of Vichy's police, and General Reinhard Heydrich, the senior Nazi official who had chaired the Wannsee Conference at which the Final Solution was planned earlier the same year. The Gestapo in Paris had promised to deliver forty thousand Jews from France in the course of that summer, and Heydrich asked Bousquet whether he was willing to help. On 16 June Bousquet agreed to a first instalment of ten thousand Jews who would be delivered from the Free Zone 'so that they can be evacuated to the East', and a formal accord between Vichy and the Germans was signed in July.

In early August Pierre Laval, the Vichy prime minister, wrote to his ambassador in Washington confirming that the regime was sending Jewish families north to be transported to Eastern Europe. 'The presence of a large number of foreign Jews, who devote themselves to the Black Market and to Gaullist and communist propaganda, is the source of difficulties which we must put a stop to,' he stated. 'In your conversations, don't forget to point out that no country, not even the United States, has agreed to receive Jews living in France.' Vichy's leaders clearly understood the gravity of what they were doing.

The round-ups – or *rafles*, as they were known, a word that still echoes with sinister connotations today – were planned with a rigorous bureaucratic attention to detail. *Préfets* of the Vichy departments were told they should be conducted in the early morning of 26 August, ideally between 4 and 5 a.m. All branches of the French police were to be involved. The *préfets* were given very precise categories of Jews who were liable for deportation (such as 'foreign Jews who had arrived in France after 1933 and were either members of a Foreign Labour Group or had been interned for illegally trying to cross the Demarcation Line' between the two zones of France). The categories of those who were exempt were tightly drawn – they included, for example, women who were obviously pregnant and the parents of children under two – and the *préfets* were also asked to supply a back-up list of 'foreign Jews aged between 18 and 40 who had arrived in France between 1933 and 1935'. It seemed, as one commentator has put it, that the Vichy authorities 'feared above all else failing to achieve their quotas and disappointing the occupier'.

Jeanne remembered the paramilitary police units known as *gardes mobiles* beginning their raid at around 4.30 in the morning on 26 August. They began hauling people out of bed in the first hotel they came to, at the entrance to the village (the building is, ironically, now the police station). The din of distress and the sound of children crying woke the whole neighbourhood, and a few families lodging closer to the centre of the resort made the prudent decision to slip away while they could. The gendarmes stayed for more than a week, searching through attics and barns and in the surrounding countryside, and some 270 Jews were picked up in the round-up. But there were still several Jewish groups at liberty by the time the paramilitary police left.

At the beginning of September the *préfets* were asked to report back on the operation to the central government in Vichy. They did so in the bloodless and elaborate language of mid-twentieth-century French officialdom, but it is apparent from these brief documents that many ordinary French men and women were as shocked as Jeanne and her family by what had been done in their names. The Ardèche *préfet* reported that 'even though people do not like the Jews ... a very substantial proportion of the population feels pity towards them because of their fate, and sees it as a matter of regret that we have had to deliver this category of refugee to the occupier'. His colleague in Marseilles wrote of 'almost unanimous disapproval of the measures taken', and in the south-western city of Béziers, where 'despite the early hour many people saw some heart-rending scenes', there was 'deep indignation'.

In some reports opposition to the deportations was put down to resentment of the Occupation rather than pity for the Jews. One stated that people perceived the operation as 'nothing more than a "delivery" imposed by the leaders of the Reich'. The *préfet* of the Haute-Savoie department (in the Alps) declared that most people were happy to see the Jews go, especially in tourist resorts where rich Jews had been flaunting their wealth, but warned the Vichy regime that 'opponents of the government, exploiting the sentimentality of the masses, have not let slip the opportunity to claim that the measures taken were dictated by the occupying authorities to a government which is too weak to resist them and that the "poor victims" were destined to certain death'. The report from Jeanne's own department, Ariège, reflects the complexity of the feelings brought into play: Ariège is one of the poorest parts of France with a strong left-wing tradition, and the *préfet* observed that people were shocked to see certain rich Jews left untouched while a group of half a dozen Jewish labourers from the county town of Foix were sent north.

The *préfet* of the nearby department of Aveyron concluded his comments with a couple of lines that offer a chilling insight into the mindset of many Vichy officials. 'For my part,' he wrote, 'I approve of a measure which has rid my department of a category of persons who had become odious and against whom I could not until now take appropriate action. Moreover a number of French Jews deserve the same fate.'

The next act in Aulus' drama was decided a long way from its remote mountain valley. In July 1942, at a meeting at Franklin Roosevelt's country house at Hyde Park in New York State, Winston Churchill persuaded the American president to agree a joint operation to invade French North Africa; Churchill did not believe the time was yet ripe for an attempt to liberate France, and Stalin was pressing for some kind of action which would divert Nazi energies from the Eastern Front (the Battle of Stalingrad, one of the bloodiest in the history of warfare, began on 23 August 1942, a few days before the dawn raid to round up foreign Jews in Vichy France). On 8 November 1942 the Allies began Operation Torch, with nine landings at three ports in France's North African colonies. On the 11th the Germans crossed the demarcation line which divided the Occupied and Free Zones of France in response, and, together with their Italian allies, occupied the whole country to protect their southern flank. A few days later the first German troops arrived in Aulus-les-Bains.

That autumn proved to be one of the turning points of the war, but for those Jews in and around Aulus who had survived the round-up of 26 August it was disastrous. Their options diminished dramatically, and for local people the risks involved in helping them increased in similar measure. At the end of November Jeanne's father was approached with a request to escort two Dutch Jews over the border into Spain. He did so successfully, and a few days later was asked to take another nine. M. Agouau said that was too many for one guide to manage safely, and Jeanne volunteered to come along as a second guide.

The escaping party were instructed to gather at the Agouau house behind the Mairie at 3 a.m. on 5 December – the neighbour's wall cast a shadow which provided cover. They were told to come in pairs, and Jeanne remembered her father giving two particular instructions: they should avoid striking the ground with their walking sticks until they were clear of the village, and they must remember that the patches of white shining in the moonlight were ice, and should be avoided. The party set off with Jeanne at the head of the column and her father bringing up the rear, and after three hours' walk they reached the Cascade d'Ars, where they broke for some food.

By coincidence the Rogalle family were also escorting a party of Jews to Spain that night, and the two groups bumped into one another by the waterfall. It must have been a heart-stopping moment. They ate together and decided to join forces for the rest of the climb. Jeanne's future husband and his father were escorting a family of Belgian Jews, a young couple with an eight-month-old baby and a grandmother in tow.

'You can't imagine how difficult, long and painful it was,' Jeanne Rogalle told me. The night was clear but it was bitterly cold. Her father knew the mountain well because the family's sheep were grazed there during the summer months, but there was no clear path, and for much of the time they were scrambling across huge rocks in the darkness. The father of the Belgian family, struggling to help the women of his party while also carrying his infant son, became exhausted. Jeanne took over carrying the baby, and towards the end of the climb her father carried the older Belgian woman on his shoulders.

It took twelve hours to reach the summit and the border with Spain. The Rogalles and the Agouaus had to turn back for fear of being picked up by the Spanish police, and by this stage the grandmother of the Belgian party was unable to walk any further. They made a shelter for her to rest in and watched the remainder of the party disappear down the mountainside in single file to an uncertain future in Spain.

The four guides took a different route back to Aulus to avoid any possibility of detection. I asked Jeanne Rogalle whether she had been frightened. Certainly, she replied, but 'we felt that in the mountains we were untouchable'. But even after they were safely back at home she worried about the fate of the two most vulnerable members of the group – the older Belgian woman and her infant grandson. The whole party had in fact been arrested by the Spanish police, who managed to find and rescue the elderly Belgian. The family was interned in the Spanish town of Sort. The Sort prison kept meticulous records, and years later they were to provide the key to a remarkable postscript to Jeanne's wartime story (which is included in my final chapter).

The behaviour of the Rogalle and Agouau families was exemplary – indeed heroic, because it entailed huge personal risk. But very few Jews were saved in this way. Most of those who were rounded up in Aulus-les-Bains on 26 August were driven to the nearby concentration camp at Le Vernet, in the plain below the Pyrenees.

I use the term 'concentration camp' advisedly. Today it is often used interchangeably with the term 'death camp' but in the 1930s it meant what it said: a concentration camp was a place for concentrating a large number of people. The term first appears in official French documents in 1939. The existence of a string of such camps along the Pyrenees is not exactly a secret, but nor was it a part of the past that official French historians were especially keen to publicize in the years after the war.

The Le Vernet camp was built along the side of the Route Nationale 20, which runs down from Toulouse to Pamiers, the largest of Ariège's urban centres. It covered fifty acres and it is estimated that as many as forty thousand people were interned there in the course of the war years, but unless you are looking for signs of it you can drive past without noticing anything at all to suggest that an especially grim episode in France's wartime story unfolded here. The camp water tower is still there, a wooden railway transport car stands at the station house, and the cemetery for those who died while interned at Le Vernet is marked by a well-tended monument. But of the rows and rows of barracks that once stood on the land to the west of the Route Nationale there is no sign at all.

Le Vernet itself is a sleepy village, typical of the region. It has a handsome old church, a school, a small shop which also serves as a café and a central square shaded by plane trees and enlivened by the sparkle of a stream that runs in a channel along one side. There are some wooden benches from which to admire the majesty of the Pyrenean peaks on sunny days. When I asked for the museum I was directed to the Mairie, and after some fruitless efforts with the bell at the front door I spotted through one of the ground-floor windows a woman bent over her desk. She responded cheerfully to my tap on the window and handed me a key to the museum, which, she explained, was just across the square. She said that she would shortly be going home for lunch, and asked me to drop the key back through the letterbox when I had finished.

The museum turned out to be no more than a single room of modest size, but the documentary evidence that has been arranged around the walls tells a harrowing story. It has been put together with a clear-eyed focus on the truth, and, while the tale is told in accessible terms and the exhibits are attractively arranged, nothing has been done to diminish the impact of their message. I reflected that French visitors must find it a difficult experience. One of the maps on display marks all the detention centres and camps that had been established by the time of the liberation of France in 1944; I counted more than thirty in the area between Toulouse and the Pyrenees alone.

To understand the story of France's concentration camps we need to take a step back, to the exodus of refugees that followed

General Franco's victory in Spain at the beginning of 1939. France was not remotely prepared for the sheer size of this wave of humanity; population movements on such a scale simply had not occurred in western Europe for many centuries. So-called *'centres d'acceuil'* were established, but these centres offered precious little by way of a 'welcome'. Many refugees had to sleep in the open air, with minimal hygiene facilities and very short rations.

Nancy Johnstone, a British aid worker who crossed the Pyrenees from Spain with a party of refugee children, was horrified by what she saw. Her group was housed in a camp on the outskirts of Perpignan; she and the children were allowed to sleep in some stables with straw to keep warm, but the men were treated 'abominably'. Their African guards (Senegalese troops and North African cavalry known as Spahis) had clearly been told that they were to be treated as prisoners rather than refugees. 'There were so many difficulties about doing relief work in Perpignan,' she recalled in a bitter passage of her memoirs. 'The chief trouble was the attitude of the French, who refused to admit that any help was needed.'

She judged that the French 'were torn between a feeling of hopeless inadequacy and pride in La Belle France. La Belle France would provide for the refugees ... She provided two miles of barbed wire; two pounds of bread between twenty-five men *after* they had been behind the barbed wire for three days; a trickle of brackish water; several thousand Senegalese with rubber batons, several thousand uncontrollable Spahis, who galloped about in a circle with drawn swords, and a number of harassed mobile guards and army officers. La Belle France also provided a number of smaller camps in the Pyrenees, including one where four thousand men were huddled on a football pitch. La Belle France omitted to provide latrines or the spades to dig them with; she omitted to provide firewood; she ignored such necessities as the most primitive hospital arrangements, leaving wounded and sick to take their chance with the soldiers and the mules on the bare ground. Admittedly it was a situation without precedent, the exodus of people, and it was impossible to say whether it was criminal carelessness, deliberate sadism or just incapacity that was to blame. It seemed a mixture of all three.'

Some on the French left saw more sinister currents at work. Jean Bénazet, a young French communist from the central Pyrenees, recorded his impressions in his diary: 'I have seen women offer their favours to *Gardes Mobiles*, who took up the offers, in return for bread. I have seen the rough reception meted out to the first fighters against Nazism and fascism. In the ditch at the Amélie-les-Bains crossroads on the road from Perpignan to Le Perthus, I have seen, under five centimetres of snow, young children who had spent the night under straw, sacks, blankets and old tarpaulins, in search of protection against the cold.

'One child was nearing its end of typhoid fever. Face to the sky, eyes staring, a Republican militiaman lay dead on a mattress in a farmyard. Alongside him an old woman was groaning in pain and a child was playing at the feet of the corpse.

'This lack of solidarity with the Spanish Republic is the death knell of the French Republic.'

As we shall see in Chapter Twelve, Bénazet emerged as an important figure in the escape lines, and his own life became an illustration of the way the impact of the Spanish Civil War in the 1930s fed through into France's drama in the 1940s.

The winter weather in February 1939 proved so cold that the camps established in the mountains had to be closed, and all the refugees were moved down from the Pyrenees. The men were sent to centres on the beaches of Roussillon – the camp at Argelès, now a popular summer resort, was especially notorious for its brutal conditions – and the women were assembled at camps inland.

A forester in Argelès later described being telephoned by the mayor one morning in February with the following instruction: 'We are going to receive Spanish refugees from Franco, and we need to build a camp on the beach. You deal in wood and you are an officer in the reserves. You're my man – get to work.' When he turned up at the beach he found a piteous scene: along with the carpenters he had been promised, it was already crowded with wounded and badly maimed Spanish soldiers ('*grands mutilés*') and amputees trying to move around on the stumps of limbs. There was practically no shelter, and most of his 'carpenters' had barely wielded a hammer before. The ground was boggy and the area was whipped by the *tramontane,* a ferocious north wind.

The refugees represented a political as well as a practical problem for the French government. French public opinion was simultaneously outraged by the suffering of those France was supposed to be helping and – in many quarters – deeply suspicious about the intentions of some of the new arrivals. Women and children were one thing, communist troops quite another. They were dirty, exhausted and dressed in rags, and rumours of pillage and summary executions swirled through the local population. Articles in the local press attacked them as 'fugitives from justice, murderers and torturers'. Later in the year, when the sun came out, there were outraged editorials about the leisurely life the refugees were enjoying at the French taxpayers' expense. 'Behind the barbed wire these former Catalan militiamen are sunbathing,' declared one. 'Dressed in "slips" these gentlemen lie lizard-like in the sun, or play volley ball as if they were on a fashionable beach.'

In order to show that they were both fulfilling their humanitarian obligations and providing proper protection to the people of France, the government in Paris decided to establish a semi-permanent network of camps and to assign them to different categories of refugee. Old people were sent to a camp in the Aude department, specialist workers to centres in Tarn-et-Garonne and Haute-Garonne, Catalans to Agde and Rivesaltes, and Basques to a camp near Oloron in the western Pyrenees. Three were established for 'hard cases', including Le Vernet, which became home to the Durruti Column of Anarchist Republican troops. The regime at these three camps remained very tough indeed. Fifty-two Spaniards died of cold and hunger at Le Vernet between March and September 1939.

In the months leading up to the outbreak of the Second World War some of the pressure on the camps was relieved. Seventy thousand Spanish refugees were persuaded that they would enjoy a brighter future by returning home, and many others found employment in France. This new source of cheap labour was especially welcome to the region's businesses and farms because so many French men were leaving to join the armed forces; in the months running up to war France mobilized a third of males between the ages of twenty and forty-five. After the Armistice the Germans were also able to benefit from access to the pool of workers; nearly a thousand Spanish Republicans were shipped off to Germany as forced labour in August 1940.

But rather than abandon the camps as they emptied, the French authorities quickly found new – and increasingly sinister – uses for the spare capacity. And it was the supposedly democratic Third Republic, not the collaborationist Vichy regime, which took the first steps down this dangerous road.

It was the government of the radical politician Edouard Daladier (a bad-tempered boozer) which first used the phrase 'concentration camp' in official documents. On 30 August 1939, with war imminent, the same government ordered the detention of all foreigners from 'territories belonging to the enemy' – which meant that thousands of refugees from the Nazis who wanted to fight for France were locked up instead (the British government, it is worth remembering, was also interning German and Austrian refugees in this period). And it was also Daladier's government which then designated Le Vernet a 'repressive camp (*camp répressif*) for foreign undesirables considered dangerous to the Defence of the Nation'.

At the time the writer Arthur Koestler was enjoying a dreamy holiday in Provence with his English girlfriend, the artist Daphne Hardy, working on his novel while she sculpted, both of them delighting in the sensual pleasures of southern France. He was already a well-established literary and journalistic figure, with celebrity status on the left: he was a former member of the German communist party, and during the Spanish Civil War he had spied on Franco for the international communist organization the Comintern, using his job as a correspondent for the London-based *News Chronicle* as cover. He settled in Paris in 1938, supporting himself by writing and editing a German-language newspaper.

Koestler was a Hungarian-born Jew and had been educated in Austria. He had become disenchanted with Communism by this stage (and indeed had just completed his anti-Soviet masterpiece *Darkness at Noon*), but a communist past put him at risk, as the Molotov–Ribbentrop Pact between the Third Reich and Soviet Russia on the eve of the war provoked deep anti-communist feeling in France. When he returned to his Paris flat from Provence in early September 1939 the concierge took him to one side: 'I am not allowed to tell you,' she said, 'but you had better leave at once. The police were here at 2.00 am this morning; they have taken away Dr Freeman [Koestler's neighbour and a German refugee] handcuffed and they wanted to arrest you too.'

Koestler made discreet enquiries among influential friends, and a radical barrister of his acquaintance came back with some depressing news. 'There is a sort of silent pogrom going on against people of the left,' he declared, explaining that it was linked to the government's desire to please Franco and keep Spain out of the war. 'I don't think they believe you still to be a communist, but they naturally know that you were condemned to death by Franco, and if the *Deuxième Bureau* [Intelligence Agency] has got a copy of the Spanish black list, which doubtless it has, you are certainly one of the first names on it.'

The young lawyer advised his friend to leave the country (Koestler was in fact doing everything he could to get a visa for Britain), adding, 'There is, of course, one thing you could try: money. Some of those German film yids have got themselves released by bribing officials in the *Sûreté*.' In his memoir *Scum of the Earth*, Koestler commented: 'Certainly, I too hated that detestable set in the *cafés* and bars around the Champs-Elysées, which was chiefly responsible for the animosity against the German exiles, but I could not see that an Aryan member of the film racket was much more attractive. It was a sad symptom that this young spokesman of the Left, member of numerous *comités* against racial persecution, should be tainted by the general contagion.'

Koestler was arrested at his flat early one morning in October. After a spell interned in the Roland Garros tennis stadium in Paris he was put on a train with five hundred others and sent south to Le Vernet. He had never heard the name before but the information from the rumour mill was scarcely encouraging: 'It was supposed to have been one of the camps for Spanish militia-men, evacuated six months ago because of unsatisfactory hygienic conditions, and serving now as a sort of disciplinary camp for unruly Spaniards and internees in general, sent to Le Vernet from other camps as a measure of punishment.' In what we would now call PR terms, sending Koestler to Le Vernet was a serious strategic error; *Scum of the Earth* is one of the best pieces of reporting to emerge from France during the war. Written without a trace of self-pity, it is a compellingly detailed description of what was done there, and rich in insights into the contradictions of French attitudes.

Le Vernet's museum records that the inmates were divided into three sections. Block A was for those sentenced for failing to produce a valid identity card or living on false papers. Block B was for political detainees and those 'holding extreme views', and Block C was for 'suspects from a national perspective', a brilliantly elastic term which George Orwell would surely have enjoyed. Arthur Koestler was sent to Block C.

The men lived in wooden 'hutments', each measuring around thirty yards long and five yards wide. There were two platforms of planks along either side of the buildings, with a narrow corridor down the centre: 'The space between the lower and upper platforms was 1 yard, so that those on the lower planks could never stand erect. On each row slept fifty men, feet towards the passage. The rows were divided into compartments by the wooden poles supporting the roof. Each compartment contained five men and was 105 inches wide; thus each man disposed of a space 21 inches wide to sleep on. This meant that all five had to sleep on their sides, facing the same way, and if one turned over, all had to turn over.' There was a little straw but nothing else – no stove, no lighting, not even tables or cutlery for meals. Some of Koestler's fellow internees had previously been interned in Germany, and judged the food and hygiene at Le Vernet 'below the level of Nazi concentration camps'.

Almost everyone in Le Vernet had been interned or gaoled somewhere before (Koestler's bunk companions included a

Hungarian poet who had done hard labour, an anti-fascist Italian who had been tortured by Mussolini's police and a Polish Jew who had been gaoled for political agitation in Krakow), and *Scum of the Earth* has some powerful passages on the way the standards of what constituted inhumane treatment were rewritten by the experience of the 1930s. 'The scale of sufferings and humiliations was distorted, the measure of what a man can bear was lost. In Liberal-Centigrade, Vernet was the zero-point of infamy; measured in Dachau-Fahrenheit it was still 32 degrees above zero. In Le Vernet beating-up was a daily occurrence; in Dachau it was prolonged until death ensued. In Vernet people were killed for lack of medical attention; in Dachau they were killed on purpose. In Vernet half the prisoners had to sleep without blankets in 20 degrees of frost; in Dachau they were put in irons and exposed to the frost.'

Koestler's indictment is all the more powerful because he was so evidently a lover of France – not just of those 'good things' it so famously offers and the *vie douce* he had recently so much enjoyed with his lover in Provence, but also of the ideals for which the French Republic was supposed to stand. He found the two faces of France at this period neatly reflected in Le Vernet's two camp doctors.

The regime at Le Vernet included forced labour, and Koestler was put into a squad charged with digging up and levelling the ground adjacent to his barracks. The work involved long hours wielding a shovel and a pick, digging out large stones and smoothing over the earth that remained. After three days he suffered some kind of collapse, and put himself on the list for a medical appointment. He was lucky: the 'good doctor', a young second lieutenant, was on duty. 'He took my blood pressure and examined me fairly thoroughly. Then he asked: "You are an author?" "Yes." "Writing for the English and American papers?"

"Yes." "*Tiens*," he said, and, turning to his orderly, "exempt from all work and also from marching."'

The 'bad doctor', a first lieutenant, was a member of the far-right French organization the Croix de Feu. He had been on duty the day before Koestler's appointment and when a fifty-year-old Turkish Jew asked for his conjunctivitis to be treated the lieutenant sentenced him to fifteen days behind bars for malingering – or making a' '*visite non-motivée*', as it was called – without even bothering to examine him. 'The next patient was a young German Socialist, suffering from a floating kidney, but with a tough and healthy appearance. He also got his fifteen days of jail and afterwards returned to work. Three months later we buried him in the cemetery of Le Vernet, with the ceremonial assistance of the Camp authorities. He was twenty-four years old. I have forgotten his name.'

Arthur Koestler was released from Le Vernet on 17 January 1940, thanks to pressure from influential admirers in Britain (at this stage, of course, the governments in London and Paris were allies). At three in the afternoon that day he was emptying latrines, and at seven he was 'sitting alone in a second-class compartment of the train to Paris, sucking a bottle of Courvoisier brandy, eating an enormous piece of garlic sausage, and from time to time touching the door handle and the window pane to convince myself that it was a real door handle and a real window pane'. He managed to escape France by enlisting in the Foreign Legion under a false identity; he secured a passage to Casablanca, and eventually reached London. In the course of the journey he unintentionally became a bit-part player in one of the great unsolved mysteries of the Pyrenean story.

While waiting in Marseilles for his transit papers to come through he met an old Paris friend, the brilliant Jewish writer and critic – he is something of a cult figure now – Walter Benjamin.

Koestler recorded that Benjamin showed him a hoard of morphine pills he had collected in case he was taken by the Germans, and he wrote in *Scum of the Earth* that his friend was 'reluctantly' persuaded to share them.

Benjamin crossed the Pyrenees on foot in September 1940 in the company of a group of fellow Jews. According to the official story, when the party reached the Spanish town of Portbou they were arrested and told that they would be returned to France, and Benjamin committed suicide to avoid this by taking all his remaining pills. Koestler clearly bought this version of events: 'At Portbou the *Guardia Civil* arrested him,' he wrote in *Scum of the Earth*. 'He was told that the next morning they would send him back to France. When they came to fetch him for the train, he was dead.'

However, there are all sorts of unanswered questions surrounding Benjamin's death. His travelling companions remembered him carrying a heavy briefcase across the mountains containing a manuscript which he described as 'more important than I am'. No such manuscript was discovered after his death. And far from being forced to return to France, the rest of the party were allowed to continue their journey to Lisbon and freedom as they had planned. A Spanish doctor's report gave the cause of death as a cerebral haemorrhage, not a drugs overdose. There has been persistent speculation ever since Benjamin's death that he was actually murdered, perhaps by a Soviet agent who had infiltrated his escaping party.

Scum of the Earth was published in Britain in 1941, which means Koestler was completing this devastating critique of French cruelty at almost exactly the same time that the Earl of Cardigan was feeling so humbled by the generosity and natural good manners of the French peasants he met on his way south.

Koestler's ordeal ended fully five months before the fall of

France and the formation of Marshal Pétain's collaborationist Vichy regime. When Vichy decided to become Hitler's partner in the persecution of the Jews, the tools for the job lay readily to hand in concentration camps like Le Vernet.

4

Ninette's Tale

Ninette Dreyfus at home in Paris

IN THE VERY EARLY DAYS of Vichy it was just about possible to argue that the regime was merely (if that is the right word) xenophobic rather than actively anti-Semitic.

Almost everything about the way France acted during the Second World War can be traced back to what happened during the First. Go to any rural French town or village and look at the list of names on the war memorial, and you are left humbled by the weight of numbers of those who gave their lives between 1914 and 1918. That is especially true in poor rural areas like Ariège, where the pull of employment in the cities has brought about so much depopulation; sometimes you feel that the names carved into the marble are the only evidence that there were ever any young people in the silent streets with their shuttered houses. France lost around 1.7 million dead in the First World War, just under 4.5 per cent of its population; the equivalent figures for the United Kingdom were 996,000, just over 2 per cent of the population. And more than 4.25 million French combatants were wounded. When the war ended France was desperately in need of manpower – and a law passed in 1919 which limited the working day to eight hours made the problem even more acute.

During the inter-war years immigrants poured in to meet the French economy's hunger for labour, and (because of the political climate in other parts of Europe) many of them were Jews. They came from the east – Russia, Poland, Czechoslovakia, Romania and Hungary – where anti-Semitism was an increasingly ugly and obvious part of life. They came from the south and west – Italy, Spain and Portugal – where unemployment and fascist politics made for an increasingly tough time for those at the bottom of the heap. And of course, with the rise of Nazism, they came from Germany and Austria. There were just over a million foreigners living in France in 1914, at the outbreak of the Great War. The figure was two and a half million in 1926, and went over the three million mark in 1934.

Official France initially welcomed the new arrivals. The nationality law of 1927 allowed any child born in France to a foreign father who had himself been born in France to claim citizenship. The same rights applied to any child of a naturalized father or a French mother, whatever the nationality of the other parent. And anyone who could show that they had brought 'worthy talents' to France could apply for naturalization after three years. But these huge waves of immigration soon provoked a backlash. One of the first steps taken by the Vichy regime – on 22 July – was to review all naturalizations of French citizens since the passing of the 1927 law. As a result fifteen thousand people had their nationality revoked. Around six thousand of them were Jews. But many French Jews found it extremely difficult to accept that any of this had anything to do with them.

Ninette Dreyfus – or the Dowager Lady Swaythling, as she had become by the time I visited her in her elegant London mews house seven decades later – came from one of the grandest and most assimilated of France's Jewish families. She was a close cousin of the Louis-Dreyfus family, bankers with an international trading empire; Louis Louis-Dreyfus, the head of the family, was known as 'King Two Louis', a pun on the old gold coins of pre-revolutionary France. Ninette lived with her parents and elder sister, Viviane, in one of the most beautiful houses in Paris; it is just off the Avenue Foch near the Bois de Boulogne, and had once belonged to the composer Claude Debussy (Debussy's daughter-in-law used to drop round for tea, paying prolonged and emotional visits to the bathroom, which she claimed was the only room in the house that had not changed).

'I didn't know I was a Jew,' Lady Swaythling told me. She was nine when the war began, and her first sense of any difference between herself and her smart Catholic schoolmates in Paris had come when they began to go through the ritual of First Communion. Ninette very much enjoyed attending these celebrations, and wished that she too could dress up in a veil and be given presents. She was somewhat put out when she was told it could not be. Viviane – who was two years older and wrote a memoir of their wartime lives – recalled that 'The terms "Jew" and "Israelite" meant almost nothing to me until the outbreak of war.

We were not Catholic, and that was it. We did not have any other religion.' Their adored nanny (or nounou, as she was known) used to take them to vespers in a local church, and if someone in the household had lost something she would ask the girls to dip into their pocket money and light a candle beneath the statue of St Anthony, the patron saint of lost objects.

There was a long tradition of near total assimilation among French Jews, going right back to the eighteenth century, when France became the first country in the world to emancipate Jews; they were granted full equality in law in 1791, two years after the *Declaration of the Rights of Man*. The tradition survived the searing experience of the Dreyfus Affair, which poisoned the last years of the nineteenth century and the first years of the twentieth (in a case that divided the whole of France, a Jewish army officer, Captain Alfred Dreyfus, was falsely accused of spying for the Germans), and there were large numbers of prominent Jews active in French public life at the outbreak of the Second World War.

During the lifetime of the Third Republic – from 1870 until the fall of France in 1940 – some fifty *préfets* or deputy *préfets* were Jews, as were roughly the same number of deputies (MPs), senators or ministers. There were dozens of senior Jewish lawyers, judges and generals. These devoted public servants had no doubt at all about their identity or where their allegiance lay. In 1933 Jacques Helbronner, a Jewish member of the Conseil d'Etat, the French equivalent of America's Supreme Court, made the unequivocal declaration that 'French Jews are French before being Jewish,' and three years later Léon Blum, France's first Jewish prime minister, said in a speech, 'I am a Frenchman who is proud of his country, proud of his history, nourished as much as anyone else on its tradition in spite of my race.' The Louis-Dreyfus and Dreyfus families (who were not in any way related to Captain Alfred Dreyfus) were very much part of this tradition.

In early 1940, Edgar Dreyfus deemed it prudent to send his wife and daughters to La Baule, a glamorous seaside resort (with a golf course) in Brittany. It was a brief but brutal experience. Mme Dreyfus wrote to tell her husband that she was unable to find a villa to rent because every door was shut in her face when she gave her name. Ninette was sent to a local private school, where the headmaster staged a public burning of all textbooks written by Jews. Her teacher tied her to a tree and told the other girls in her class to file past and spit at her. 'That', she said to me, 'was France BEFORE the Germans came.' Ninette started crying when the time came for school each morning. Her mother sat her down for a life lesson: 'Better to know who you are,' she said. 'What it is to be a Jew.'

After this unsuccessful experiment the family was reunited in Paris, just in time for the great exodus to the south as the German army approached. The Dreyfus party joined the columns of refugees in a chauffeur-driven Chrysler, and settled first in Marseilles. They would in the end be forced to flee across the Pyrenees like so many others, but the way they tried to preserve a life in the country they regarded as home reflected the experience of the thousands of people who saw themselves, in Helbronner's words, as French before being Jewish. Being forced to accept that France – or at least the Vichy government which claimed to speak for France – took a different view was an extremely difficult and painful psychological process. It meant reinventing your identity. Many people lost their lives because they were unable to believe that people they regarded as fellow French citizens could act in the way they did; Jacques Helbronner himself died in Auschwitz.

When Marshal Pétain, newly endorsed as Vichy's leader, visited Marseilles in 1940 he was being hailed by many people as the only man who could save France. M. and Mme Dreyfus came out on to the balcony of their hotel suite to join the general brouhaha which greeted him, crying with emotion, waving their handkerchiefs and making themselves hoarse with shouts of '*Vive Pétain.*' Louis Louis-Dreyfus, who was a senator, was among those who voted full powers to Pétain in the Grand Casino at Vichy, which served as a temporary parliament building. The official leaders of Judaism in France were equally enthusiastic: the Central Consistory of the Jews of France moved to Vichy with the new government, and in September 1940 the body representing the country's rabbis sent a supportive telegram to Pétain assuring him that 'ever inspired by the commandments of Judaism, it exhorts the faithful to serve the fatherland, promote the family and honour labour'.

With the benefit of hindsight, it is obvious that anti-Semitism lay at the very core of the Vichy project. In August the regime repealed a decree issued in 1939 which banned the publication of anti-Semitic propaganda. And on 3 October Vichy promulgated the infamous *Statut des Juifs.* It was a formal repudiation of the fundamental Republican principle that all citizens of France should be treated equally: for the first time a specific group of people were given a legal identity and barred from serving in widely drawn areas of public life, including politics, the law, the foreign service and senior branches of the home civil service.

All of this was done on Vichy's own initiative; it was not dictated by the Germans. Vichy followed up on the *Statut* by introducing more than a hundred pieces of anti-Jewish legislation during the year that followed. In June 1941 there was a second *Statut* which drew a very broad definition of who should be considered Jewish: if you had three grandparents who were Jewish, or two if you were yourself married to a Jew, you were, for Vichy's purposes, a Jew, and this applied irrespective of your religion (so candles to St Anthony did not count).

The anti-Jewish regime in the Occupied Zone was of course

even tougher; Jews were forbidden to visit public places such as cinemas, swimming pools and parks. They were banned from most professions and, in time, from owning radios, telephones and bicycles. In early 1942 they were subject to an overnight curfew, followed by an ordinance which restricted the time when they could shop to the hour between three and four in the afternoon. These measures may have been imposed by the occupying Germans, but in Paris and the other cities of the northern zone they were enforced by the French police, which was still under Vichy's control. The only decision which Vichy really baulked at was the Nazi diktat, in May 1942, that all Jews over six years old should wear a yellow star emblazoned with the word *juif*; in the face of widespread public opposition to the move, Marshal Pétain's government refused to follow suit, although in December the same year it did order that *juif* or *juive* should be stamped on ration books.

Important differences between the treatment of French Jews like the Dreyfus family and 'foreign' Jews remained. French Jews, for example, were not subject to detention of the kind the Jews at Aulus-les-Bains were forced to endure; the law allowing *préfets* to intern Jews in their departments was introduced on 4 October 1940 (the day after the promulgation of the *Statut des Juifs*), and it referred to the internment of foreigners 'of the Jewish race'. Many French Jews were able to live in relative freedom in southern France, and in the case of the Dreyfus family it remained a privileged life for a surprisingly long time. After their sojourn in Marseilles they rented the Villa Rochelongue in Cannes, just across from the famous waterfront known as La Croisette.

Ninette Dreyfus was on the threshold of her teens and remembers the months in Cannes as a happy time of her life – she felt it was an adventure, and had a strong sense of being caught up in a moment of history. The headmistress of her lycée, of whom she became a close friend in later years, was a de Gaulle supporter, and hosted glamorous gatherings of like-minded members of the Cannes film set at the school in the evenings. There were some anti-Semites in her class and she got into a few fights, but she encountered nothing like the open hatred she had experienced in Brittany. Her sister Viviane recalled being teased for having a shrill Parisian accent, but nothing worse. When her maths teacher announced that she was being forced to leave her job because of the racial purity laws everyone in the class was outraged.

In Cannes Viviane read deeply, debated Proust with her family and fell in love for the first time. She experienced the pain of separation when her boyfriend left to fight with the Free French (she learnt much later that he had been caught in the Pyrenees trying to cross into Spain, and died just after being liberated from hard labour in a salt mine). She remembered a pleasure-seeking world where people tried to ignore the realities around them. 'We played golf, we went on picnics as we had always done,' she wrote. 'Around us, everyone behaved as if nothing untoward was happening, as if there was no war and we were not pariahs.'

But of course there was a war, and the way things were developing in France did not augur well. In March 1942 the Germans forced the Vichy regime to appoint a new commissioner for Jewish affairs, Louis Darquier. Darquier, or Baron Darquier de Pellepoix as he liked to style himself (he pinched the title from an aristocratic Darquier family in Gascony which had nothing to do with his own), was said to have 'the correct conception of the Jewish question' – in other words he was violently anti-Semitic. He also had a particular hatred for rich Jews, of which the Louis-Dreyfus family was such a powerful symbol. The headquarters of his Commissariat aux Questions Juives were established in the former Louis-Dreyfus Bank building at 1, Place des Petits-Pères near the Bourse in Paris. From the offices where King Two Louis and Ninette's father Edgar once worked, Darquier issued a memo banning the use of the word 'Israelite'. 'The use of this term is due to Jewish influence,' he wrote, 'which, by banishing the word "Jew", has managed to achieve, finally, the first principle of Jewish defence, which is to pretend that the Jewish problem is only a religious problem. At the Commissariat for Jewish Affairs, a Jew must be called a Jew, and you must not write Monsieur Levy or Monsieur Dreyfus, but "the Jew Levy" and "the Jew Dreyfus".' Lady Swaythling believes her family was 'top of de Pellepoix's list'.

When the whole of France was occupied by the Axis powers on 11 November 1942, Mme Dreyfus dished out sachets of cyanide to her husband and the children. 'If you are taken and they are going to shoot you,' she told them, 'don't forget, at the last minute, but only at the last minute, to shout *Schweinkopf* at them – pig's head.' Viviane recalled a heart-rending moment when, on a rainy Cannes day that winter, she found her mother sitting alone in the drawing room of the villa, gazing at her feet and apparently lost in contemplation. She asked what was wrong; 'her voice came very low, just the shadow of her voice: "Nothing. It's raining. And I am Jewish."'

In fact the family's situation improved for a while, because Cannes was initially occupied not by the Germans but by the Italians. The Italian attitude to Jews was a good deal friendlier than that of the Vichy regime, let alone that of the Nazis. The Italian occupiers had no taste at all for persecution – rather the reverse, in fact, and escape to Italy began to look like an attractive proposition.

But the course of the wider war was to make that impossible. The Axis powers surrendered to the Allies in North Africa in May 1943. A few days later the first bombs fell on Rome, Sicily was invaded in July and the first Allied troops reached the Italian mainland in September. On 8 September Italy formally capitulated and an armistice signed with the Allies secretly a few days earlier was published. The Italians disappeared from the French Riviera, and with them went any hope that Jews there would be protected from the Germans.

The Dreyfus family arrived in Nice in the hope of leaving for Italy on the very eve of the Italian capitulation. When the news that the Italians were withdrawing reached them in their hotel the family went into hiding; they spent a night in a garage as German troops poured into the town. The next day they managed to get what must surely have been one of the last trains out, and headed back to Cannes, thus narrowly escaping one of the most savage of all the round-ups of Jews during the Occupation.

Throughout the spring and summer of 1943 the Vichy government had been under pressure from Berlin to strip as many French Jews as possible of French nationality so that more of them could be deported to the death camps. Darquier de Pellepoix, Berlin's enthusiastic ally, wanted to 'de-naturalize' all Jews who had been given French citizenship after 1927. But both Marshal Pétain and the Vichy prime minister, Pierre Laval, had begun to worry that Germany was going to lose the war, and had concluded that they needed some evidence of having stood up to Hitler by way of an insurance policy. On 24 August Pétain refused to sign Darquier's proposed bill, and declared that he was unable to understand 'the sending of Jews of French nationality when there were so many other Jews in France'.

The German reaction to this (scarcely robust) exhibition of French independence was to start rounding up Jews indiscriminately, making it as plain as could be that they had ceased to have any regard for Vichy's laws. Alois Brunner, Himmler's man in France, took personal charge of the Nice operation, and carried it out with extreme brutality. Viviane Dreyfus remembered scenes of chaos as the family made their way to the station. 'In every road we saw brutal mass arrests,' she wrote. 'People were being arrested in hotels, in shops, in churches, on the pavement, on the highway. Chance decided everything.' Carmen Callil, in her classic *Bad Faith: A Story of Family and Fatherland*, described what happened next: 'Brunner was a sadist, indiscriminate and thorough. His torture headquarters were in the Excelsior Hotel; he packed its leafy courtyard with trapped Jews. Every other dwelling in Nice was searched, every hospital, bus, train and car, day and night. Brunner arrested any Jew he could find, and anyone who, to him, looked Jewish. Checking penises was his method, which meant many Jews escaped, and many circumcised Catholics and Moslems went to Auschwitz.'

From Cannes the Dreyfus family took a train to Pau and the Pyrenees, using false papers. Three and a half years after Ninette had first been confronted with the reality of French anti-Semitism, the family were now living clandestinely. There was no longer any room for the pretence that being French came first; Edgar Dreyfus and his family reached Pau as Jewish refugees, not scions of a rich Parisian banking dynasty.

Hiding in the Pyrenees while they waited to cross into Spain, the Dreyfuses again found – ironically – the best of France. The family first rented rooms above a bakery in the countryside outside Pau; Ninette remembers getting up early to help the baker with his morning rounds. Food in the mountains was plentiful, a thrill after the pinched world of rationing; 'from six in the morning, with the farm workers, we devoured *cassoulet*, goose *confit*, cheese, omelettes, real bread with real butter and real jam, real coffee with real sugar', wrote Viviane. No one denounced them, whatever suspicions they may have had about a family which claimed to be from Valenciennes but knew nothing about the place. (They had in fact never set foot there.)

When they moved into Pau itself they were put up by a French family, and were introduced to the neighbourhood as 'our cousins from the north'. It took time to find good guides to take them over the mountains. And they waited in a city full of fear; there were sudden roadblocks, round-ups, and arrests by both the Germans and the collaborationist French military police force known as Le Milice. Edgar and Viviane made the crossing into Spain first, on horseback. Ninette followed with her mother and a cousin. The area around the border was a restricted zone; the three of them were driven into the mountains in an ambulance, with Ninette posing as a TB victim and her cousin as a nurse.

When I interviewed Lady Swaythling her main memory of the trek across the mountains was the mud. She and her mother were told they must travel in the rain, as it made it more difficult for German sniffer dogs to follow their scent. Whenever the party heard a noise they had to drop on to the soaking ground. By the time they reached Spain she had lost her shoes, and her hands and feet had been viciously torn. It was a very long way from Debussy's lovely garden by the Bois de Boulogne. After the family had been reunited, Ninette's parents treated her to a manicure on the way down to Madrid. The manicurist wept at the sight of her hands.

Ninette later discovered that seven members of her family who had stayed behind in Paris died in Auschwitz.

– 5 –

Fanny/Joan's Tale 1

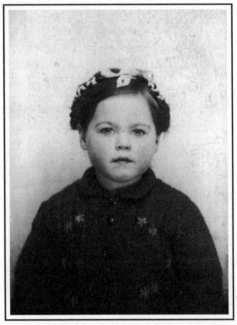

Fanny Zimetbaum, from her identity card

Lady Swaythling's story was one of those that came to me
serendipitously: her goddaughter put us in touch with one
another after hearing me mention my Pyrenean walk at a literary
festival.

Another graduate of a Pyrenean crossing now living in
London is Joan Salter, and she was part of the reason I set out on
this journey in the first place. She was carried across the

mountains as a tiny child, and began researching her wartime experiences comparatively late in life. She is a close friend of my literary agent, Vivienne Schuster, and the connection inspired my BBC programmes and this book. If Ninette Dreyfus's story reflected the wartime experiences of French Jews, Joan Salter's was an equally vivid and characteristic reflection of what it was to be a 'foreign' Jew then. And it began as the story not of Joan Salter but of Fanny Zimetbaum, which is what she was called when she was born – the reason for her change of name is an essential part of her story, and we shall explore it later.

Her father, Jakob Zimetbaum, first arrived in France looking for economic opportunity. Born in the Polish city of Tarnow, at the age of seventeen he was sent to Antwerp by his father to learn the skills of gemstone cutting from a distant cousin, but he found the work hard and the culture oppressively religious. Paris was altogether more alluring, and Jakob set himself up there as a freelance gemstone salesman, working the city's nightclubs and casinos with, as Joan put it, 'something to offer a man on a winning streak for the attractive lady on his arm'. He diversified into fashion, making copies of the designs on display at the couture fashion shows and using the family garment business back in Poland to produce high-quality copies for sale in Paris. By the 1930s he was rich.

He met Bronia, Joan's mother, in 1937. Though she too was from Poland (she was born in Warsaw), she had moved to Paris five years earlier with her first husband, who died of tuberculosis after little more than a year of marriage, leaving her pregnant with a daughter, Liliane. Foreign Jews in France tended to be less assimilated and more religiously observant than French-born Jews, and the couple went back to Poland for a traditional wedding. Bronia had evidently been influenced by her years in Paris: when Jakob's mother and aunt took her for a ritual bath at the Tarnow *mikvah* on the eve of her wedding she thought they were trying to drown her and pulled off their wigs.

The couple planned to honeymoon in Vienna, but delayed their departure slightly to mark the festival of Purim with Jakob's family. It was a lucky decision: this was March 1938, and had they gone to Austria they would have been caught up in the Anschluss, the absorption of Austria into the Third Reich.

The newlyweds returned to Paris, and Joan's album of photos from this period shows her mother as an elegant, fashionably dressed figure. But with the outbreak of war the following year the comfortable, sociable lives the couple had grown used to came to an end. Jakob was most emphatically not one of those Jews who was complacent about what Nazi aggression might mean; from the autumn of 1939 he devoted all his ingenuity and resources to staying one step ahead of the deadly game of being a Jew in wartime Europe. At the end of that year he converted his wealth into easily negotiable items like gold and gemstones, and hid it in caches around Paris. He then moved the family to Brussels, where Fanny/Joan was born in February 1940.

Jakob's decision to move the family to Brussels was based on the belief that the Germans would not bother to invade Belgium on their way into France. It was a serious strategic error, but, on the basis of the facts available to him, not entirely foolish, for Belgium had declared itself neutral in the hope of staying out of the conflict (and of course most of France's military top brass badly misread Germany's war plans too). Jakob was detained by the Germans when Belgium fell in May and, by the sort of weird administrative logic that war sometimes produces, deported west, to Angoulême and then Bordeaux, after the German Armistice with France. Six months later he and a group of other Polish Jews were put on a train heading back east, destined for a labour camp.

It was an ordinary train and their guards became engrossed in a game of cards. As the train slowed down outside Paris Jakob tried to persuade his fellow detainees to jump. They refused but he went ahead, and the decision almost certainly saved his life. On reaching Paris Jakob picked up some valuables from one of his caches (hidden in a graveyard) and made his way back to Brussels to rejoin the family. The next step in this dizzying game of cat and mouse was to return to Paris. Bronia and the children did so 'legally' (she explained to the authorities that since her husband had been deported she was unable to support herself and needed to live with her sisters in the French capital) and Jakob, now a fugitive without proper papers, crossed the border clandestinely.

The family split as a way of minimizing risk – Bronia and the children lived with her sisters while Jakob hid in a cousin's apartment in the Boulevard Voltaire, near the Place de la République. After he had come frighteningly close to capture in the summer of 1941 (the German army came through the area searching for Jews, and Jakob only escaped by bribing the concierge to say that the apartment was empty) he decided to head south to the Free Zone while leaving the rest of the family behind in Paris. This decision must also have seemed logical at the time; as a man on the run without papers he was at acute risk of deportation in the Occupied Zone, but no one at that stage of the war imagined that the Germans would deport women and children as well as men.

Like Arthur Koestler, Bronia Zimetbaum found the two faces of France reflected in two very different French officials. Each week she had to report to the local police station with her daughters so that they could have their registration as aliens checked. According to the account passed on to Joan 'this took place in a small room manned always by the same two policemen: one a kindly young man, the other known for his hostility and rudeness to foreigners'. One week in the summer of 1942 she found the queue for the 'nice' policeman so long that she decided to risk the nasty one, but the children began raising a ruckus. According to Joan, 'My sister's demands to be picked up and for me to be put down resulted in the pair of us screaming at once, causing absolute fury from the man behind the desk.' Bronia gave up and waited outside until the queues had shrunk and the children had calmed down.

When she returned the 'nice' policeman was free, but he refused to accept that her name was on his list, even though she could see it there. The young man asked his colleague to look in another room for a different list, and while he was gone he gave Bronia a warning: 'Madame,' he said, 'tomorrow they are starting rounding up women and children. Your name is on that list. If you have anywhere to hide, go.'

The Rafle du Vélodrome d'Hiver, or Vél d'Hiv, on 16 and 17 July 1942, was another infamous moment in France's Second World War history. More than thirteen thousand Jews were picked up, more than four thousand of them children. They were told they could bring a blanket, a jersey, a pair of shoes and a couple of shirts with them, but nothing more. Many of them were detained in the Vélodrome, a sports stadium near the Eiffel Tower built for cycle racing, ice hockey and the like, where they were held in appalling conditions (it was a ferociously hot period of the summer) before being sent to Auschwitz.

Although the operation was to take place in the Occupied Zone, Vichy was still – nominally at least – in charge of the French police who would be largely responsible for carrying it out. The Vichy police chief, René Bousquet, managed to secure agreement from the occupying German authorities that his officers would have to arrest only foreign Jews, and that French Jews would be left to the German military; the idea that this distinction repre-sented some kind of moral victory is itself a condemnation of the

Vichy mindset. In all other ways the Vichy regime cooperated fully with the Nazi plan for the round-up. Under the original proposals children under sixteen were to be spared from deportation (this was partly to preserve the fiction that the deportees were destined to provide labour). Pierre Laval, the Vichy prime minister, argued that it would be kinder to keep families together – even though he must have had a pretty clear idea of the fate awaiting both children and parents at the end of their journeys.

Bronia left her boarding house shortly after 5 a.m. on the morning of 16 July. She learnt later that the Gestapo turned up half an hour after she had gone. Her landlady had contacts in the Resistance, and she and the children were taken down to the demarcation line in a laundry van. They were smuggled across into the Free Zone, and the family were reunited in a village near Lyons. They had been saved by an astonishing combination of good fortune and kindness.

As Joan began to research the story of their escape relatively late in life, there are periods where the details are hazy. She knows that her father was interned again – this time in a camp near Annecy – and the dates suggest he may have been caught up in the round-ups of August 1942. However, most of those taken then – like the Jews of Aulus-les-Bains – were sent north to the Drancy holding centre near Paris and then on to the death camps in fairly short order. Jakob Zimetbaum had time to establish a relationship with some of his Corsican guards, and managed to bribe them to let him escape. He was taken by motorbike to Perpignan, one of the gateways to the Pyrenean crossings.

The story of Jakob's survival suggests he was an extremely savvy operator. In Perpignan he invested some time in research; dressed as a French peasant he sat around in the city's bars, drinking coffee and smoking, while he listened to other Jewish refugees negotiating with guides for a passage across to Spain.

He concluded that it was a dodgy racket, and that many of the *passeurs* were taking the money and turning in their clients to the authorities. Jakob moved on and eventually crossed the mountains successfully by a less well-trodden route further inland.

Jakob gave some of his very few remaining gemstones to his guide as a down payment for escorting Bronia and the children across too. Joan does not know exactly when they made the journey, but the scraps of memory passed on by her mother suggest the winter of 1942/43, just after the Axis occupation of the whole of France.

Her mother did not talk much about the experience, but she remembered the cold and the snow. Fanny/Joan was two years old, and her mother had to carry her. Bronia did pass on one terrible memory to her daughter – a memory that must have weighed heavily on the family: when the infant Fanny started to cry, their guide suggested she should be killed because the noise might alert German patrols.

– 6 –

Tales of Children

Children of the Château de la Hille

IF YOU HEAD BACK TOWARDS St Girons (where the Chemin begins) from Le Vernet you will weave through a hilly landscape dotted with romantic medieval names – age-old towns and villages like La Bastide-de-Sérou, Montbrun Bocage and Montégut-Plantaurel. Plantaurel is the generic name for this range of the Pyrenean foothills, and as you approach the village of Montégut you will see signs to Le Musée des Enfants du Château de la Hille.

This museum is even more difficult to find than the one in Le Vernet – it is tucked away in a small industrial park just off the main road. It is only open two mornings a week and is really no more than a small collection of photographs, books and manuscripts. I sought it out because Joan Salter had alerted me to the story of the children who made their home here during the Second World War, and, as the old French guide books used to say, *il vaut le détour*; the story, though haunting, is in its way just as uplifting as the Le Vernet story is depressing.

For Ruth and Betty Schutz it began in Berlin on 28 October 1938, when three men in SS uniforms banged on the front door of their apartment and took away their father. Along with some seventeen thousand other Polish Jews living in Germany he was expelled to Poland in one of the earliest organized deportations of the Nazi regime. The family never saw him again. The girls' mother, Bertha, began to look desperately for a way to escape from Germany.

Kristallnacht, the notorious night of officially sanctioned violence against Jews and Jewish property across Germany, was a fortnight later, and prompted the British government to agree the so-called Kindertransport programme, under which nearly ten thousand Jewish children from Germany, Austria, Poland and Czechoslovakia were given asylum in Britain (leaving their parents behind, of course). The first trainload left Berlin on 1 December 1938 and the programme went on right up until the outbreak of war – the last group of children left Germany the day Hitler's troops crossed the border into Poland.

Despite her best efforts, Bertha failed to secure a place on a Kindertransport for her girls, and in February 1939 she took a remarkable decision: she put Ruth and Betty on a Kindertransport train heading for Belgium without any papers and without any arrangements for a foster family to receive them. Ruth was thirteen and Betty was nine – Bronia, the baby of the family, stayed with her mother. Betty Bloom (as she became) wrote later that the plan was Ruth's idea. When I spoke to Ruth – now living on a kibbutz in Israel, and a mother and grandmother herself – she wondered at the emotional toughness her mother displayed. Bertha's decision almost certainly saved the children's lives.

There was a bad moment at the border – a Belgian official told the girls to get off the train because they did not have the necessary passes, but they sat tight – and no one quite knew what to do with them when they reached Brussels. Eventually the Jewish Refugee Committee arranged for them to be placed in a hostel with forty-five other girls who had also pitched up in Brussels without family or contacts to look after them.

Life in the Home General Bernheim was reasonably comfortable but it must have been an unsettled – and indeed unsettling – existence; all the girls had their own stories of families left behind, many of them in traumatic circumstances. Inge Joseph, another young resident of the hostel, wrote later, 'My new friends and I were like Gypsies. Our mothers and fathers were in Germany or Austria, our sisters and brothers scattered about in Belgium, Poland, Palestine, Britain, and the United States, and we were not sure where we would be living next weekend, next month, or next year.'

Ruth and Betty were still living in the Home General Bernheim when Germany invaded Belgium on 10 May 1940. The hostel was in the countryside near the border, and they could soon hear the sound of battle. On 15 May the hostel director, Elka Frank, managed to secure places for her charges on a goods train out of the country. They were given little time to pack, and many of them arrived at the station wearing several layers as the most efficient way of carrying their clothes. Elka Frank did not tell them where they were going – indeed it is unlikely she had anything more than a vague notion herself. Both Betty and Ruth remembered Brussels station as a scene of chaos as people struggled to get away ahead of the German advance. The Belgian capital fell two days later.

The party of girls was joined at the station by a group of some fifty Jewish boys in similar circumstances. The children were packed into goods wagons, the boys in one and the girls in another. For four days they headed west and south. Ruth told me she remembered seeing some wounded soldiers – she thinks they were British – returning from the front. Near Dieppe the train was bombed and several people in another carriage were killed. For Betty the worst moment was having to relieve herself in a leather shoulder bag her mother had given her as a going-away present.

The train journey ended in Toulouse, and from there they were taken south-east in lorries to the village of Seyre, roughly equidistant between the river Ariège and the Canal du Midi, the great 150-mile waterway which connects Toulouse to the Mediterranean. Their lodging was a barn belonging to the local squire (no one can quite remember how this arrangement was arrived at), and conditions were extremely primitive. They slept on straw, and drew their water from the village pump. Food was scarce. Ruth had become friends with Inge Joseph (who was the same age), and Inge's wartime memoir is – like so many others – dominated by a near obsession with meals. 'One topic of conversation', she wrote, '... gradually dwarfed everything else; food. Our biggest worry with each passing day was whether there would be enough to eat. To compensate for our empty stomachs, we found ourselves conversing endlessly about the food of our early childhoods ... "What I would give to smell the chicken roasting in the oven for Shabat dinner," Ruth dreamed, "and the noodle pudding was so rich. Sometimes, for tea, my grandmother made linzer torte. I can still taste the raspberry jam."'

During the freezing winter of 1940–41 many of the children fell ill with hepatitis, scabies and boils (Betty Bloom remembered her sister's legs being covered with the things). Elka Frank, who had accompanied her charges on the train journey south, tried to treat the girls' open sores with yoghurt from local farmers and managed to get hold of a small supply of gasoline which she combed through their hair to control their lice.

Life only really looked up when the Swiss Red Cross was persuaded to take on financial responsibility for the children. The organization's director in Toulouse was a rather dashing figure called Maurice Dubois who drove a red Bugatti open-topped sports car and had a penchant for natty suits with knickerbockers; he and his wife scoured the area for more suitable accommodation, and in early 1941 they settled on an empty castle in the Ariège department. The Château de la Hille was to be home for many of these orphans of war for nearly four years.

Château-building aristocrats in this part of France did not bother with the fussy ornamentation that you find in the grand palaces of smarter regions like the Loire Valley – Ariège is poor, and life here has always been rough. The Château de la Hille is an old-fashioned, no-nonsense castle, built at the end of the sixteenth century in the immediate aftermath of the feuding wars between the counts of Foix and Toulouse. It is very obviously designed to keep out enemies and the elements.

When the Swiss Red Cross took the building on in 1941 it had been empty for twenty years – all the furniture had been locked into the chapel, and there was no plumbing or sanitation. Some of the older children were sent ahead to make the place habitable. The teenage boys built a water cistern and knocked up tables, benches and beds, while the girls sewed sleeping bags and bedding. It was high summer before the château was ready for the general move.

Inge Joseph, who had stayed on at Seyre to help look after the younger children, recorded her first impression of their new home: '... it was about 3 p.m. when we began the two-hour walk from the train station to the castle ... Suddenly, like a glow emanating from some roadside woods, the castle appeared. It was truly an old medieval fortress, naturally a pale tan, but nearly yellow in the sun, and surrounded by a high stone wall. It had the remnants of a drawbridge and a tower neatly constructed at each of the four corners of the building.

'From just across the road, we could hear the cascading waters of a hillside brook, and the smell of pine and willow trees perfumed the air. As we walked up the long lane, leading from the road to the château, the castle seemed to grow majestically, making me feel very small and human. I felt I was not the only member of our ragged group who was wondering how long it would be before we met our fairy-godmother and prince charming.'

The château offered a sense of security and belonging after a year of being buffeted across Europe by the hurricane of war, and most of the children very quickly took to the somewhat wild, Hogwarts-like life they could enjoy there. Reading and listening to accounts of their time at the château reminded me of the years I spent boarding at an old-fashioned and eccentric Sussex prep school in the 1960s. The children ate either in the castle ballroom – complete with parquet floor and chandeliers – or, in warmer weather, at trestle tables in the courtyard. They slept in dormitories, and during the summer months there was a bell at 7 a.m. summoning everyone to group exercises. The field along-side the château was used for football matches and tug-of-war competitions.

There were around a hundred children, ranging in age from six to seventeen. With minimal adult supervision they formed a kind of self-organizing extended family – 'an idyllic self-contained village', Inge Joseph called it. Betty wrote that 'in spite of all the hardship the spirit of comradeship, morale and self-discipline in the château was exceptionally high'. The children gathered firewood from the surrounding forests and tended the vegetable garden. They were divided by age into three groups, Les Grands, Les Moyens and Les Mickeys. The older children looked after the younger ones and gave them what education they could – Ruth remembered teaching multiplication.

Sebastian Steiger, a Swiss Red Cross teacher who joined the staff there later in the war, described it as a place of enchantment, a fairytale castle with its towers and battlements and windows that you could never quite count. The day he arrived, the courtyard echoed with the joyful shouts of children. (He went back years later and found that without this music it was a miserable place, with 'dead windows and cold walls'.) He climbed on to the piano stool in the salon to look out of a window (Betty Bloom remembered the piano as an 'unimaginable luxury') and was bowled over by the view of the Pyrenean peaks 'so cleanly drawn against the sky'.

Next to a ruined building known as the Moulin Neuf, a short hike from the castle, the Lèze, which in the summer months is a lovely, languorous river, pools into a lake where the children could escape the southern heat. Betty Bloom learnt to swim there. Nature is generous in this region of France: if you drive through it in high summer today you will see fruit trees groaning with unpicked apples and pears. In July 1942 one of the château children, seventeen-year-old Edith Goldapper, wrote in her diary, 'It's the harvest time for fruit; the avenue of cherry trees entices us and we go down in relays all day. What a delight it is to lie in the grass eating cherries fresh from the trees!'

They must have missed their parents. Steiger had to deal with an outbreak of serial bed-wetting among the youngest children, and teenagers like Ruth and Inge worried about the other members of their families, especially those who had not managed to escape from Germany. But most of the photographs which have survived show happy, energetic boys and girls with healthy-looking suntans. 'The sheer beauty of the place nearly always stirred at least some positive energy in me,' Inge wrote, 'even during the worst moments. Walking around and through it, I imagine myself a medieval baroness. Viewing the surrounding countryside with its rolling hills and splendid forests and farm-land was like looking over Van Gogh's shoulder.'

There was even time for romance – although of a very chaste kind. Inge fell in love with a young man called Walter Strauss, and on her sixteenth birthday, 19 September 1941, he presented her with a four-colour pencil, a wooden pencil case he had made him-self, and a photograph inscribed 'To Inge, with much fondness, Yours Walter'. Writing many years later she described it as the happiest day of her life; 'no other day since has come close to the sense of total joy and fulfilment that I felt . . . as I slowly, very slowly opened the white tissue paper wrapping and fingered the special gift'.

Steiger was put in charge of Les Moyens, children aged from ten to fourteen, who were especially rowdy. They ran him ragged until he discovered an abandoned dump-truck on rails hidden beneath a pile of debris in the grounds; he put his charges to work digging it out, and when they had repaired the rails they enjoyed propelling themselves down a short slope at high speeds.

There were expeditions to the local sights. Betty Bloom remembered an excursion to the great cave of Le Mas d'Azil, still a favoured destination for schoolchildren today. Steiger took Les Moyens on a hike to an abandoned monastery and they discovered an underground monastic burial ground, a catacomb-like cellar stacked with coffins. Some of them had broken open, revealing the skeletons within, and when a flight of bats brushed the children's heads they all fled. 'That was fantastic,' said one thirteen-year-old as they relaxed under a chestnut tree later; 'the dead were terrifying.'

It is a great tribute to those who looked after the château that the teenagers were able to enjoy that childish pleasure in a frisson of fear. For most children the fun of fear lies partly in the way it reinforces the sense of security that underpins their lives. These children were living precariously, and had very good and real reasons to feel threatened themselves. In his memoir of his time at the château, Sebastian Steiger reflected on how odd it was to be living out this gentle idyll in the shadow of war; he and the other staff would tune into the BBC in the evenings for news of the fighting, but their days passed in the settled, hazy peace you can still find in what the French are pleased to call *la France profonde*.

On 26 August 1942 the reality of the war came to the château with a vengeance. The gendarmes turned up in the small hours of the morning here, just as they did at the nearby mountain resort of Aulus-les-Bains; as part of the general round-up of foreign Jews that day, all the boys and girls over fifteen at the château were to be taken to Le Vernet for deportation. The group were told to gather in the dining hall before leaving, and Inge Joseph recalled that it was where Walter Strauss had given her sixteenth birthday present to her. 'My seventeenth birthday was only three weeks away. My mind churned along with my stomach. People in concentration camps often died. How did it happen? Did they starve? Were they beaten? Or shot?' Some forty teenagers were piled into trucks in the castle courtyard and taken away.

Mademoiselle Rosli Naef, the Swiss director at the château, was not always popular with the children. She had spent several years working at Lambaréné, the missionary health centre in

Congo founded by the celebrated theologian and Nobel Prize winner Albert Schweitzer, and she was intolerant of weakness. She apparently regarded most illnesses (including, in one instance, a case of tuberculosis) as malingering. When one of the girls began menstruating and anxiously asked Mlle Naef about it she was told to use toilet paper and not let it interfere with her chores. The director could also be a somewhat distant figure; Edith Goldapper recorded in her journal that Mlle Naef refused to appear in public on her birthday, ruining the children's plans to surprise her with presents and a specially written poem.

But she was definitely the sort of woman you needed in a crisis. As soon as the police had left she went to the post office in Montégut to telephone Maurice Dubois, the senior Red Cross representative based in Toulouse, and furnished him with a full list of those who had been taken. The following day she pitched up at Le Vernet and managed to talk her way in to confront the camp commander – no small feat itself, and a testament to her remarkable force of will. The commander allowed her to stay in a hut reserved for the French Red Cross. Her presence alone was some comfort to the children; Edith recorded that 'we wouldn't leave her alone for a second . . . she gave us a sense of being safe'.

Maurice Dubois's reaction later earned him recognition as a Righteous Gentile at Yad Vashem, the holocaust memorial in Israel. He immediately took a train to Vichy, and, through the good offices of the Swiss embassy, secured an interview with a senior official in the Ministry of the Interior. He reminded the Vichy bureaucrat that the Swiss Red Cross had arranged for some three thousand French children to be looked after by families in Switzerland, and informed him that their future had been put in doubt by the action of the French police at the Château de la Hille. Confronted with this threat (which M. Dubois probably did not, strictly speaking, have the power to make) the Vichy official caved in, and sent an order to Le Vernet for the release of the children.

When the order came through they were packing their bags for the transport north to Drancy, where they would probably have spent a couple of days before being sent on to Auschwitz, where the gas chambers had begun operating in May that year. Rosli Naef appeared in their barracks and told them to leave their suitcases and to help the other deportees pack their clothes. They watched the others leave for the train (Edith noted that 'the poor things managed to rejoice in our liberation, even though their own future was so uncertain'). The children gave all the food they had to the deportees; they were anyway too strung out to eat themselves. Inge Joseph recorded a slightly different version of these events but she included a striking image of Rosli Naef which rings very true: as the doors of the cattle trucks taking the deportees north were slammed shut, 'I saw Rosli walk out to the train, moving as if in slow motion from car to car, collecting cards, letters and packages, presumably to be sent on to relatives.'

That evening one of their Swiss teachers (a M. Lyrer, who was remembered with great affection by all those who recorded their time at the château) arrived with some jam from the orchards at La Hille. One of the group, Kurt Moser (who would later be arrested in the Pyrenees while trying to escape into Spain), played the harmonica to celebrate their freedom. The following morning, after giving a pot of jam to the woman in charge of their barracks, they left Le Vernet. They were put on a train and the Montégut grocer picked them up from the station. The younger children ran up the road to greet them.

Les Grands had spent only four days at Le Vernet, but the experience – such a rapid transition from a kind of paradise to hell, and then back again – had marked them, and it hung like a shadow over life at the château. Ruth's main memory of the camp was the humiliation of the open latrines. The local farmers would leave huge quantities of damaged or overripe fruit at the camp, and it was the closest the detainees came to fresh food; as a result many of them suffered from diarrhoea. 'For a young girl . . .' Ruth said, and let the thought trail off. Edith wrote that 'I never got used to life at the château again. I had been changed.'

The German occupation of the whole of France in November 1942 meant that the children were again at risk. The château was an ideal setting for games of hide-and-seek; now the game was played in deadly earnest. The children found a loft above the chapel which had been used to store onions; it was windowless, so no one looking at the building from the outside would know it was there, and it opened on to M. Lyrer's panelled bedroom. The boys camouflaged the entrance by adding an extra section of panelling, and it proved an effective bolt-hole. The older children slept there at night (undeterred by the lingering smell of onions and a few mice) and during the day Les Mickeys were recruited as lookouts. Steiger was at the château when the gendarmes turned up with a list of four teenagers they wanted to arrest; they had to leave without finding any of them. The lookouts spotted the police watching the buildings from the woods that evening, and Les Grands stayed hidden until the all-clear was given the following day.

Some of the older teenagers began to leave, and after the shock of the Le Vernet incident the Red Cross officials were happy to help and encourage them. Ruth was one of the first to go. On New Year's Eve 1942 she and a friend headed to Lyons, where M. Lyrer had given them the name of a priest who could supply them with false papers. Their contact had been arrested by the time they got there, and they moved on to Annecy (which is just on the French side of the border near Geneva) in the hope of crossing into Switzerland. However, the Swiss had sealed the borders and were sending back refugees over sixteen. They gave up and moved again, this time to Grenoble, which at this stage of the war was under Italian occupation, and had become something of a magnet for Jewish refugees because of the more tolerant Italian attitude towards Jews. Ruth eventually managed to make contact with a Zionist youth movement called the MJS, which was dedicated to rescuing Jewish children, and she went underground, living under a false identity.

Ruth's friend Inge Joseph also left over that Christmas period, following an escape plan conceived by Rosli Naef. Inge was acutely conscious of how close the château was to the Spanish border ('From rooms on the second floor,' she wrote, 'we could sometimes make out the Pyrenees dividing us from Spain and, as would become ever more apparent, separating us from freedom') but Mlle Naef wanted her to head in the other direction – towards the Alps and her own native Switzerland. The director put together a party of five – including Inge and her boyfriend Walter Strauss – and arranged for them to be fielded by the Swiss Red Cross team at Annemasse, just across the border from Geneva.

The five teenagers travelled by train across southern France, and found their way to the Swiss Red Cross home in Annemasse without too much difficulty. But their attempt to cross the border went dreadfully wrong. The guide they had been given abandoned them before they reached the crossing point – it was snowing, and he was worried about leaving tracks – and they got lost. Walter Strauss went ahead to scout the ground and was picked up by the French police. (It later turned out that they had managed to cross into Switzerland and then back into France.)

When Walter failed to return the remaining members of the group decided – after some debate – to follow in his footsteps. They spotted some lights and followed them to a house. Feeling wet and miserable in the snow (they were, after all, only teenagers) they decided to knock on the door. The building was occupied by German soldiers, and all four of them were taken into custody. Three members of the party broke down relatively quickly and admitted who they were and where they had come from, but Inge spoke good French and refused to abandon her cover story: she was, she insisted, a local Swiss girl who lived on the road between Geneva and Lausanne, and she had got lost in the woods. She was interrogated several times and then threatened with execution.

Inge was clearly someone of great resource and courage. When she was allowed to use the lavatory she spotted an open window and jumped out into the snow. She somehow made her way back to the Swiss Red Cross building in Annemasse, and the director gave her another guide who succeeded in getting her over the border the following day. But she was caught by the Swiss police and sent back to France, where she was promptly arrested again. She and Walter were reprimanded by a French court and sent back to the Château de la Hille. Nothing was heard of the remaining three members of the party until much later; they had in fact been deported and died in the camps.

The episode left Inge with a terrible sense of guilt, and there was worse to come. Not long after Walter's eighteenth birthday, in February 1943, the police called for him at the château. He was taken to another French concentration camp called Gurs (the biggest of them, at the Atlantic end of the Pyrenees) and later deported. He died in Auschwitz. Inge herself was sent to live under an alias with a French family and was the only one of the five who survived into adulthood.

There were other disasters. Another group (including Klaus Moser, the young man who played the harmonica to cheer everyone up at Le Vernet) were betrayed by a guide while trying to cross the Spanish border in the Pyrenees and deported. In all, twelve of the children of the Château de la Hille were sent to the camps, and only one of those survived the war. Those are grim statistics (and every death and deportation was keenly felt by other members of the château 'family'), but given the circumstances in which the children were living the total is really remarkably small. Another twelve of Les Grands left the château to join the Resistance, and one of them was killed in combat.

Ruth's work for the MJS involved acting as a courier taking very young children to the Swiss border. In September 1943 she sent a note to M. Lyrer asking him to bring Betty to Annecy. The two girls spent an afternoon by the lake eating ice creams and enjoying the sun, and Ruth placed her younger sister in the care of a young family and a guide who had been paid to smuggle them all across the border. Betty spent several tough months in Swiss internment camps near Geneva, and wrote later that 'what upset me most of all was that, contrary to La Hille, there was no co-operation between the detainees. No one bothered about the children like myself, not even the family I had crossed the border with, with no schooling or medical attention.'

Ruth's own departure was prompted by a coup of real daring. The MJS discovered that a Jewish couple had hidden their baby in an orphanage just before being arrested and deported. The Germans got to hear about it too, but before they could pick up the child Ruth disguised herself as a German officer, showed up at the orphanage and demanded to be given the child. She then took the baby to a safe house where she was hidden; Corinne, as she was called, survived the war and is now living near Tel Aviv – as Ruth told me with justifiable pride.

After this adventure the MJS decided that France had become too dangerous for Ruth. She took a train to Carcassonne (passing not far from the Château de la Hille), and another on to Quillan, and from there was escorted into the Pyrenees. Her route took her to Andorra and ran slightly to the east of today's Chemin de la Liberté, but it covered very similar high-mountain terrain. The journey took several days, and she can remember that after the food ran out the group was given sugar lumps and mountain water to get through the final stages.

They slept during the days and walked at night, and she remembered above all the total blackness of the nights; even today there are large areas of the mountains where you see no electric light at all after sunset, and Ruth was struck by the strangeness of being in such vast unpopulated spaces in the middle of Europe. Her memory of the journey had acquired an almost dreamlike quality by the time I interviewed her. But then the whole of the Château de la Hille story is a little like a dream – amid so many nightmares.

Today the Château de la Hille is an upmarket B&B, offering well-appointed rooms for tourists and a range of facilities for weddings and parties. Its website promises 'relaxation, rest, charm and comfort', and potential clients are enticed with the promise that there is 'a golf course within fifteen minutes' drive'.

7

Belgians, Bravery and Betrayal

Nadine

SINCE I TURNED FIFTY I have developed a distressing tendency towards mulishness. I think I was a reasonably biddable child, and it is as if I am making up for that by being a decidedly stubborn middle-aged man. My episodes of grumpy contrariness are usually provoked by officialdom thinking it knows what is best for me.

A fitness check before setting off on the Chemin seemed

perfectly sensible – it is a tough walk and it is quite right that the BBC should feel responsible for the physical well-being of those who work for it. But when people lectured me on what I should wear I began to dig my heels in. I was questioned closely about my 'sock policy'. One layer or two? Fabric? Texture? Weight? Synthetic fibre or natural wool? Then my email account was deluged with websites offering all sorts of super-light, hideously coloured and very synthetic 'technical' vests and underpants. I responded airily (and, I admit, somewhat mischievously) that the plus-fours and long woollen stockings I wear when shooting pheasants would do fine. This was not thought to be amusing.

In the end I did compromise a little; a very light waterproof jacket that could be folded away almost as discreetly as one of Clutty's silk maps seemed a worthwhile investment. But the vests and underpants were non-negotiable, and I am happy to report (for the benefit of any reader with fogey-ish tastes who may be contemplating the walk) that a pair of moleskin plus-fours and a soft cashmere sweater are the ideal kit for enjoying the cool of the evening in the high mountains.

So what a delight it was to spot Bernard Holvoet's ensemble on the St Girons bridge on that first rainy July morning of the Chemin. Bernard is a regular on the walk, and with his cape, his fedora hat and his steel-rimmed spectacles, he stood out sublimely from the clashing cacophony of 'high-vis' jackets. Indeed he looked as if he had stepped from a time before such colours were even invented; he would have been much more comfortable in a grainy black and white photograph of pre-war winter sports enthusiasts. Bernard was regarded with admiration and affection by the Chemin regulars, and stories of his benign eccentricities and considerable intellectual accomplishments circulated in hushed tones; it was said that he had never cooked a meal because his oven was full of books.

In another flamboyant rebuke to the modern health and safety culture, Bernard's habit was to sustain himself through the trek with a diet of fine Belgian chocolates and cigarettes. During the previous year's Chemin he had run out of chocolate early on, and ordered a resupply from the *chocolatière* in St Girons; it was delivered to the lunch stop at the Col de la Core, more than four and a half thousand feet above sea level.

The year I did the walk the cigarettes took their toll: Bernard conked out on the afternoon of Day Three, and was found lying on his back on the mountainside, observing that he had always wondered where he would die. I felt pretty rough that afternoon too, but Bernard's heart rate had shot up to a shocking level, and the next morning we had to leave him behind at the Refuge des Estagnous. The guide in charge of our group told me – rather dismissively, I thought – that Bernard had had a *crise de foie*, a crisis of the liver, that brilliantly sweeping – but medically meaningless – French term for overdoing things a bit. I am happy to report that after a couple of days of recuperation he was able to make his way off the mountain.

Bernard Holvoet's interest in escape routes was inspired by his grandfather, a Belgian count called Jacques le Grelle (or 'Jérôme', to give him his code name), who in 1943 played a key role in MI9's efforts to repair the Comet Line after it had been infiltrated. Bernard first did the shorter commemorative walk known as the Randonnée Comète au Pays Basque, or Comet Line Hike in the Basque Country, which traces Dédée de Jongh's favoured route to Spain at the western end of the Pyrenees. Through that he came to know the team who run the Chemin. He said he regarded the other regulars as a 'big family', and that the annual Chemin was one of the high points of his calendar.

Bernard said that when he laid a wreath in his grandfather's honour he always asked himself, 'What would I have done?' The question of how one would have responded to the choices that confronted those who worked on the escape lines inevitably comes into your mind when you walk the Chemin. For Brits it is slightly queasy-making, because we were never tested by the experience of occupation. For Bernard the question was especially acute because – as we shall see – his grandfather made the brave decision when the likely consequences were all too apparent.

Bernard is a fervent Anglophile. 'What brings me here,' he explained, 'is those who flew for our freedom when the rest of the world had given up.' He said that whenever he went to a commemoration the British veterans 'always say how grateful they are for those who risked their lives and their families' to help them escape. But Bernard takes the view that gratitude should flow in the other direction; that for people like his grandfather 'their lives were all they had to give' as a way of thanking Britain (and especially its aircrews) for fighting on.

Today we have largely lost any sense of a close bond between Belgium and Britain – partly, perhaps, because of our prejudice against those 'Brussels bureaucrats' who, if you read the British tabloids, you might think make up the whole Belgian population. But the relationship loomed very large indeed in the lives of both nations through the world wars.

It was of course Germany's violation of Belgium's neutrality that formally brought Britain into the First World War (Britain was bound to protect Belgian neutrality under a treaty of 1839), and because of its position across the Channel British governments have always viewed the country as strategically important. Belgium's military performance in the early days of the Great War earned it widespread admiration in Britain. Its tiny army managed to hold up the German advance for nearly a month, giving Britain and France a critical breathing space. Popular feelings were summed up by Asquith, the prime minister, in the House of

Commons. 'The Belgians have won for themselves the immortal glory which belongs to a people who prefer freedom to ease, to security, to life itself. We are proud of their alliance and their friendship. We salute them with respect and honour. We are with them heart and soul, because, by their side and in their company, we are defending at the same time two great causes – the independence of small States and the sanctity of international covenants.' Britain gave sanctuary to some 200,000 Belgians during the years of the Great War.

The British reaction to Belgium's performance in the Second World War was rather different. Many people took a harsh view of the fact that Belgium had sought to escape conflict altogether by returning to neutrality on the outbreak of hostilities in 1939, and an even harsher view of the speed with which the country capitulated to the Germans in May 1940. There was a small fascist party called the Rexists which actually welcomed the arrival of the Nazis, and so too did the Flemish national party known as the VNV. The Belgian MP and prominent anti-Nazi activist Roger Motz, in a pamphlet published in London towards the end of the war, conceded that in the aftermath of defeat Belgium had had some difficult questions to answer. 'Had she offered only formal resistance to the Nazis? Had she brought about the encirclement and subsequent annihilation of the French armies of the North and of the British Expeditionary Force by appealing for help too late? Had the King of the Belgians warned his Allies that he would be forced to sue for an armistice? Were the Belgian authorities not responsible for the confusion on the roads along which endless streams of refugees greatly hampered the progress of the Allied armies? Had not members of the fifth column in Flanders shot British soldiers in the back?' And so the list went on.

The number of Belgian refugees who reached Britain during the Second World War was much smaller than the number who came during the First – partly because the speed of the German victory limited the opportunity for escape across the Channel, and partly because the Vichy regime agreed to stop Belgian refugees in France leaving for Britain as part of the Armistice agreement with Germany. But at eighteen thousand the number was still significant, and there were more Belgians in Britain than anywhere else in the 'free world' apart from the Belgian Congo. Many of the new arrivals were desperately keen to join the war effort, inspired by determination to free their country and restore its reputation. In August 1940 Churchill formally declared Belgium a British ally, along with two other countries which had also declared neutrality but found themselves under German occupation, Holland and Norway. In October a Belgian government-in-exile set up shop in Belgravia's Eaton Square.

Roger Motz was appointed minister of information in the Eaton Square government and in 1942 he published a pamphlet called *Belgium Unvanquished*. Printed on wafer-thin 'economy standard' wartime paper, it is an evocative physical artefact as well as offering an intriguing insight into the mindset of the time. *Belgium Unvanquished* is a piece of propaganda designed to cement the alliance between Belgium and Britain by playing to popular feeling on both sides.

In an appendix called 'Making Fun of the Germans' it includes an anecdote which is bound to touch anyone who, like me, is inclined to sentimentality about the BBC. Motz estimates that 98 per cent of the Belgian population listened to BBC broadcasts from London during the war, and he goes on: 'A German officer asked a Belgian the time. The Belgian pretended not to under-stand; a little girl was passing and shouted to him, "It's a quarter past seven." The officer, very intrigued at finding that this little girl could tell the time without looking at a watch, said to her, "Little girl, how do you know it's quarter past seven?" and the kid replied,

"Don't you see that there's nobody in the streets? This is the time for the broadcast from London. Everybody is at home."'

But the real heroes of the book are the RAF, not the BBC. Motz makes great play of Belgian enthusiasm for bombing raids, and repeatedly stresses the way the air war gave Belgians an opportunity to register their resistance to occupation. 'Recently six airmen met their death in the course of an engagement in which four German planes were brought down near Wavre,' he wrote. 'In spite of German orders to the contrary, an immense crowd attended the funeral service for the British victims. Masses of flowers came from all parts, and on the graves a cross bearing this daring inscription was placed: "In gratitude to those who have given their lives for our liberation". A little later another plane was brought down by anti-aircraft guns near Gembloux. All members of the crew were killed. On the day they were buried all the shops were shut and the crowd pressed closely behind the students of the Agricultural Institute who were lining the streets. Behind the coffins of the airmen a large crown was carried; on it was a ribbon bearing the inscription "to our heroes". Very often these demonstrations of pity exasperate the Germans, who fire blank cartridges into the crowd . . .'

The American journalist William Shirer painted a similar picture of Belgian feelings in a report from Ostend at the height of the Battle of Britain. Shirer was asked by the owner of his hotel to share a bottle of wine with the family. 'Some local Belgians joined us,' he recorded, 'and we had a good talk. It was touching how the Belgians kept hoping the British bombers would come over. They did not seem to mind if the RAF bumped them off if only the RAF got the Germans too.'

José de la Barre, a young underground operative who fled Belgium when her intelligence network was blown, added her own colourful flourishes to the picture when she arrived in

London in early 1943. In a powerful interview with the United Press about life under the Occupation she described her compatriots listening out for the sound of 'the RAF roaring through to bomb German towns' at night. 'Many Belgians,' she said, 'lie awake and feel joy in their hearts, while their gaolers trembled.' She also recalled being on a train when it was buzzed by a British plane: 'as one, all the Germans rushed out and flew for nearby shelter . . . but . . . nearly all the Belgians waved frantically to the RAF airmen, who, seeing so many civilians, waved back and passed on. In the joy, no one thought that a bomb might drop.'

José de la Barre must have cut a glamorous figure on her arrival in London – she was young, aristocratic and attractive – and she noted in the book she published about her experiences much later in life that the interview received 'wide coverage'. Her message no doubt made her very popular with her hosts. 'Since 1940,' she declared, 'men, young and old, of every occupied country, have tried to get across Europe to reach a land of freedom. Women have also tried, and I am one of the lucky ones among them who have had the joy to get safely to England. I have just arrived after two and a half years under Nazi rule and every day I feel the joy of being free – but sometimes I am still astonished when I find that I can speak my mind without having to glance around me, without the fear of the Gestapo.' It was not a bad manifesto for the ideals the Chemin de la Liberté celebrates and the escape line movement as a whole. (José de la Barre's own journey across the Pyrenees was particularly tough, of which more later.)

From an early stage, providing help for evading and escaping servicemen was very closely associated in the public imaginations of both countries (and indeed in reality) with the ideal of self-sacrifice. *Belgium Unvanquished* includes the following passage:

'On 7th April, 1941, a German council of war in session at the Brussels Palais de Justice sentenced thirteen Belgians to various punishments for sheltering British soldiers. One man, M. Edgard Lefebvre, and one woman, received the death penalty; sentences ranging from one to eight years' imprisonment were inflicted on the other accused people. As soon as this was known in England, Mr Arthur Francis Ayeling, British Chargé d'Affaires with the Belgian government in England, paid a visit to M. Pierlot, the prime minister, and conveyed to him on behalf of the British people and Government feelings of profound gratitude for the courageous behaviour of the Belgian patriots. The English newspaper *The Times* wrote in this connection, "This example of devotion recalls the numerous deeds of courage and self-denial performed by the Belgian population during the last war."' Roger Motz's pamphlet ends with an appendix listing fifty-eight people who had been executed in Belgium between August 1941 and January 1942 and he adds, 'One will notice the frequency with which the death penalty is inflicted on those who helped British airmen.'

That background may help explain the quite extraordinary courage displayed by those who worked on the Comet Line and helped escapers and evaders in general. Resistance in Belgium of course took other forms as well; José de la Barre, for example, was involved in gathering intelligence about airfields and coastal defences, and groups like the MNB (Mouvement National Belge) and the Liège-based AL (Armée de la Libération) distributed underground newspapers and ran sabotage campaigns. But this heavily populated and highly industrialized country had very little of the sort of wild landscape which offered such rich opportunities to the French *maquis*. Helping Allied airmen, however, was a task almost everyone could contribute to, and in northern Europe the RAF was for a long time the only visible sign of defiance against the

Germans. The sort of work the Comet Line did went to the heart of the Belgian understanding of resistance to the Occupation.

And the sense that Comet was animated by a particular spirit of mission, comradeship and self-sacrifice runs through much of the literature that has been generated by its story. In a Comet Line history written in 1947, while the passions of the war were still very much alive, Cécile Jouan speculated on the motives of those involved: 'We who lived it, this adventure in forbidden territory, we shall never forget it,' she wrote. 'Was it a taste for danger that drove us on? There was plenty of that. But what was at the heart of it? A malicious delight in irritating the occupier? That was part of it too, of course, but only a little. Above all it was the joy, the thrill of feeling useful, the camaraderie of battle and the exaltation of this unforeseen conflict, in which all our weapons were born of love.' 'Don't thank us,' the Cyclone (Dédée de Jongh) would say later, 'we who had the joy of battle without being forced into it by the call of duty.' One of her comrades wrote, 'It wasn't hatred that kept us together. Of course we loathed the occupier, but the great driving force behind what we did was . . . yes, it really can be said like this, a love of our own and the joy of saving others.' M. R. D. Foot, in a survey of the Resistance written thirty years later, evoked the memory of the First World War British nurse who was such a source of inspiration to the de Jongh family; Comet, he wrote, 'carried on Edith Cavell's tradition of 1914–15 with glorious devotion'. The Comet Line volunteers were twentieth-century Cavaliers in their flair and passion.

The number of people involved in the line's work was huge. After the war one of those who ran the Brussels end of the operation told Rémy (the French Resistance hero who wrote an early history of Comet) that he aimed to have some sort of contact in every village in the country – so that, for example, any local doctor would know whom to alert if he was asked to treat a wounded Allied airman. Many of these helpers would not have thought of themselves as being part of any formal structure – and indeed the name 'Comet' did not emerge until quite late on in its life. I have focused on the fate of a few of the best-known and most senior members of the line to illustrate the qualities that made it so resilient; every time an individual or group was arrested or killed others came forward to fill their places.

If reading the succession of sad stories that unfold over the next few pages feels a little like being hit repeatedly with a hammer, my apologies; the German pressure on the line was relentless.

Andrée Dumon (code-named 'Nadine' to avoid confusion with Andrée de Jongh), the young Comet Line escort who was given such a scare over her papers while taking a group of airmen to Paris, has a special place on this honour roll because she was one of the earliest members of the line to be captured, and spent longer than most in the hands of the Nazis. She also outlived most of her comrades and gave an interview for our BBC series in 2011.

Nadine was betrayed by a member of another underground group in August 1942, a man who had visited her house a couple of times. Her father was picked up with her at their home. She tried to escape from the kitchen through the back door while her father attempted a getaway over the roof, but the house was surrounded by German soldiers and both were taken into custody.

Nadine was just shy of her twentieth birthday when she was caught, and her capacity to resist and survive can only make one feel humble. She was initially sustained by the confidence – misplaced, as she later discovered – that the Germans would not kill a woman, and for the first two days of interrogation she refused to say anything of substance at all. She was then confronted by the man who had betrayed her, and seventy years later she could still vividly recall the courtesy with which the Germans treated him, offering him a chair and a cigar as she was brought into the room, and his cringing subservience in return. He confirmed her identity but she continued to deny everything.

Her interrogation – with beatings and threats of execution – continued for several weeks. She remembered that it lasted until at least late September because of the pear tree outside the window of the interrogation room; one early autumn morning when the pears were ripe she interrupted her interrogator's threats to remark lightly on how delicious they looked through the open window, which of course enraged him. Nadine said she was helped by a confidence that 'the war will last a very long time, but we will win'. Eventually her Gestapo interrogators gave up.

Nadine Dumon spent a year in St Gilles prison outside Brussels before disappearing into what was known as *Nacht und Nebel*, or Night and Fog. The phrase – a reference to a Wagnerian spell – was designed to be terrifying; those who were shipped off to Germany under the programme simply disappeared from the records, and their relatives were denied any information about where they had gone or what had happened to them.

There was a moment of great happiness on the first leg of the journey: Nadine's father – whom she had not seen since the day of her arrest – was moved east on the same transport, and a kind German soldier allowed them to travel together for some of the way. They were separated at Cologne and briefly reunited at Essen; when Nadine spotted him in a line of male prisoners she held back from kissing him because she calculated that by avoiding undue attention she would have a better chance of being able to get close to him in the future. But they were separated again and that was the last time she saw him (Eugène Dumon died in the Gross-Rosen concentration camp in 1945).

Nadine was moved between several prisons and camps – including a castle in Poland, where she made an unsuccessful

escape attempt. After that she was sent to the women's concentration camp of Ravensbrück and finally to Mauthausen in
Austria, a camp for 'Incorrigible Political Enemies of the Reich'
which operated on the principle known as 'extermination through
labour'.

The journey from Ravensbrück to Mauthausen took four days
in cattle trucks without food or water. They arrived at five in the
morning and the train stopped in fields some way from the camp.
Nadine, who had prided herself on being *'sportive'* (she had been
a keen basketball player and gymnast at school), was so weak by
this stage that she crushed her joints when she jumped out of the
truck. She knew that if she lay on the ground she would be shot,
and she somehow managed to get to her feet.

It was a moonlit night, the ground and the pine trees covered
with snow. When she described the scene seven decades later she
could still conjure up the brightness of the stars and the silver of
the river Danube. Walking was heavy work in the drifts and she
lost her breath. The temptation to give up became almost overwhelming. She was intoxicated by the beauty around her, and that
somehow lured her towards the release of death; 'I'll lie down and
they'll shoot me and it will be finished,' she thought. But then she
'heard a voice' telling her mother how she had died, and it stirred
her on. 'They *cannot* say that to my mother,' she said to herself, 'it
cannot happen.' With the help of two friends she made it to the
camp.

The new arrivals had to wait for three hours in the snow
before the camp woke up. They were stripped and checked for
lice, and Nadine was so obviously ill that the German guards
painted her with two huge red 'K's, one on her front and one on
her back, to indicate that she was *krank*, or sick. A French prisoner
warned her that the marks were a sure and swift passport to
death, and together the two of them managed to scrub them off.

Nadine was still alive when Mauthausen was liberated in May 1945, more than two and a half years after her arrest. For many years she was unable to speak about her experiences in the camps, but at the time of her interview for our BBC series she had begun to give talks to schoolchildren. Nearly ninety, she continued to be troubled by an arresting dilemma: as a member of the Resistance, she had always told those above her that she could never kill . . . and yet she had taken such huge risks to return airmen to Britain so that they could kill again. She is a tiny woman, and watching her standing stiffly to attention at a ceremony organized by the Escape Lines Memorial Society I marvelled that such a slight frame could endure so much.

The Gestapo officers who questioned Nadine often focused on what she could tell them about Frédéric de Jongh. By this stage Dédée de Jongh had in fact already moved her father south to take control of the operation in Paris, fearing for his safety in Brussels because of a brush with the Gestapo earlier in the year. He left in the nick of time; the two men who took over the Brussels operation – Charles Morelle and Henri Michelli – were arrested within six days of his departure. Both were deported to Germany; Michelli survived the war but Morelle died at Dachau on 18 May 1945, just after the liberation of the camp by the Americans.

The next to step into the breach in Brussels was Baron Jean Greindl, also known as 'Nemo', another of those figures who have been written about and remembered with a kind of awe. Airey Neave speculates that his code name was a reference to the commander of the *Nautilus* in the Jules Verne novel *20,000 Leagues Under the Sea*, and interprets his physical appearance in characteristic style: 'His firm nose and mouth suggested vigour and resolve. He had fine, humorous, grey-blue eyes. His long, sensitive hands suggested a sharp intellect.'

When the war broke out he was in his mid-thirties and had

spent much of his life running a coffee plantation in the Belgian Congo. In 1942 he took over the Cantine Suédoise, a soup kitchen for children run with the support of the Swedish Red Cross, under the patronage of a Swedish lady called Mme Scherlinck. The Cantine served as useful cover for his Comet work, and over the summer and autumn of 1942 he developed the Brussels operation energetically.

But in November that year the line was infiltrated by two German agents who turned up claiming to be American bomber pilots. They were taken to a safe house belonging to a family of Comet helpers called the Maréchals. The Maréchals were natural resisters; their marriage was a product of that close alliance between Belgium and Britain during the First World War. Georges, the father of the household, had served in the Belgian army and met his English wife, Elsie, while he was in London recovering from a bout of pneumonia, which he had picked up in the trenches in 1917. Together with their daughter, also called Elsie, and their son Robert they had looked after no fewer than fourteen airmen during the previous couple of months. But this time something felt different.

During lunch one of the 'Americans' aroused suspicion by asking to use the *Kabinett*, using the German word for the lavatory. When young Elsie asked them what sort of plane they had flown they replied that it had been a Halifax, which was of course a British rather than an American bomber. When she pressed them on the size of the aircrew they gave the answer 'Four' – the correct number was six. Mother and daughter discussed their suspicions while they did the washing up, and Madame Maréchal told her daughter to visit Nemo at the Cantine Suédoise to ask for advice on what to do.

Not long after young Elsie's departure the two 'Americans' turned a gun on her mother and revealed their true identities. The younger Elsie, meanwhile, had made contact with Nemo and was instructed to watch the two men carefully and report back. When she returned home she was immediately arrested too, as was her brother when he got home from school and her father when he got back from work. Nemo became concerned about the lack of news from the Maréchals and sent another helper, a young lawyer called Victor Michiels, to reconnoitre their home. According to Rémy, Nemo extracted a firm promise from Michiels that he would under no circumstances try to enter the building. But after half an hour of watching the young lawyer became impatient. The road was quiet and he could see no sign of surveillance, so he rang the doorbell. When the door opened Michiels found himself looking down the barrel of a German revolver; he made a run for it but was shot and killed in the street. The sting at the Maréchals' netted a good trawl for the Germans: over the next two days nearly a hundred people connected with the Comet Line were arrested. Nemo himself escaped the net.

And worse was to come. Comet was dealt an especially damaging blow by the arrest of its leader, Dédée de Jongh, the young woman who (as I have described in Chapter Two) had become such a powerful source of inspiration to those who worked on the line. It seems to have been the result of a simple act of betrayal by a local farmworker rather than a sophisticated Gestapo operation; the man was angry because Dédée suspected him of stealing from her rucksack on earlier trips, and had stopped using the farm where he worked as a resting place on her route over the mountains.

Stan Hope, the flight sergeant who had spent such a cheerful Christmas in Brussels with his friend Maurice and his family, was one of the three airmen Dédée escorted south on her final journey to the Pyrenees, in January 1943, a couple of months after the infiltration of the line in Belgium. She also took her father with her on that journey because she had become increasingly concerned about his safety in Paris, and had decided to send him to London. The group had a first-class compartment to themselves, and Stan recalled that Dédée and her father talked together for most of the way.

In Bayonne they left the station separately and the three airmen spent the night in different safe houses (courtesy of Tante Go's organization). The next day they took another train to St Jean-de-Luz, where they were greeted by a torrential downpour. The weather was so bad that Dédée was forced to accept that a man of her father's age simply could not hope to manage the arduous climb over the mountains, and Frédéric de Jongh was left behind with Tante Go.

Stan Hope and the two RAF men with him continued on the journey into the mountains, and that evening the guide Florentino joined them at the farmhouse near Urrugne which had served as Dédée's last French staging post for more than twenty missions (she had by this stage escorted nearly a hundred and twenty airmen to freedom). Florentino ruled that the rain had made the river Bidassoa impassable, and it was agreed that the party should delay its departure until the following day.

If I was writing an opera set in Occupied Europe, I would make the sound of heavy vehicles a leitmotif. It was so often the overture to disaster or tragedy. Stan Hope heard lorries on the road below the farmhouse at around midday on 15 January; he and his fellow RAF evaders had been playing with the children of the household and were eating their sandwiches upstairs in the expectation of a long, tough walk. He made a flip comment along the lines of 'Here come the Gestapo.'

It was in fact the German military police. They lined everyone up against a wall and told them they would be shot as saboteurs. One of the RAF men managed to produce his dog tags and their captors relented. They were marched down the mountain towards St Jean-de-Luz. Stan described it as a 'horrible experience'. 'To think I had got so close,' he said, 'I could practically see Spain, and then I was caught.'

The group were first imprisoned in Bayonne and then taken to Bordeaux. Stan told me he was beaten up, but not tortured. He was shown pictures of a Basque guide (presumably Florentino) and asked to confirm his identity, but he fended off the questions by saying 'They all look alike to me'. He said he 'respected' the officer from the Abwehr (German Military Intelligence) who questioned him during this period: 'I didn't like what he did to me, but he had a job to do and I don't think he enjoyed doing it.' After a couple of weeks in Bordeaux Stan was brought back to Bayonne, and he caught a glimpse of Dédée at the station; he was sporting a black eye as a result of the beatings and she gave him a thumbs-up to show solidarity. They were all put on a train to Fresnes prison, just outside Paris.

Stan Hope was kept in solitary confinement for some four months at Fresnes. The rations – mostly soup, bread and ersatz coffee – left him constantly hungry; 'You had a pain all the time,' he said. He found a piece of metal in his cell which he could use to scratch on the walls; he spent hours writing out menus, 'breakfast menus, dinner menus, supper menus, every kind of food you can think of'. His two forms of exercise were walking up and down the cell and killing the fleas which infested it.

From time to time he was taken to the Gestapo headquarters in the Avenue Foch in Paris and subjected to further interrogation about those who had helped him while he was on the run. His Gestapo interrogator frightened him badly ('A real horror,' Stan said to me during our interview, 'I hope they got him after the war'). Dressed in civilian clothes, he spoke English with an American accent, and constantly threatened Stan with torture. In the end, exhausted, frightened, weak and badly destabilized after so long in solitary confinement, Stan yielded some information about the family who had looked after him in Brussels.

Talking about the moment he broke distressed him greatly when I interviewed him; it is to his credit, and a mark of real courage, that he was able to confront the memory at all. He said that he wanted to kill himself afterwards, but could find nothing in his cell that would fit the purpose. His Brussels hosts were arrested, and Maurice, the young man with whom he had shared such happy times during his first days on the run, was deported to Germany and eventually shot. Maurice's body was later recovered and reburied in Brussels. Stan Hope showed me a treasured photograph of his grave.

Tante Go tried several times to spring Dédée de Jongh from prison before the Germans established her identity, but to no avail. Dédée does, however, appear to have been helped by the delicate appearance that had made it so difficult for her to persuade the British authorities to take her seriously when it all began; like the pipe-smoking British diplomat in Bilbao, her interrogators could not quite believe that such a slight young woman could be running such a complex and hazardous enterprise. After interrogation at several prisons in south-west France – including one called, appropriately, the Maison de Chagrin, or House of Sorrows – she was taken to Fresnes prison in Paris along with Stan Hope. He was eventually sent to a prisoner-of-war camp, while she disappeared into *Nacht und Nebel*, and, like her agent Nadine, did time at Ravensbrück and Mauthausen. Her astonishing toughness got her through, and she too survived to be released by the advancing Allies in April 1945. She went on to fulfil her most cherished childhood ambition, working for most of the rest of her life with the sick in the Belgian Congo, Cameroon, Ethiopia and Senegal. She died at the age of ninety in 2007, having been elevated to the rank of countess.

By the time of Dédée's arrest Nemo was looking for a replacement so that he could leave the line and escape to London himself, but he stayed in Brussels for just too long: three weeks after she was picked up in the Pyrenees the Gestapo called for him at the Cantine Suédoise. He was sentenced to death and kept imprisoned in the stables of an artillery barracks. In September 1943 he was killed when an American bomb hit the building during a raid on a nearby airfield – a horrible irony after all the risks he had taken to get Allied aircrews home. A fortnight after his death an order came through from Berlin for the execution of eight other members of the Cantine Suédoise operation – they were shot at the Brussels rifle range on 20 October 1943.

This grim roll call of arrest, interrogation, deportation and – often – death went on throughout 1943 and into 1944. Frédéric de Jongh was picked up in Paris in June 1943 as a result of the treachery of a particularly repulsive figure called Jean-Jacques Desoubrie, also known as Jean Masson.

Masson came into contact with the leaders of the Comet Line in the spring of 1943. He was working with the Resistance in northern France, and Frédéric de Jongh recruited him to help escort airmen on the Brussels–Paris leg of the journey south. Masson seemed remarkably adept at procuring the right passes, and on 15 May 1943 he successfully escorted a party of seven airmen to Paris, proving his credentials to the satisfaction of Frédéric and the other Comet regulars in the French capital.

Three weeks later Masson set up the sting operation which led to Frédéric's arrest. He arranged for as many of the key figures in the Paris network as possible to be at the Gare du Nord to meet the latest group of airmen he was escorting. Robert Aylé and his wife Germaine, who ran a safe house in the Rue de Babylone, were among those in the reception party. When the party arrived Masson shook hands enthusiastically with Frédéric to make sure the waiting German police officers identified the right man – a modern version of the Judas kiss. A fiction that Masson was being arrested too was maintained at the station, but the truth came home to Frédéric and his colleagues as they were waiting in a police cell. Airey Neave has left a dramatic description of the moment:

'There were steps outside, and they braced themselves to meet their ordeal, but it was Jean Masson. He stood at the door, smiling. There were no handcuffs on his wrists, as there had been at the Métro.

'"Jean!" exclaimed Robert eagerly.

'Jean Masson spat on the floor in front of them. Then he came closer.

'"Well, you fools!" he sneered.

'His face was the most unpleasant any of them had ever seen. It was exultant, repellent in its triumph.

'Robert was the first to speak:

'"You filthy bastard!"

'Jean Masson laughed. He minced across the floor in a kind of ecstasy, and disappeared.'

Cécile Jouan similarly described Masson at this moment as 'beaming, with pride in his triumph written all over his face'.

Masson was the illegitimate son of a Belgian doctor and a French woman who abandoned him at an early age. His last words (he was eventually arrested by the Americans and executed by the French in Lille in 1949) were '*Heil Hitler*', which suggests he was a true believer in the Nazi cause. His treachery cost Frédéric de Jongh his life as well as his freedom: the former Brussels schoolmaster faced a firing squad with two other Comet stalwarts at the Mont-Valérian fort in Paris in March 1944. The secular idealism which had inspired him in pre-war days had by now given way to religious faith; he died having been reconciled with the Catholic Church during his imprisonment.

It was after Frédéric de Jongh's arrest that Bernard Holvoet's grandfather became part of the story.

Count le Grelle, a reserve captain in the Belgian army, escaped across the Pyrenees in the autumn of 1941, and, after eight months in Spanish prisons, made his way to London, where he volunteered for intelligence work. He broke his back during parachute training and had to spend a further eight months in hospital, but in 1943 MI9 asked him to return to Occupied Europe to rebuild the Comet Line.

A meeting in Madrid was arranged between le Grelle and 23-year-old Jean-François Nothomb (code name 'Franco'), who had taken over Dédée de Jongh's role after her arrest. Le Grelle then set up shop in Paris, reorganizing the Comet Line's northern sector, while Franco continued to manage the southern half of the line. Le Grelle survived less than three months in the job; in January 1944 he and Nothomb were both arrested by the Gestapo. Le Grelle was interrogated and tortured (for seventeen nights in a row, according to his grandson Bernard). Both men were sentenced to death, but the machinery of repression was becoming somewhat rusty by then, and neither sentence was carried out. Nothomb was sent to several concentration camps, and, according to the historian Oliver Clutton-Brock, he survived because 'the warrant for his execution never caught up with him'. After the war he became a Catholic priest and did missionary work in Latin America. Count le Grelle was liberated by the Americans from a prison camp in Germany in 1945.

At the end of Cécile Jouan's book *Comète – Histoire d'une ligne d'evasion* there is a moving honour roll of the Comet Line members who gave their lives. There are 155 names on the list, ranging in age from twenty to seventy-three. She concedes it is difficult to be precise about numbers, and it is of course sometimes hard to define who could properly be described as a member of the line. Rémy notes that when Baroness Chaudoir was arrested her maid was picked up with her. The baroness had allowed her home to be used as a safe house for pilots (and showed her mettle by defiantly smoking cigars in her cell in St Gilles prison in Brussels), but the maid could scarcely be blamed for her mistress's decision to engage in clandestine activity. The maid was given a gaol sentence anyway and died in a German prison. (The baroness, who was in her mid-sixties at the time of her arrest, was deported to Germany and died herself in March 1945, tragically close to the end of the war.)

Thirty-seven of the women on Cécile Jouan's list died at the Ravensbrück concentration camp; others are recorded as having simply 'disappeared' in Germany, so the Ravensbrück total may in fact be higher. Ravensbrück was a place of particular horror which, even today, after so much research into the mad logic of the Nazi regime, is still not fully understood. The idea of a concentration camp designed for women was quite simply beyond the imagination of those directing the war in Britain and the United States. In her account of the fate of the British SOE operatives who were sent to Ravensbrück, the journalist and historian Sarah Helm wrote that 'Many of the crimes committed here were crimes not so much against humanity as very specifically against women, gynaecological experiments, forced sterilizations, forced abortions, to name but three.' She described the subsequent war crimes trial against Ravensbrück staff as being 'in a category of its own' because 'the fact that many of the accused were also women only contributed further to the macabre nature of the case'.

The camp was built on SS-owned land. It was initially a labour camp, and served a number of enterprises contributing to the German war effort – including a factory owned by the well-known German company Siemens. Some of the Ravensbrück women were, for example, employed to produce parts for the unmanned V2 rockets that were used to attack London in the last days of the war. But many of the inmates were given tasks with no purpose beyond keeping the camp machine ticking over, and during the final months of its existence killing rather than labour became Ravensbrück's real business.

One of the most vivid accounts of camp life was left by a Comet Line helper called Denise Dufournier. Unlike most of the best-known figures in the organization she was French, not Belgian, and came into contact with Frédéric de Jongh in Paris through the good offices of a French Resistance figure called Marie-Elisabeth Barbier. Her main task was to find safe houses, clothes and papers for Allied airmen on their way through Paris. She was caught during the general Paris round-up that followed Frédéric de Jongh's arrest in June 1943 and moved from Fresnes prison to Ravensbrück in January 1944. Her book *La Maison des Mortes* (The House of the Dead) was written and published in 1945, within months of her release from the camp.

Dufournier brilliantly described the way normal values were inverted in the world of the camp, so that, for example, the entire health care system seemed designed to make the inmates ill. When they arrived they were made to stand naked in the snow for several hours, waiting to be examined by a doctor who smoked a cigarette while 'with a smile of satisfaction he watched the steady flow of the *Stucke* [a German word for livestock, which the guards used to describe the prisoners] who would become his prey'. The dentist checked everyone's mouth for gold that could be extracted if they died, and the new arrivals were given a product which was designed to reveal traces of syphilis; it caused an outbreak of pustules on the faces of apparently healthy women, and Dufournier wrote that at night 'the corridors were full of poor women doubled up with appalling pain caused by the old sores that the drug had revealed'.

Typhoid and dysentery were widespread; healthy women were sometimes made to share beds with those suffering from the former. There was a prison block set aside for tuberculosis cases. One day the senior nurse appeared there and declared that the camp authorities had received a consignment of medicine from the Red Cross which would help them. She asked those who were having trouble sleeping at night to raise their hands and then arranged for them to be given a dose that, in Dufournier's words, 'was so effective they never woke up again'. And it was a camp doctor who, in the last weeks of Ravensbrück's existence, selected those who would be gassed (a gas chamber was constructed at the camp in February 1945; it is a grim tribute to the Nazi determination to keep killing people that they were still building new facilities just three months before they lost the war).

A group of Polish women in the camp were subjected to a particularly gruesome series of medical experiments designed to test a drug which the Nazis hoped would be useful in battlefield medical treatment: their legs were cut open and infected with bacteria, bits of wood and glass to simulate the effects of gunshot and shrapnel wounds. Dufournier became friends with one of them, a woman called Hella. 'From time to time,' she wrote, 'bits of bone would come out of her leg. I helped her once when she was trying to pull out a lump herself.'

Unsurprisingly this kind of thing made the inmates extremely suspicious of everything the medical staff did. Another Comet Line volunteer who was sent to Ravensbrück described the following incident to Rémy: 'One day the nurses appeared with big syringes. Some women were so frightened they jumped out of the windows. I said to myself, "We'll see – I put myself in God's hands", and I allowed them to inject me just below my breast . . . What was in the syringe, I'll never know. But what I do know is that the women who jumped out of the window were executed in front of us.'

When women died at night their bodies were stacked in the washrooms waiting for collection. Denise Dufournier was part of a work detail designated for painting duties, and she wrote, 'When we arrived at the washrooms to pick up our tools in the morning we usually had to make our way through the corpses laid out on the floor. One day we had to paint the walls of a washroom in their company. The smell was heart-stopping.' In the final months of the camp's existence the death rate was so high that the bodies were stacked by the dozen on top of one another. Passing the crematorium one day while picking up a consignment of new paint, Dufournier and her team witnessed the ashes of the dead being loaded on to a lorry and then spread on a field by the side of the camp lake. 'It was the crowning glory of this masterly organization,' she observed. 'In the interests of efficiency those prisoners who had become useless while alive would, all the same, thanks to this final arrangement, be used to fertilize the earth.'

In the winter of 1944 the two Elsie Maréchals, the mother and daughter who had been tricked by German agents posing as American pilots, were also sent to Ravensbrück, and they en-countered the corpse-collecting cart on its daily round as soon as they entered the gates. 'I couldn't believe what I saw,' the younger Elsie remembered later. 'Piled in anyhow were bodies, naked, thin – just bones – with the limbs dangling everywhere, with mouths and eyes wide open, abandoned in a miserable death. That's what we saw when we arrived.'

Like Denise Dufournier, young Elsie was struck by the

inversion of civilized values in Ravensbrück. After being transported from one prison to another all over the Reich, she and her
mother had become friends with a group of other prisoners, and
she remembered being angered by the sight of 'women of all
ages, especially the eldest ones, with their poor fleshless bodies
with empty skins, trembling with cold and fear, brutalized, being
forced to run like young ones up to the shower! The old ladies of
our group, dignified and of good education, had no respect. Just
the contrary, they were regarded as useless. Poor Mme Davreux,
so thin, Mme Chaudoir, Mme Van Kampenhout, these were really
old people – Mme Davreux was eighty.'

Mme Davreux died in Ravensbrück, and her daughter
Madeleine asked young Elsie to help her heap the corpse on to a
pile of other bodies. 'They had shaved her hair,' Elsie
remembered. 'She was a very dignified lady with hair down to her
waist. I took her by the feet and she [Madeleine] took her by the
shoulders and I said to myself "That's your mother, your dear
mother, and there's not a tear, not a sign of sadness in your face,
nothing. That's what we have become – without emotion for anything any more . . ." And we got her down there and that was that.
She lost her mother and I still had mine.'

Denise Dufournier's *La Maison des Mortes* has none of the
Cavalier spirit that characterizes so much Comet Line literature.
There are moments when the love of life and devotion to France
that sustained her shine through, but in her preface Dufournier
states plainly that her purpose is to awaken 'righteous anger' in
the reader. She lays down the most terrible curse on the German
race. 'Would that a great poet will be born,' she wrote, 'who,
inspired by some talent for evil, will celebrate, in grandiloquent
song, the epic of this soulless people, so that every man born to
this race, his children and his children's children, and so on down
the generations, shall hear, without interruption and forever, sung

in their hearts from morning until evening and from evening until morning, from the day of their birth to the moment of their death, this great plaint of Despair, heavy with remorse and always beginning again as soon as it is over.'

After the war Denise Dufournier married a British diplomat and their daughter, the artist Caroline McAdam Clark, lives not far from my home in south London. Caroline McAdam Clark told me that Ravensbrück scarred her mother for ever, and was 'an ever-present part of our lives, a kind of running sub-text, something that was always "there"'. She remembered that when her father was posted to Vienna fifteen years after the end of the war her mother 'couldn't stand hearing German all around her again'.

8

The Officer and
the Legionnaire

Harold Paul Cole

T O SUCCEED ON THE ESCAPE LINES you needed cool courage, a quick and inventive mind, and the capacity to maintain a false-hood with complete conviction. Harold Paul Cole possessed those qualities in abundance. But the talents that made a good agent also made a good traitor. Cole lived and told so many lies – some of them for good and some of them for ill – that it is almost impossible to work out what sort of a man he really was. He projected so many different versions of himself to so many people that the layers of deceit are simply too thick to penetrate. And even today, many decades after his death, some of the dark mysteries that surrounded his name remain.

His contemporaries reacted to him in very different ways. Cole first came into the life of the Pat Line in early 1941 when he began bringing groups of British evaders and escapers to Marseilles from northern France. Captain Ian Garrow – still leader of the line at this stage – is said to have been an enthusiastic admirer, at first at least. Garrow is reported to have praised Cole's 'uncanny ability' to get through the demarcation line between Occupied and Free France. Helen Long, the niece of one of Garrow's key helpers, records in her history of the line that Garrow said, 'No other courier is as successful as he is. Lots of chaps swear they owe their lives to him. He amazes them with his outrageous, cheeky schemes for outwitting the guards along the way.'

By contrast Donald Caskie, the Scottish minister running the British Seamen's Mission in the Vieux Port at Marseilles, claimed he disliked Cole before he even met him. 'I had a premonition about "Cole",' he recorded in his autobiography. 'It was strengthened by his demeanour when we met. In meetings with agents, one was always aware that there was, of necessity, a missing dimension to their personalities, something withdrawn. We did not talk about our private lives . . . But we were not on our guard against each other. The suppressed dimension had become an instinct. Cole lacked that instinct and to me he was insincere . . . Cole was, I felt, a half man, and when the unresolved half was defined he might be a traitor.'

Caskie put his insight into Cole's true nature down to the 'Celtic gift' of second sight he believed he possessed as a Highlander. 'A wicked man,' he wrote, 'has an existence, secreted

MI9's Brigadier Norman Crockatt (**left**) favoured officers with 'sparkle' – such as the ingenious 'Clutty' (**below**), the agency's technical officer. Clutty's flying boots looked like ordinary shoes when the leggings were removed, and his silk maps became standard issue for aircrews.

Above: Spanish refugees from the Civil War crossing the Pyrenees into France. In early 1939 there was an exodus of more than half a million people. They were crammed into hastily constructed camps such as the one at Le Perthus, south of Perpignan (**below**).

Above left: Buses outside the winter sports stadium in Paris during the round-up of Jews – including whole families – in July 1942. The following month Le Vernet camp (**below**) became a transit point in the first mass deportation of Jews from the Vichy zone. The camp water tower (**right**) still stands.

Frédéric de Jongh ran the Paris operation until his arrest in June 1943.

Elvire de Greef, often known as 'Tante Go', with her beloved Gogo who gave her the alias.

Baron Jean Greindl, or 'Nemo', ran the Brussels operation until his arrest in April 1943.

In 1943 23-year-old Jean-François Nothomb took over from Dédée de Jongh and her father and ran the line until he was betrayed in January 1944.

Nancy Wake, the 'White Mouse', escaped across the Pyrenees after Pat O'Leary's arrest, and later returned to France as an SOE agent.

The Reverend Donald Caskie ran a safe house for British soldiers at the Seamen's Mission in Marseilles.

Captain Ian Garrow, escape line pioneer.

A rare wartime glimpse of the elusive Pat himself, under cover in Marseilles in 1941.

Above: The Milice strutting their stuff on the Champs-Elysées. They were enthusiastic Nazi allies in the fight against the 'terrorists' of the *maquis* (**below**).

To meet German demands for labour Vichy first appealed for volunteers to an exchange programme for French POWs (**left**), then introduced forced deportations under the hated STO (**above**).

Above: Vichy police chief René Bousquet at his trial in 1948.

Left: *Maquisards* entering Toulouse in August 1944.

Ceremony at the Barrau barn on Day One of the Chemin de la Liberté (**left**).
With one of the guides on the evening of Day Two (**right**).

Day Three was the toughest test (see pages 308–311).

Spectacular views from the Refuge
des Estagnous.

Solace for sore feet on Day Four –
Spain at last.

among his other lives, that is evil and egotistical. In this way I sought to analyse the conflict I sensed in Cole. The evil that he did pushed itself through the surface of his disguise . . .' This may sound a little fanciful, and Caskie was of course writing with the benefit of hindsight, long after the full Cole saga had unravelled. But Cole did indeed lead several different lives, and some measure of the 'evil and egotistical' appears to run through all of them.

Caskie wrote that Pat O'Leary, like Garrow, initially stood up for Cole because of his record. Helen Long, however, recorded that O'Leary took an immediate dislike to him. O'Leary, she wrote, remembered their first meeting like this: 'I heard the way this man spoke to Ian; and the way he presented his case. To me from the first moment I set eyes on him . . . he was a nobody. No good at all. And most certainly not the sort of person for us to be in harness with.' Helen Long's book was, of course, also written with the benefit of hindsight.

Oddly – and it is a fact that has contributed to some of the conspiracy theories about Cole – no one back at MI9, with which Garrow was by then in contact, seems to have bothered to check Cole's army record when he appeared on the scene. After the war O'Leary received an apology for this 'lamentable effort'. In the Lille area of northern France, where Cole first established contacts with the Resistance and began collecting escapers and evaders, he apparently presented himself as a captain in the British Secret Service. He affected the clothes and mannerisms of the officer class (a penchant for plus-fours, a moustache and liberal doses of 'old-chappery' in his conversation) and Peter Janes referred to him as 'the Officer' in the account of the journey south in his diaries.

He was no such thing. Cole was in fact a sergeant in the Royal Engineers and a conman. Born in 1906 in east London, he had trained as an engineer, but had several convictions for petty crime and confidence trickery to his name by the time he joined the army in 1939. In early May 1940, on the eve of the German attack on France, he was under guard at a military depot on the outskirts of Lille accused of theft (it seems he had tried to abscond with the sergeants' mess fund). When the German offensive began he was 'allowed to escape', but was taken prisoner by the Germans when they arrived in Lille on 20 May. He escaped from the Germans near Namur and returned to Lille, where he was taken in by a woman named Madeleine Deram, whom he described as his mistress.

Garrow and his colleagues knew nothing of this seedy past, and it is unsurprising that they were impressed by Cole's ability to deliver results: he was soon bringing parties of airmen down to Marseilles in large numbers, and on a regular basis – 'five to ten and sometimes more British servicemen at intervals of ten days to two weeks', according to Oliver Clutton-Brock in *RAF Evaders*.

Cole's ability to get through a sticky situation is perhaps best illustrated by the way he talked himself out of trouble while trying to bring Flight Lieutenant 'Taffy' Higginson across the demarcation line in the summer of 1941. The two of them were stopped and questioned by a German officer and a sergeant. Higginson, who spoke no French, was carrying a briefcase containing a change of underwear and some chocolate, and he gave this account of what followed:

'He [Cole] told the officer I was simple minded . . . But the sergeant still pointed at me.

'"I am sure he is English. He is not speaking." The officer told me to turn out my briefcase on the road. By this time, because of the heat and excitement, the chocolate had spread all over contents of the briefcase and looked an absolutely frightful mess. Cole, with tremendous presence of mind, said:

'"Look, I told you he was out of his mind, look what he has done in his briefcase!"

'The officer turned away in disgust and told me to clear off, which I did.'

Higginson was awarded the DFC and DFM for his flying exploits and later became a squadron leader. He was an influential and enthusiastic defender of Cole's reputation after the war.

But in the early autumn of 1941 Pat O'Leary began to ring serious alarm bells about Cole's reliability when he discovered that a week after asking for a very large sum of money (50,000 francs) to have a new group of pilots brought south Cole was still at large in Marseilles – at large and living high on the hog. According to Helen Long, O'Leary made this discovery when he bumped into a woman friend of Cole's at a Marseilles restaurant; she told him she was meeting Cole and a group of friends later that night for a party, and added, 'It is going to be one hell of a party! You know what Paul's parties are like!' A couple of days later Cole himself appeared with two 'pilots' in tow; when O'Leary questioned them privately they admitted they were French and had been coached by Cole to play the role of escaping airmen. The conclusion that MI9's money was funding Cole's private pleasures – his reputation for womanizing crops up everywhere, and at about this time he had become engaged to a nineteen-year-old French girl – seemed inescapable.

Garrow sent O'Leary and another of his lieutenants north to Lille to investigate what Cole had done with the – by then con- siderable – sums he had been given for expenses over the previous months. Some of the money was supposed to be destined for François Duprez, who worked for the Lille town hall (he was, in fact, the contact who had originally provided Cole with his false identity papers) and who had been nominated as the line's northern banker. When O'Leary turned up at the Duprez family home M. Duprez denied receiving any money at all. 'He [Cole] has never handed any money over to me for banking in the name of the line,' he stated flatly.

At this point things began to unravel with a speed and complexity that would do credit to a piece of highly imaginative thriller writing.

Pat O'Leary and his colleague persuaded Duprez to travel south to Marseilles so that he could repeat his evidence to Garrow, and headed south themselves to warn Garrow about what was going on – only to discover that Garrow had been arrested in their absence. Captain Garrow was picked up by the Vichy secret police, and though there is no suggestion his arrest was connected with Cole, Pat O'Leary found himself facing two crises simultaneously: the loss of the line's leader, and Cole's embezzlement. He agreed to take on leadership of the line himself (at which point it acquired the name by which it is known today) and decided to confront Cole with the evidence against him.

His opportunity came at the end of October when Cole arrived in Marseilles with his largest party yet – seven airmen and six soldiers – and his young fiancée. On the Sunday after delivering his party Cole was invited to a meeting at the home of George Rodocanachi, the Greek doctor who had allowed Garrow and O'Leary to use his Vieux Port apartment. The confrontation that followed was made all the more surreal by the presence of three ladies – including Mrs Rodocanachi's sister – taking tea in the drawing room, quite oblivious to the interrogation that was being conducted in one of the other rooms.

Initially Cole denied everything, but when Duprez himself appeared he confessed all. Some kind of scuffle took place (according to some accounts Cole tried to escape) and Pat O'Leary punched Cole in the face and laid him out. Cole was then locked in the bathroom while O'Leary and the other organizers of the line debated what to do with him; his crime at this stage was theft, not treachery, but he was clearly unreliable and his knowledge of the line and those who worked on it made him a very serious risk.

The discussion was interrupted by a noise from the bathroom. O'Leary's group opened the door just in time to see Cole disappear through the bathroom window, across a perilous drop into the courtyard and in again via the window of another part of the apartment block. They tried to follow him but once he was out of the building he was safe – a daylight chase through the streets of Marseilles was obviously not an option. In a letter to his MI9 contact, Donald Darling, O'Leary wrote, 'If God is just, my dear Donald, that son of a bitch Paul will fall by my hand – I swear it and will take care of it.' Long after the war Ian Garrow stated that he had already reached the conclusion that Cole should be killed at the time of his arrest, and had consulted Dr Rodocanachi about how to do it discreetly ('a massive injection of insulin ... Thereafter a gentle push into one of the side basins of the Old Port' was apparently the advice that came back). But Garrow was of course detained before he had the chance to do anything.

Cole was nothing if not resilient. Despite this debacle he made one more journey south with a group of escapers (two British sergeants and a Pole) but he abandoned them in Toulouse, and it has been reported that he relieved the men of 6,000 francs before he left them.

But there was worse to come. On 6 December Cole was arrested by the Germans in Lille. The circumstances are not entirely clear, but the consequences were deadly: Cole was turned.

The first of the Pat Line helpers to be arrested as a consequence was Duprez, the 'banker' whose evidence had revealed Cole's embezzlement. He was picked up at his desk at the town hall the following day. Cole would later claim the Germans had recognized Duprez's signature on his false identity card. That may possibly be true, but Cole certainly seems to have been deeply involved in the arrests that followed; in several cases he turned up himself with members of the German GFP (Geheime Feldpolizei) posing as Allied airmen.

Six Pat Line helpers in northern France were picked up on 8 December. One of them was a priest, the Abbé Pierre Carpentier, who was a pivotal figure in the Pat Line because he was able to forge the documents needed to travel south over the demarcation line. On the afternoon of the 8th Cole arrived at his home in Abbeville with the GFP men in plain clothes (according to some accounts of this incident there may have been at least one genuine pilot with them too) and asked for a set of identity cards and passes. The Germans followed the *abbé* when he went to borrow some ID cards and subsequently arrested the suppliers of the cards as well as the *abbé* and his mother. Cole and his new German friends then moved on to Paris, where several more Pat Line helpers were added to the haul.

In March 1942 Pierre Carpentier smuggled a statement out of his prison cell stating that he had been 'ignobly betrayed' by Cole. He gave a detailed account of his memory of what had happened and also stated that his German interrogators had told him Cole revealed much more than he needed to in order to make the position of those he had shopped even worse than it already was. The *abbé* was beheaded in Germany in the summer of 1943.

But even this dreadful litany of perfidy left unanswered questions. Cole did not betray everyone in the Paris network, and he does not seem to have betrayed anyone at all in the south – even though he and the Pat Line leadership had parted on less than cordial terms. Why not? There have been suggestions that Cole really was a British intelligence officer, and equally that he was a German double agent all along. And his subsequent career and death only added to the mystery surrounding him.

Cole escaped from the Germans and married his fiancée, Suzanne Warenghem, in Paris in April 1942. He was then arrested again, this time in Lyons by the Vichy French, who put him on trial for espionage. He was convicted and sentenced to death, but the sentence was commuted to life imprisonment and when the Germans took over the whole of France they set him free to work for them as an intelligence agent again.

In April 1945, after fleeing east with his Gestapo minders, Cole presented himself to the Americans claiming to be a British intelligence officer called Robert Mason, and spent several weeks enjoying the privileges of a captain's rank before MI9 finally caught up with him. He was interrogated in Paris (even the officer who questioned him said he had an 'incredibly likeable personality') but escaped yet again before he could be tried.

He managed to dupe one more woman into helping him out. 'Monsieur Harry', as he now styled himself, told Pauline Herveau that he was an army doctor awaiting demobilization and persuaded her to put him up in a flat above the bar she owned in Paris. Some local people told the police there was a suspicious character hanging about Billy's Bar, and when two officers turned up to investigate, Cole tried to shoot his way clear. But the French detectives were too quick for him; one of them, a Resistance veteran, shot him through the heart. It was a suitably theatrical end to his many lives – although such was his reputation that some of those he had known refused to believe he had really been killed; there was an enduring rumour that the Billy Bar incident was a put-up job by British Intelligence, who used it – so the conspiracy theory runs – as a cover for spiriting Cole away to yet another incarnation.

The Cole episode inflicted terrible damage but it did not shut down the Pat Line. O'Leary remained at liberty and continued to run things. Life became more difficult when the Germans crossed the demarcation line and occupied the whole of France in November 1942, and at that point O'Leary moved his operation from Marseilles to Toulouse, that bit closer to the Pyrenees. In December Ian Garrow was rescued from gaol and escaped across the mountains to Spain and on to Britain. And in January 1943 a new courier called Roger Leneveu was recruited to the line.

Leneveu was also known as Roger the Legionnaire because he had – at least so he said – spent several years serving with the French Foreign Legion. He came to the Pat Line well recommended for his previous work with the Resistance and, like Cole, he quickly established a reputation as a good courier. But he was in fact a double agent working directly for the Germans from the first. In mid-February 1943 one of Pat O'Leary's most trusted helpers was arrested with a party of airmen at Tours – just after a meeting with Leneveu in Paris. A fortnight later, on 2 March, Pat O'Leary agreed to a meeting with Leneveu at a café in Toulouse; he believed the young Frenchman might have information about what had gone wrong, and appears to have gone to the meeting without suspecting that anything untoward was afoot. Marie-Louise Dissard, a Toulouse *résistante* with whom O'Leary was staying at the time, stated later that when she told him the time of the appointment he replied, 'That's perfect; I will come back at one thirty . . .' for a lunch meeting.

The denouement in the Café Super was another moment in Pat O'Leary's extraordinary life which reads like a screenplay. O'Leary arrived at the rendezvous 'in his usual ghostlike way' (as John Nichols and Tony Rennell put it) and sat down facing the door as he always did. Airey Neave described what happened next:

'Then he said to Roger:

'"Now tell me quickly, do you know who has been giving us away in Paris?"

'"Yes," said Roger, grinning, "I know him very well."

'Something cold and hard was pressed into O'Leary's neck and a voice said, "Don't move!"'

Pat O'Leary spent the rest of the war in German camps. At one of them, an SS camp called Natzweiler in the Vosges mountains, he had a cameo role in the sad fate of four women SOE agents who were brought there for execution. One of them had worked on the Marseilles escape line early in the war; O'Leary recognized her and was able to make very brief contact with them by shouting through their cell window. But he could do no more than that, and the executions went ahead. O'Leary had to watch impotently as the smoke billowed out of the crematorium chimney afterwards. He survived the war and at the time of Cole's death he was in Paris recovering from his camp experiences. He was called in to identify Cole's body.

After betraying O'Leary, Roger Leneveu continued with a successful and fruitful career as an escape line infiltrator and traitor during 1943, the last full year of the German occupation of France. In 1944, he was liquidated by the Resistance.

Françoise and the Americans

François – smoking her way through liberation

MARIE-LOUISE DISSARD, THE WOMAN who had been looking after O'Leary in her apartment at the time of his arrest, seemed the least likely underground mastermind imaginable. But she was in fact an extremely shrewd operator, and in May 1943 MI9 confirmed her as the new head of what was left of the Pat Line. The anecdotes that float around her memory are rich and varied; separating the wheat of truth from the chaff of legend is difficult, not least because she died alone and – despite a rich bounty of decorations in the immediate aftermath of the war – apparently forgotten by her compatriots. Perhaps the legends are not chaff at all, but speak as eloquently of her true nature as the hard facts; like Paul Cole, Marie-Louise Dissard had a supreme talent for creating a version of reality that suited her purposes. Unlike Paul Cole, she used it entirely for good ends.

Françoise – to give her her *nom de guerre* – was nearly sixty when the war broke out. She had worked as a secretary in the Toulouse Mairie and as a teacher in her youth, but between the wars she established a couture dress shop in the Rue de la Pompe called The Modern Mannequin – a *'magasin de frivolités féminines'*, as it was described at the time – where she made clothes for the *haute bourgeoisie* of Toulouse and costumes for the city's theatre. Her own taste in clothes was distinctly theatrical; she favoured large straw hats decorated with coloured feathers, flowers and even fruit, carried capacious handbags of the Lady Bracknell variety in satin or velvet, and her dresses were described as 'extravagantly ecclesiastical' in a 1970s tribute in the French magazine *Résistance*. Françoise leant heavily on a cane when she walked, and her shoulders were stooped with rheumatism.

Another of Françoise's props was a violin case. She had it with her on a visit to one of her moles in the city administration. After the man had given her a full rundown of that day's police patrols (she was expecting the arrival of a group of evading airmen) she opened the case with a flourish to reveal a leg of mutton. 'If all goes well, Monsieur Sauret, I shall give this to my children this evening,' she declared. The 'children' – four British airmen – were safely on their way to the Pyrenees a few hours later, no doubt feeling well fed.

Françoise played on her eccentricities very successfully to

secure her cover. On one occasion she is said to have talked her way through a checkpoint by knocking back most of a bottle of rough red wine, dirtying her hands and face and behaving like a bag lady; she approached one of the Germans manning the checkpoint muttering endearments in the strongest Toulouse accent she could manage and breathing boozy fumes all over him. She felt up his uniform, commenting on the quality of the cloth in a drunken manner until he pushed her through.

In September 1942 a Vichy police report dismissed any idea that she might be a threat to security: 'Madame Dissard,' it stated, 'a former employee of the city council, with a business at The Modern Mannequin, is steeped in socialist doctrine and thoroughly signed-up to the British cause, openly declaring her Anglophile feelings and endlessly expressing her enthusiasm for that country's victory. It is generally said that she does not enjoy full command of her mental faculties and it is beyond doubt that she can exercise no influence whatever on those around her because no one gives any credit at all to what she says.' At the time the report was written Françoise was already renting a safe house on behalf of the Pat Line and delivering regular food supplies for the clandestine tenants. One cannot help wondering what the report's author thought when it emerged, at the end of the war, that she had helped no fewer than 250 airmen to escape over the Pyrenees.

Françoise was especially attached to her cat, and Mifouf looms large in the memoirs and diaries of those who stayed with her on the way to the Pyrenees. Fred Greenwell, a bombardier on a Lancaster which was shot down during a raid on Germany in February 1944, described Françoise as 'a humorous, good natured, chain-smoking, indomitable woman with a huge cat'. He wrote that 'From the moment I came under the control of Françoise and her network I felt a lessening of tension and pressure.' And he remembered the time he spent under her wing as 'three golden days to rest and recuperate' which 'paid rich dividends when we came face to face with the Pyrenean peaks a few days later'.

Another RAF man, Squadron Leader Frank Griffiths, was expecting to meet 'a luscious blonde of some twenty summers' and was clearly somewhat put out to find instead a sexagenarian who 'had two prominent top teeth and smoked incessantly. She carried a bag with her into which she was continually diving and producing things like a conjuror.' But he was full of admiration for her professionalism. Françoise escorted him from Annemasse, near the Swiss border, to Toulouse. There had been several Resistance attacks while she was away from the city and they found the station crawling with French and German police – every passenger was being searched and questioned. Griffiths recorded that Françoise 'went up to a gendarme and created a minor disturbance – about what I do not know – which drew attention to herself while I walked out of the station'.

She showed similarly quick wits when she was arrested while escorting a party of four airmen down to Perpignan to begin their climb across the mountains. She described the incident in an interview she gave in 1946, and her interviewer judged that it illustrated 'the ingenuity, courage, and sang froid which is characteristic of Françoise'. When a German police patrol boarded the train to check documents, Françoise instructed her airmen to hide in the loo. Unfortunately the Germans were thorough: 'They called the conductor and asked him to open the door to the WC. Françoise was standing nearby, and one of the aviators said "Françoise". Thereupon the Germans accused Françoise of travelling with these men, and being in charge of them. She denied this. The Germans asked her how it was that this man knew her name, she said he did not. They had NOT called her

Françoise, but asked her if she was *française*. After much questioning they decided to let her go.'

What followed illustrates the very ambiguous nature of relations between the Vichy authorities and the occupying Germans by this stage of the war. Françoise became aware that she was being followed when she got off the train in Perpignan and she sought sanctuary in – of all places – the local police station, where 'she bluntly told the Police Captain that she was sick and wanted a car to take her to Narbonne. In the meantime the two Germans who had been following her entered the Police precinct and asked if they had seen a woman of Françoise's description. The Police Captain left his office (Françoise was inside) and told the Germans that he had not seen such a woman. The Germans appeared satisfied and left. At this moment there was no need to further feign sickness, and Françoise admitted that the Gestapo was after her. The Police Captain arranged for two of his men to conduct Françoise to Narbonne, with orders that if stopped by the Germans, they were to say she was under French arrest. Françoise was able to regain Narbonne without further mishap.'

The 1946 interview – from which that account is taken – is the only material I have encountered which comes directly from Françoise herself. Most of what I have read about this intriguing figure comes from the memories of others, and because evading airmen only spent a little time with her on their way through to the Pyrenees, their accounts give us frustratingly brief glimpses of what she was like. Flight Lieutenant Earl Woodard, for example, the navigator on an American B17 bomber shot down over France in the spring of 1944, got a sense of the steel beneath all that eccentricity. 'We watched quietly while Françoise, the leader of this underground organization, bargained with the mercenaries who were to lead us through the mountains,' he wrote. 'She was not a young woman, perhaps sixty-five years old, very much in charge and respectfully called "the Queen of the Pyrenees".'

Nancy Wake, the Pat Line helper known as the White Mouse whom we met briefly in Chapter Two, spent rather longer with Françoise than most escapers. She was staying in Françoise's Toulouse apartment at the time of Pat O'Leary's arrest, and had to spend several weeks there because her attempts to escape across the Pyrenees were frustrated by a series of mishaps. In her auto-biography she described her host like this: 'She was a wonderful person and I loved her dearly. She was very ugly. It was hard to tell her age as she did nothing to improve her looks . . . Françoise was a chain smoker. She was never without the bamboo holder and cigarette in her mouth. She used to drink black coffee all day long but managed to keep the holder in the corner of her mouth and drink at the same time. I don't know whether she undressed at night because she always appeared in the morning looking exactly the same as she did the night before . . . She also adored her cat, Mifouf. I often heard her telling Mifouf what swine the Germans were. Without a doubt Françoise was one of the most fantastic personalities I have ever met.'

While Nancy Wake was staying in the Toulouse apartment Françoise organized a mass breakout from Castres prison. She persuaded a prison guard to give a bottle of drugged wine to the chief guard, and once the man had passed out her accomplice used his keys to release ten prisoners (a Canadian, an American and several Frenchmen) by the front gate (which he carefully locked behind him). The party were brought to the apartment, where Françoise and Nancy tried to clean them up. In her auto-biography Nancy Wake recalled the days that followed as 'hilarious'; the city around them hummed with sound, 'Milice, police, gendarmes and police cars screaming, chasing all over the place for the ten men', while the escapers were 'sitting in Françoise's flat in their birthday suits, wrapped in blankets or anything that could keep them warm, while I washed and scrubbed day after day'. The laundry work took some time as the clothes had to be dried discreetly inside the apartment, and Nancy wrote that to pass the time 'Françoise and I used to play cards with the men until the early hours of the morning, drinking pints and pints of black coffee.'

Françoise went on helping airmen up to D-Day and beyond, and on one night sheltered no fewer than eighteen of them in her apartment. Indeed, so many airmen came through Toulouse that for a period in 1943 and again in 1944 Françoise used a rented house in the city's suburbs, the wonderfully named Villa Pamplemousse (Villa Grapefruit), to accommodate them all. Fred Greenwell was struck by the number of American airmen being looked after there. 'The big house was run on the lines of a transit camp,' he wrote, 'and there were several Americans hiding there. I was the sole British representative.' In Ian Garrow's early days in Marseilles British soldiers like Peter Janes were his line's main clients – by the time Françoise took over the line from Pat O'Leary, American airmen were arriving in ever greater numbers.

The United States Eighth Air Force began to establish itself in Britain in the spring of 1942. It was a low point in Allied fortunes. Most of Western Europe was under German occupation or in Axis hands, and the two significant exceptions, Vichy France and Franco's Spain, were anything but sympathetic to the Allied cause. The Japanese had overrun the eastern and Pacific territories of the British, the Dutch and the French, and had occupied the Philippines. In Russia the Germans were advancing with what looked like unstoppable momentum. And the campaign in North Africa was in the balance. Allied strategy relied more heavily than ever on a bombing campaign.

The speed and size of America's contribution were awe-inspiring. In February 1942 the Eighth Air Force presence in Britain consisted of seven men and no planes; by December 1943 it had reached 185,000 men and 4,000 planes. Eight RAF bases north of London were handed over to the United States Air Force and more than a hundred additional bases and supply centres were constructed, most of them in East Anglia. 'By late 1943,' the American military historian Donald Miller wrote, 'the Eighth would transform these lands of tall churches and small villages into a great land-based aircraft carrier.'

The presence of so much firepower alone was a lift to British spirits. In an article for the *Smithsonian Magazine* John Keegan, the British military historian, recalled the inspiring sight of American bombers leaving East Anglia on a mission: 'Squadron after squadron they rose to circle into groups and wings, and then set off south-eastward for the sea passage to their targets, a shimmering and winking constellation of aerial grace and military power, trailing a cirrus of pure white condensation from 600 wing-tips against the deep blue of English summer skies. Three thousand of America's best and brightest airmen were cast aloft by each mission, ten to a "ship".'

Casualty rates in the Eighth Air Force were, like those in the RAF's Bomber Command, terrifyingly high. Two-thirds of airmen were killed or captured by the enemy. In the autumn of 1943 fewer than one in four could expect to complete the twenty-five combat missions that made up a full tour of duty. And by the end of the war 26,000 members of the Eighth Air Force had been killed – a higher figure than the total for the entire United States Marine Corps. Donald Miller tells a chilling story about the air base at Thorpe Abbotts in Norfolk: 'One replacement crewman arrived . . . in time for a late meal, went to bed in his new bunk, and was lost the next morning over Germany. No one got his name. He was thereafter known as "the man who came to dinner".'

The big difference between the RAF and the Eighth Air Force was that, unlike the British, the Americans bombed in daylight. Their bombers were heavily armed – the use of the name 'Flying Fortress' for the B17 was no idle boast, the plane carrying up to twelve .50 Browning machine guns – and flew in a tight defensive formation known as a 'combat box' (a little like an aerial version of the old British infantry squares which proved so effective at the Battle of Waterloo).

Forming up into the V-shaped formation could be hazardous; many airmen lost their lives in aerial collisions above East Anglia as their pilots tried to manoeuvre their huge 'ships' into battle order. And any plane which fell out of formation – if, for example, it was hit and lost power – could, in daylight, expect merciless treatment from the Luftwaffe. Larry Grauerholz, a navigator on a B17 which was hit during a raid on Bordeaux in 1944, told me, 'Once you leave formation the German fighters are waiting for the cripples, and they shot us up like a pack of bees.' His pilot ditched the plane in a marsh on the Atlantic coast.

And the wisdom of daylight bombing looked especially questionable in 1943 when the Americans joined the British on raids deep into Germany. There was no fighter with a range long enough to reach the targets, and the bombers flew many of their missions without escort. The development of the Mustang as a long-range fighter changed that, but the level of bomber casualties in the summer of 1943 was very high indeed. Daylight bombing was certainly no panacea.

On the other hand, jumping out of a plane in daylight had all sorts of advantages over jumping out at night. After talking to some of the Americans sharing his shelter with Françoise in Toulouse, Fred Greenwell concluded it was one of the reasons so many Americans seemed to be getting away success-fully. 'Night time parachuting,' he wrote, 'seemed to require more luck and was a much more hazardous affair than jumping in day time!'

Greenwell knew from experience just how hazardous a night jump could be. When he baled out of his Lancaster over Alsace-Lorraine, which at this stage was part of Germany (having been reclaimed by the Germans after the fall of France), the darkness made it very difficult to get a sense of what sort of landing he could look forward to. 'I looked down and was puzzled,' he recalled later. 'The moonless sky above me was star-studded and clear of cloud and at briefing "Met" had forecast cloudless sky throughout – yet I seemed to be about to descend into a large mass of solid cloud. There was no point in trying to guide the parachute in any specific direction and in any case, my hands were too cold. I imagined a church spire pointed underneath my feet and resigned myself to my fate. Further descent brought the realization that my "solid cloud" was a white blanket of snow stretching in every direction. Further down and for "church spires" read "fir trees" – countless thousands of them – their tops standing out like knitting needles.' His parachute caught on a tree and he had to wrench it free of a branch before hitting the ground. One of the American pilots he met in Toulouse, in contrast, 'had practically dropped into the arms of a member of the *maquis*, who had watched his descent and waited for him to land' when he baled out in daylight.

By the spring of 1943 many people living under German occupation had begun to hope they would soon be free (the German surrender at Stalingrad in February that year was a big factor in breaking the myth of Nazi invincibility) and were increas-ingly willing to take risks. According to M. R. D. Foot, 'the great day raids by the USAAF over German-occupied territories were often followed with passionate interest by crowds of spectators on the ground, who stood by to help at the fall of a parachute'. One American airman said that when he was shot down near Toulouse in August 1943 a crowd of no fewer than thirty people surrounded him: 'A man had brought civilian clothes with him. In four minutes I looked like any one of the Frenchmen and my suit and flying equipment had disappeared,' he reported.

The American chapter of the Pyrenean story includes one drama which reads like the script of a Hollywood blockbuster and involves someone who in today's terms definitely ranks as an A-list celebrity. On 5 March 1944 a 21-year-old fighter pilot called Chuck Yeager was shot down near Bordeaux; in the fullness of time he would go on to be the first man to break the sound barrier, and the world's most famous test pilot.

The future hero of *The Right Stuff* evidently had no time for old world courtesy; once he had recovered from baling out and treated some minor but painful wounds, he introduced himself to a French woodcutter by jumping him from behind and shoving a gun at him. 'With eyes the size of quarters,' Yeager recalled in his autobiography, 'he stares at the pistol I am waving in his face. He speaks no English, so I talk at him like Tarzan: "Me American. Need help. Find underground." He jabbers back in excited French.' His captive proved to be friendly, and Yeager was put in touch with the Resistance fighters of the local *maquis*.

The *maquis* were by this stage generally well supplied by Britain, and Yeager's group were energetically engaged in blowing things up. They promised to send him over the mountains as soon as the snow had melted sufficiently, but for several days he lived with them in the woods 'constantly on the move, making camp twice a day to eat and sleep. But never staying in one place for longer than a few hours.' Yeager was present for a drop of ammunition and explosives from the RAF. Having learnt a bit about the art of handling fuses and timing devices from his father on the farm back in West Virginia, he was put to work. 'When they see I know what I am doing,' he wrote, 'I am put in charge of cutting up cords of plastique and attaching them to fuses – a terrorist bomb-maker. The work is fun and interesting.'

Yeager was eventually put into a truck with a group of other airmen and dropped off in the mountains. The driver gave them each a knapsack containing bread, cheese and chocolate, and pointed at a mountain path which climbed south in the general direction of Spain. Yeager and another airman, a B17 navigator called Pat Patterson, broke away from the main group because they wanted to push ahead, but they soon got horribly lost in the mountains. They climbed seven thousand feet in heavy, wet snow, with regular stops for breath in the thinning atmosphere; 'The Pyrenees make the hills back home look like straight-ways,' he wrote. 'The climb is endless, a bitch of bitches.' After three days, 'staggering like drunks' and 'almost ready to give up', they found a mountain refuge where they collapsed and slept.

As Yeager tells the story in his autobiography, they were woken in the most dramatic way imaginable (Yeager wrote the book with the help of a professional writer, who clearly knew how to give a story colour). A German patrol spotted one of his companion's socks drying on a bush in front of their cabin: 'The bastards ask no questions. They just unsling their rifles and begin firing through the front door. The first bullets whine above my head and thud into the wall; I leap through the rear window, Pat right behind me. I hear him scream, and I grab hold of him and yank him with me as I jump on a snow-covered log slide. I am spinning round, ass over teakettle, in a cloud of snow, and it seems like two miles down to the bottom of that flume. We splash straight down into a creek.' After hauling the now unconscious Patterson out of the water Yeager inspected the damage; his companion had been shot in the knee and a single tendon was all that connected the two halves of his leg. Yeager cut through it with his penknife and bound up the stump with a spare shirt.

He waited until nightfall and then began climbing in what he hoped was the direction of the frontier, carrying Patterson over his shoulder. At the summit he saw below him 'the thin line of a road that must be in Spain'. He pushed Patterson over the edge of a ridge and the wounded navigator rolled down the hill. Yeager followed, riding down the steep slope with a stick between his legs 'just as I did when I roller-skated down the steep hill behind my house, using a broomstick as a brake'.

Yeager left Patterson in full view by the road in the hope that he would be picked up by a passing motorist and began to walk. At the first village he reached he gave himself up to the police. Patterson was indeed found by the Guardia Civil and survived – he was repatriated to the United States. Chuck Yeager was treated for his injuries in Spain and, once the formalities had been sorted out with the Spanish authorities, returned to Britain. Normally airmen who had been shot down and made it home were banned from further combat missions on the grounds that if it happened again they were in danger of being captured and giving away information about the people who had helped them before. Yeager argued that as the area of France where he had been shot down had now been liberated the rule no longer applied, and he was allowed to resume combat missions in the final phase of the war. On one occasion he 'killed' five enemy aircraft in a single day.

But most of the American airmen who crossed the Pyrenees were, like so many of their British allies, ordinary people in extraordinary circumstances rather than superheroes. Scott

Goodall is a retired British writer who has been involved in the Chemin de la Liberté since its very early days, and the bulging files at his handsome old farmhouse just outside St Girons are full of correspondence from all over the United States. There are letters from veterans of the Pyrenean crossing who want to establish contact with the people who helped them, letters from families who have done the walk in tribute to the older generation, and all sorts of memoirs and diaries, many of them typewritten on yellowing pages.

The experiences they record are often much less lonely than the kind of solitary ordeal which men like Stan Hope and Bob Frost endured when they hit the ground. If you parachuted in daylight it was more likely that you would be reunited with your fellow crew members. Earl Woodard baled out of his dying B17 over Normandy in April 1944. Almost immediately 'two or three Frenchmen appeared and hurried me off to a wooded area nearby. One of them accompanied me far enough to point out a hollow tree in which to hide.' He was collected a few hours later and within a week had been reunited with four other members of his crew (the rest had been picked up by the Germans). The group remained together all the way through the journey to the Pyrenees, Madrid and eventually Gibraltar.

Woodard's memoir, *The B17 of La Goulafrière*, gives a hint of the sort of cultural confusion which arose in contacts between the French and the sometimes noisy arrivals from the New World. One of the plane's crew was a flamboyant chancer called Jack Hotaling, who had been a fireman in Los Angeles before the war and had enjoyed a brief relationship with a Hollywood star called Paulette Goddard (she later enjoyed the 'patronage' of Charlie Chaplin). Hotaling behaved as if Occupied France was a film set.

Sometimes his adventures were heroic. On landing he was

picked up by the owner of a stud farm and hidden in a hayloft. When he was reunited with Woodard a few days later he gave him a dramatic story of what happened next: 'Within minutes two Germans on motorcycles zoomed up the drive and, parking in the courtyard, began searching for the American whose parachute descent they had been watching. According to Hotaling, as the Germans walked into the barn he dropped on to the first to enter, breaking his neck. The farm's owner, Monsieur Marguet, made certain the second met the same fate! The Germans were quickly dispatched in an unused well behind the house and their vehicles submerged in a nearby pond.' Woodard and the other surviving members of the crew regarded this as a tall story until M. Marguet confirmed it.

But more often Hotaling's adventures were romantic. M. Marguet was not at all pleased when the American airman tried to per- suade his beautiful daughter Yvette that he would make her a star if she was willing to come to Hollywood. While the rest of the crew holed up in an old brick barn, Hotaling spent his evenings in the company of Noelle, an attractive woman who ran a dance hall in a nearby village, and cheerfully talked his way out of trouble when he was stopped by a German patrol after curfew. Some of the locals told Woodard and the other members of the crew that Noelle was a lesbian and that Hotaling's attentions would get nowhere. At times the Woodard diary reads like a soap.

Another member of the crew remembered a difficult evening when he and Hotaling were required to share sleeping quarters with a local poacher. 'Hotaling was appalled when the old poacher with whom we were staying removed his boots,' he recalled. 'His feet were filthy and Jack told him he should wash them. The old man thought that was the funniest thing he had ever heard. The more Hotaling insisted the more the old fellow laughed.' There was a similar cultural chasm over drinking habits. Earl Woodard recorded that their host 'expressed considerable concern for my health when I asked for a drink of water'. The French offered wine instead. Another evading airman, Robert Vandegriff, recalled a similar experience: 'We had a couple of empty water bottles so as we were thirsty we asked the French boy to get us some water. A great look of surprise came into his face, and he told us that the water was no good to drink, but he would get us some cider. We assured him that water was all we wanted, but nothing would do but cider.'

The co-pilot on Vandegriff's flight, a Lieutenant Toft, was six foot four inches tall, and 'it was hard for the French to get clothes to fit him. His arms stuck out of his coat, the pants lacked about six inches of being the right length, and the shoes, although about his size (which is a small packing case), had nails in the soles which didn't do his sore feet any good. Toft, in his odd assortment of clothes, didn't look much like a U.S. Army officer.' Larry Grauerholz ran into similar difficulties when he reached Toulouse and faced the prospect of a Pyrenean climb (he was a graduate of Françoise Dissard's network). 'The main problem was getting shoes,' he told me. 'American feet are bigger than European feet, and we had to get rid of our military shoes because they were a dead giveaway. I made the crossing in a slipper and a sandal.'

Larry Grauerholz was the only American airman we were able to interview for our BBC series; he was a lively ninety-four when I spoke to him, and came into the studio with his wife Ruth, who was eloquent on the subject of the dreadful condition of his feet when he returned to the United States after the slipper-and-sandal episode. The two of them made a trip to the Pyrenees in 1999 to revisit his wartime haunts, and his children completed the Chemin de la Liberté. But along with the diaries and Christmas cards with American stamps, Scott Goodall's files are also bulging with letters of condolence and death announcements in American local papers; a 2007 cutting from the obituaries pages of a St Louis paper, for example, pays tribute to the memory of Earl Woodard, who 'flew numerous bombing missions over France and Germany . . . and escaped on foot over the Pyrenees'. By the time I walked the Chemin de la Liberté the American presence, once substantial, had faded away altogether.

But the contents of Scott Goodall's files are a tribute to the strong sense of connection with France and the French which so many of these young Americans took home with them, and the letters and diaries matter because they preserve memories of acts of heroism which might otherwise have been forgotten, simply because of the sheer scale of the human drama of the Second World War. One of my favourites concerns Paule Viatel, yet another remarkable woman who, like Françoise, was working the territory between Toulouse and the Pyrenees. I like the story because you can only really appreciate her physical achievement if you have done some serious Pyrenean walking yourself.

Paule Viatel had been a figure of some significance in the Resistance long before she began helping airmen, and was driven to south-west France as a consequence of one of the greatest Resistance disasters of the war, the arrest of Jean Moulin, or Max, de Gaulle's personal representative in France, in a Lyons suburb in the summer of 1943. Moulin was arrested at a high-level meeting of Resistance leaders, and one of those picked up with him, Bruno Lart, had been using Paule Viatel's apartment in Lyons. That of course made her a target, and she decamped to Toulouse, where she combined intelligence work for the British Special Operations Executive with helping people who wanted to cross the Pyrenees.

One of those she guided on his way was an American pilot called Clayton David. He'd been born a country boy and fell in love with the region on his train journey along the Pyrenees: 'The date was 10th April, a beautiful spring day. As the train made its way along the side of the mountain range, we could see the beauty of the countryside. My farm experiences reminded me then of all the work that farmers had to do to get their crops started at that season of the year. The fields, vineyards, and orchards blended into the mountains capped with snow that glistened in the sunshine,' he wrote. After the war he went back to track down Paule Viatel. He became interested in her story and wrote an account of her underground career in his memoirs.

About a month after getting Clayton David away, 'Claire' – as Paule was code-named – was escorting a group of eight people near St Girons when disaster struck. 'A front-wheel drive vehicle which she knew approached them. Suddenly the vehicle spun round in a cloud of dust, forcing her and her men into the ditch. Four men sprang out of the vehicle with machine guns and revolvers drawn. Claire recognized the fifth man who was now standing behind the other four looking like a beaten dog. It was Maréval . . . who had helped her set up the network.

'They were all ordered out of the ditch, and Claire was separated from the others. She was searched, interrogated, threatened and beaten. They knew she was the leader, but they beat everyone in the group with gun stocks as they were taken to a nearby farmyard.'

At the farm they were all – including Maréval – locked in a room. Claire confronted her betrayer, who claimed to have agreed to cooperate with the Germans only after being arrested in Toulouse, taken into the woods outside the city and beaten. She remarked rather caustically that he seemed to have escaped without any bruises. While they were locked up the party of Germans who had arrested them were hunting down and shooting the local blacksmith, who was her contact for the next leg of the journey into the Pyrenees.

On their return the Germans told the farmer's wife to make

them pancakes, and Claire sensed them relaxing. She asked to be allowed to get some fresh water so that she could wash herself – she was covered in blood after her beatings – and while the bathroom door was closed she slipped out of a window and ran away. 'She expected to hear shots, but there were none,' Clayton David continued. 'She ran through the country, through woods, yards and paths. Worn out, she kept going down hills and up slopes. Anything to put distance between her and the farm where her companions were being held.'

By nightfall she had reached the village of Salies-du-Salat, a good ten kilometres as the crow flies from where the party had been picked up, and much further than that across this kind of country, with its hills and valleys. When a car passed she threw herself into a ditch and lost her shoes, so she had to continue barefoot. She was turned away when she asked for help at a house in the village and walked on through the night. She rested through the following day and walked through a second night before realizing that, having eaten nothing at all and still suffering from the beating she had received, she was now in urgent need of assistance.

At six in the morning on her third day on the run, 'bloody and beaten . . . with clothing torn by the efforts of her escape', she knocked on the door of a household which, thankfully, was willing to help. They patched her up and she was able to complete the final leg of her journey to Boussens – thirty-five kilometres from the point at which she escaped – where she knew a contact who could get word of her plight to the Resistance in Toulouse. A Resistance car took her back to Toulouse and not long afterwards she was brought out to London, where she was assigned to the BBC.

When Clayton David had met Claire as an evading airman she was working closely with another agent called Jean-Baptiste

Arhex, a Basque who lived near Pau, towards the western end of the Pyrenees. When the American made contact with her again forty years later he found that the two of them had married and were living comfortably in Paris. Claire told Clayton David that as a result of her narrow escape she was never able to face the smell of pancakes again.

– 10 –

Tales of Resistance

Charles de Gaulle at the BBC

IN 1994, AS A DYING (WE NOW KNOW) François Mitterrand prepared to relinquish the Elysée Palace after fourteen years in power, the journalist Pierre Péan published his book *Une Jeunesse Française*. Its revelations about the young Mitterrand's years as a far-right political activist in the 1930s and as an official in Marshal Pétain's Vichy regime – a *fonctionnaire maréchaliste* – came as a deep shock to supporters of this grand old man of the left, and prompted national soul-searching. The book's title is clever and suggestive: it hints at the idea that a flirtation with extremism and a pragmatic accommodation with the realities of power were simply part and parcel of the coming-of-age experience shared by everyone growing up in France then.

Paul Broué, a little younger than the future president but of the same generation, lived his own *jeunesse française* during those years; it was very different, but it too reflected the experiences of thousands of young Frenchmen during the 1930s and 40s. Today Paul Broué can often be found minding the desk at the Musée du Chemin de la Liberté behind the old station in St Girons, surrounded by black and white photographs and documents telling the story of the *passeurs* who guided people over the mountains. He is a modest and mild-mannered man, and there is nothing in his slightly owlish looks or in his pottering demeanour to suggest a heroic past linking him to the displays, but he is in fact a living exhibit; he escaped this way himself in 1943.

Paul Broué grew up in the mountain town of Seix, where I bought the walking pole which helped me so much on the steeper passages of the Chemin. Set in a deep valley and straddling the river Salat, it is a gateway to the high peaks and passes which today offer summer hikes and winter sports; in the 1940s it was the starting point for some of the most demanding routes to the Spanish border. Paul's parents ran a *pension*, a bed and breakfast, for mountaineers and skiers. 'It was a household where we didn't like *les Boches* very much,' he recalls. Paul's uncle lost a leg fighting the Germans during the First World War and his father was wounded in the calf by shrapnel. Paul's mother was a nurse, and his parents met while Broué senior was recovering in hospital.

Paul can remember hearing the big guns booming across the mountains from Spain in the final stages of the Civil War, and during the Retirada, the great flight from Franco's forces in

February 1939, he and his schoolmates helped hand out chocolate, jam and sweets to refugee children. Paul's father was deeply affected by the outbreak of a new war against Germany in September 1939, and he died of a heart attack that Christmas. Paul was sent to finish his studies in the pretty medieval town of Mirepoix, and left school with a qualification as a lathe operator. He was offered a job in a smelting works in Pamiers, the commercial centre of the Ariège department, but he turned it down because he was warned that it would make him eligible for work in Germany.

One of the most popular beauty spots in the Seix area is the Cascade d'Ars above Aulus-les-Bains. In the right conditions the walk there is stunning, and easily manageable as a day trip. From the main road you wind south and upwards towards the waterfall. Early in the season you are liable to find the path blocked by the detritus of spring avalanches – whole trees, sometimes, and wedges of deep snow – and towards the top the route requires more of a scramble than a walk, but with a steady pace you can reach the falls in less than two hours. They plunge nearly seven hundred and fifty feet in three stages, and on a bright day the great gouts that spurt over the ridge at the top catch the sun; from below it looks as if someone is chucking fist-sized diamonds over the rim. There is a natural clearing at the foot of the Cascade which makes a perfect picnic spot.

One morning in the summer of 1942 Paul cycled up the road from Seix with his mother, sister and a group of friends to do the trek. On the way they passed an unusually large number of police; the gendarmes were mustering for the round-up of Jews at Aulus-les-Bains. Paul and his party had no idea of the significance of what they had seen until a couple of days after their summer outing.

History touched Paul's life again when the Germans occupied the whole of France in November that year. Not long afterwards he received a letter from one of his old teachers at Mirepoix. Knowing that the family was anti-fascist and that Mme Broué ran a *pension*, M. Rouquette asked whether they would consider looking after a young man heading across the mountains. Paul and his mother agreed, and took their first step on the road to being *résistants*. Their home soon became a regular staging post on the route to Spain.

Mme Broué somehow managed to provide lodging and food for escapers even though she also had two Germans billeted in the *pension*, and the teenage Paul took on the job of guiding people on the short journey up the road to the hamlet of Moulin Lauga, where they would hide until the last German patrol of the day had come down from the mountains.

Paul's time as an escape line helper was interrupted when the French authorities sent him to work as a night guard on a railway line in the valley along the river Ariège nearby. Resistance attacks on the railways were becoming increasingly common, and the Germans were putting pressure on Vichy to secure this vital means of communication – so Paul was at this stage working very much in the interests of the regime's collaborationist policies. However, the job turned out to be a pleasant interlude; he was with a group of friends, and they did not take their duties too seriously, sleeping through their shifts whenever they could. The family they were staying with spoilt them and made sure they never ran short of cigarettes. When the summer came they spent their days swimming in the river, and they were well paid. 'It was a fine life,' Paul says, and the war seemed a long way away.

But Paul had for some time nurtured a dream of escaping to join the Free French forces in North Africa, and as 1943 advanced the danger of being deported for work in Germany became ever more acute. In July Paul decided that the time to leave had come. Equipped with a rucksack containing – among other necessaries –

a sautéed rabbit and a change of socks, he joined a party of eight others hoping to make it across the border. Two of his companions had escaped from the concentration camp at Noé (a smaller version of Le Vernet, about an hour's drive from the mountains) and another two were trying to escape the work transports to Germany – one of them, a certain Albert Dougnac, had been hiding in a barn for months.

Their guides took them on a route which roughly followed today's Chemin de la Liberté. They set off at 4 a.m. in fog and rain, and Dougnac, who had been unable to take much exercise during his time in hiding, began to tire at around four and a half thousand feet. The party had to slow down and they were still well within range of German patrols at daybreak. It was not until three in the afternoon that they reached the Refuge des Estagnous. The refuge was rather less salubrious in those days than it was when I stayed there while walking the Chemin, but it was at least dry and they could make a fire. The snow was falling steadily, even though it was July.

For the final leg of the journey by this route you have to climb a couple of hours down from the refuge to a mirror-green mountain lake, then up out of the gorge to another lake before beginning the ascent to the pass below Mont Valier. The weather had cleared on the morning Paul Broué and his companions set out, as indeed it had when I did the journey. The way the peaks of the mountains float in reflection on the surface of the lakes is mesmerizing, but there is a hint of menace in all that chilly beauty. Our guide told us a story that had been passed down to him by an old *passeur* in his village when he was a child. A big party of city folk from Marseilles were once brought this way, he said, and one of them was a woman wearing high heels. The guide snapped them off before the final climb, but she slipped on some ice and plummeted to her death in the upper lake.

Between the two lakes there is a steep climb of around a hundred metres up a rock face. Today there are guide-rails hammered into the rocks and a rope to hang on to, but Paul Broué and his companions had to scramble up unaided. He and several others suffered vertigo and panic attacks, and the guides had to threaten them to keep them going. One member of the party was 'encouraged' with the help of a knife which the guide poked through his trousers.

Paul Broué and his companions reached the frontier at the pass where today's Chemin walkers cross into Spain. They paid their guides 2,000 francs each – the two members of the party who had escaped from the concentration camp at Noé were exempt because they had no money. Paul was picked up and interned by the Spanish. After two days of detention in Sort he was transferred to a prison in Lérida – where he 'celebrated' his twentieth birthday – and then on to the detention camp at Miranda de Ebro. It was three months before he was released (thanks to the Red Cross) but he eventually managed to make his way to North Africa, where he joined the Armée Française Nationale as a commando. In September 1944 his unit landed in St Maxime on the Mediterranean coast and fought their way through eastern France and into Germany (they crossed the Rhine in April 1945) until they met the Russian army coming in the other direction.

Paul went on walking the Chemin de la Liberté into his eighties, and he was still an enthusiastic participant in the ceremonies before and after the trek when I did it. His wartime journey from passive to active resistance, from being a spectator willing to take a few risks to being a fighter committed to driving out the Germans, makes him a truly representative hero of his times. If, as a young man just out of school, you had the chance to spend a few months in a jammy non-job in the mountains with some friends, why not take it? Like Paul Broué, most French who resisted slipped into it over a period, rather than waking up one morning with a burning determination to risk everything for the glory of France.

The idea that something called 'the French Resistance' was born fully formed when Charles de Gaulle made his famous 'appeal' to the French people from London on 18 June 1940 is of course a myth – both in the sense that it is untrue and in the sense that de Gaulle used it to help form France's understanding of its own past.

De Gaulle's address might very easily have become a footnote in history (along with his idea of an Anglo-French fusion). At the time of the fall of France he was the most junior general in the French army and he had been a member of the government for only twelve days. After shuttling between London and the French government in the final days of the Battle of France he finally left for exile in London aboard a British plane on 17 June 1940. He was, as one of his biographers has put it, 'unknown and virtually alone. He had no following and no organization. He lacked all prestige. Indeed, apart from his will and character, his only assets lay in the receptiveness of his British hosts to the improbable proposition that France, in his person, should be given an opportunity to fight on.'

De Gaulle's arrival in London was greeted with some scepticism in British government circles. Churchill had met him and admired the way he had so stubbornly argued the case against an armistice with Germany, and the prime minister agreed to allow him to use the BBC to broadcast to France on 18 June. But the British Cabinet met that morning without the prime minister (who was working on his own 'Blood, Sweat and Tears' speech) and decided that the broadcast should not go ahead because it might alienate Marshal Pétain's new regime. Churchill was tipped off about the decision, and in the course of the afternoon the members of the Cabinet were persuaded to reverse it. In the early evening de Gaulle, who had apparently been quite unaware of all this, turned up at Broadcasting House in a taxi. The BBC – famously – did not consider the speech sufficiently important to record.

De Gaulle later wrote that Churchill was 'the great artist of a great history'. He might just as well have been describing himself. De Gaulle's BBC broadcast was above all an act of imagination; it offered the French an alternative narrative for the traumatic experience they had just endured. De Gaulle told his compatriots that it was technique, not national spirit, which had allowed the Germans to triumph. 'It is the tanks, aeroplanes, the tactics of the Germans that are causing us to retreat,' he declared. He also offered them hope, and a vision of the future. 'This war is not limited to the unfortunate territory of our country. This war is not over as a result of the Battle of France. This is a worldwide war. All the mistakes, all the suffering, do not alter the fact that there are, in the modern world, all the means necessary to crush our enemies one day. Vanquished today by mechanical force, in the future we will be able to overcome by a superior mechanical force.' The idea of 'resistance' until the day of reckoning comes in the closing paragraph: 'Whatever happens, the flame of French resistance must not and will not die.'

But what did resistance mean in the France of 1940? What, indeed, could it mean? It certainly did not at this stage mean young men wearing berets and armed with tommy guns blowing up bridges. The writer Jean Texcier formulated some rather more realistic principles in a document called *Conseils à l'Occupé* (Advice for the Occupied), a project he conceived in Paris a couple of weeks after de Gaulle was putting together the text for his appeal in London.

Returning to a now occupied Paris at the beginning of July

1940, Texcier was disgusted by the spectacle of the German conquerors 'bursting with happiness' and crawling all over the place with their cameras to take pictures of the historic landmarks of their prize, and he was even more revolted by the way his compatriots were responding to the new reality. He watched young women 'partial to a little novelty, initiating small talk [with the occupiers] in the cafés', and read newspaper editorials which 'vaunted the benefits of the disaster, lecturing the French and cynically telling them that France was at last rid of its true enemies'. Provoked by this 'atrocious spectacle', he published – secretly, of course – what he called a 'small manual for dignity'.

The *Conseils à l'Occupé* makes no mention of fighting; it is more of a guide to correct form when dealing with an occupying enemy. 'Make no mistake,' Texcier writes in *Conseil 1*, 'they are not tourists.' So when a German sought to engage one in conversation one should (*Conseil 5*) 'politely give him to understand that what he has to say is of no interest to you'. If one of your favourite shops puts up a sign saying 'German spoken here', change shops, Texcier advises, and instead of turning out for the concerts the Nazis put on in public squares you should, he instructs, 'head for the countryside and listen to the birds'. There are shafts of irony too: 'If you see a young woman discussing business with one of them,' reads *Conseil 10*, 'don't be offended, because the young man will only get what he wants because of his worthless money – and remember that with such a young woman three quarters of Frenchmen would be no more delicate than this young blond from the Black Forest.' The underlying message is that an occupied people should keep their spirits free until they can realistically hope for something more concrete. 'Flaunt your indifference,' Texcier writes in *Conseil 21*, 'but keep your rage safe and secret. It may be useful one day.'

The *Conseils* were circulated clandestinely and found a sympathetic audience, but the time when rage would prove useful was a long way off. In thinking of this stage of the war one must, according to the historian Julian Jackson, 'cast aside romantic images of groups feverishly deciphering coded messages from London, unpacking parachute drops, or sabotaging trains. In 1940–41, there were no contacts with London, and no parachute drops; most early resisters had no idea how to sabotage a train or the means to do it. Equally, the hackneyed phrase he or she "joined the Resistance" is entirely inappropriate to 1940–41. Before it could be joined, the Resistance had to be invented.'

Many of the early resisters were, like Texcier, intellectuals, and while they might not be very good at laying sticks of dynamite on railway tracks they were able to write. One of the first formal resistance organizations was called, rather charmingly, the Groupe du Musée de l'Homme, and was established in the summer of 1940 by a circle of mostly left-wing intellectuals associated with the anthropological and ethnographical museum and research centre in Paris. One of its most successful enterprises was to set up an underground newspaper called *Résistance* in the first winter of the German Occupation. It was edited by Jean Cassou, the Toulouse Resistance leader I quoted in my introduction.

Emmanuel d'Astier de La Vigerie, the author of the 'Plaint of the Partisans', was a very different figure from the *intellos* of the Groupe du Musée de l'Homme. An aristocratic former naval officer turned journalist and poet, he had been mixed up in monarchist and far-right politics before turning to the left during the Spanish Civil War, and had been an enthusiastic opium smoker (a fact which did not stop him becoming France's first post-war interior minister). But he too found the production of a clandestine newspaper the most effective form of resistance; his La Dernière Colonne organization began publishing the paper

Libération (no relation of today's left-wing daily of the same name, which was founded by Jean-Paul Sartre in the 1960s) in the summer of 1941.

Newspapers and anti-German propaganda sheets began popping up all over France, and Julian Jackson argues that they created the first real Resistance structures. 'A newspaper required money, printing facilities, paper and ink,' he wrote; 'it had to be collected and distributed. As circulation expanded, these became full-time tasks, and false identity papers had to be forged for those who performed them. In this way the newspaper *Libération* changed the priorities of the group which had created it. La Dernière Colonne became *Libération*.' Very often these newspapers had bellicose-sounding names – like *Combat* and *Franc-tireur* (literally a 'free shooter', and so used to describe irregular troops or guerrillas) – but their real business was propaganda and the information war. Often the papers gave their names to the groups that had founded them, and over time members of those groups did indeed begin to acquire a military character; that was certainly the case with Combat, which, under Henri Frenay, went on to become one of the most important resistance movements in southern France.

This early resistance to the Occupation was spontaneous and organic; it grew in the fertile soil of M. R. D. Foot's 'small but uncommonly tough segment of the newly conquered population who refused to accept defeat'. Those involved were united in their opposition to the German presence on French soil, but often agreed about little else; the resistance movements embraced communists and monarchists, Catholics and anti-clerical Republicans, far-right supporters of groups like the Croix de Feu (of which the young François Mitterrand had been a member) and Action Française and left-wing trade unionists – the full multi-coloured political spectrum which had made the politics of the Third Republic so fractious in the inter-war years was represented.

The very different political backgrounds of the early Resistance leaders dictated very different attitudes to the Vichy regime and its leader, Marshal Pétain. Henri Frenay, for example, was a serving officer in the army when he first began to put out feelers for sympathizers who would join his movement, and at one point he actually worked in Vichy for the Deuxième Bureau, the regime's intelligence arm. His *Combat* newspaper did not directly criticize the marshal until May 1942, when it declared, 'All is clear now. The Pétain myth is over . . . All France is against you.' By no means all the underground papers condemned Vichy's anti-Semitic Statute on the Jews in October 1940, and some resisters would certainly have sympathized with Vichy's Jewish policies.

The picture was further complicated by differences between groups in the occupied north and the 'free' south. The north was a much more dangerous place to operate. Several members of the Musée de l'Homme group, for example, were arrested at the end of 1940, barely six months after they had established their organization. By the spring of 1941 the group had been destroyed altogether and its newspaper had been closed down. Because of the greater level of risk, resisters in the north tended to be more secretive and security-conscious. In the southern zone things were altogether more relaxed, and – again Frenay's career is an illustration of this – there was even a degree of discreet co-operation between resisters and the Vichy security services.

The process of forging these disparate groups into a unified force which could have a real impact on the course of the war began with a visit to London by Jean Moulin, the man who more than any other came to stand as the emblem of the resistance movement as a whole.

At the time of the fall of France Moulin was a high-flying civil servant, the youngest *préfet* in France, responsible for running the Eure-et-Loir department south-west of Paris. When the victorious Germans arrived at his offices in Chartres they tried to force him to sign a document which falsely accused Senegalese troops of a civilian massacre. The Senegalese had in fact fought gallantly to defend the city, and it appears that a number of them had been killed by the Germans after surrendering. The Germans wanted Moulin's endorsement of their version of events to cover up the crime.

Moulin was shown the remains of a group who had very obviously been killed by a bomb, and immediately dismissed the idea that this grim spectacle was evidence of an atrocity by the Senegalese. He was badly beaten and locked into a cell with the mutilated remains of one of these alleged 'victims' of the African troops. After what he later described as 'seven hours of physical and moral torture' he concluded he was 'at the limits of my resistance' (that word again) and attempted suicide with a piece of broken glass in his cell. He was found covered in blood by his German guards, patched up and returned to the prefecture, the contested document still unsigned.

The incident was allowed to drop, and Moulin returned to his duties as *préfet* of the department, but in November 1940 the Vichy government fired senior officials who were considered insufficiently enthusiastic in their support of the new regime, Moulin among them.

Moulin spent some nine months in southern France after his dismissal, and made contact with several Resistance leaders, including Frenay, who persuaded him that the movements badly needed money and weapons. It seems he originally meant to travel to the United States, where Pierre Cot, a pre-war socialist minister for whom Moulin had worked, had set up shop, hoping to use it as a base for encouraging resistance in France. But at some point Moulin decided to travel to London instead, and in October 1941 he had his first meeting with de Gaulle.

Moulin was the first *préfet* to join de Gaulle, and, now in his early forties, had a natural air of authority and competence. The general was impressed both by his personality and by the detailed report he was able to make on the state of the resistance movements in the southern zone and their needs. Moulin laid out a plan for exploiting the military potential of the movements and for using them to help with the transition to a post-war era. De Gaulle sent him back to France with a mandate to unify the Resistance and to persuade its leaders to accept his authority.

Both these tasks proved formidable. Julian Jackson has argued that it was even more difficult to persuade the various Resistance groups to work together than it was to persuade them to accept de Gaulle as their leader. But heroic efforts by Moulin (or 'Max', as he became known in Resistance circles) eventually bore fruit. In January 1943 he persuaded the three main Resistance organizations in southern France to unite in the United Movement of the Resistance, or MUR (Mouvements Unis de la Résistance), with a single military structure known as the Armée Secrète. Later that spring he took the process a stage further with the establishment of a France-wide council called the Conseil National de la Résistance, which brought together the main resistance movements in northern and southern France, French political parties which were operating underground and representatives of the trade unions. At the first meeting of the CNR (in a Paris flat on 27 May) the sixteen-man body voted to recognize de Gaulle as the head of a French provisional government.

Jean Moulin did not long survive his new creation. A month later he was betrayed – in circumstances which have never been fully cleared up – while attending a meeting of Resistance leaders in the Lyons suburb of Caluire. He was tortured for some three weeks but appears to have revealed absolutely nothing to his interrogators. It is not clear whether he died from his wounds while being moved to a camp in Germany or was personally beaten to death by Klaus Barbie, the Lyons Gestapo chief. But the network he left behind was strong enough to survive his death and sufficiently united and well organized to give the term 'the Resistance' real meaning.

The other critical factor in the formation of the Resistance – the one, indeed, which probably did more than anything else to turn young men of Paul Broué's generation against the Vichy regime – was the apparently insatiable demand of the German Reich for labour.

During 1942 Fritz Sauckel, the German minister for labour, became increasingly insistent in his demands that Vichy should provide more manpower for the factories that were essential to the German war machine. Pierre Laval, Marshal Pétain's prime minister, tried to maintain at least the illusion that Vichy had some independence from Berlin by proposing a programme known as the Relève.

The word means 'relief' – in the military sense of one set of troops relieving another – and the Relève system allowed specialist French workers to volunteer for a tour in Germany in exchange for the return of French prisoners captured during the fall of France. The policy was announced in June 1942 and the first men released under the scheme arrived back in France in August. But the Relève was more than a little skewed in the Germans' favour, with three French volunteers being needed to secure the release of one French prisoner of war, and Sauckel was still pushing for more workers. It was becoming ever more diffi-cult to argue that Vichy offered any kind of protection against Berlin's bullying.

The process of introducing the Relève coincided with the

August round-up of Jews which, as we can see from the reports from *préfets* which I have quoted in Chapter Three, provoked a strong reaction among many French men and women who until that point had been content to make the best of the bad world in which they found themselves. Then came the German occupation of the whole country in November that year. H. R. Kedward, in his study of resistance in southern France *In Search of the Maquis*, argues that this sequence marked a turning point. 'However persuasive the BBC and the Resistance press were in producing a language of deportation and slave labour,' he wrote, 'it was the cumulative impact of [these] three events which gave the words such emotive power; first the Relève itself, secondly the mass deportation of Jewish men, women and, especially, children, thirdly the impact of the Nazi occupation of the southern zone . . . The pressure of the Relève, the racial persecutions, and the investigations and arrests after November brought the language of deportation and the facts of authoritarianism into village squares, and rural towns which had existed since 1940 in relative isolation from the German Occupation and from state inter-ference.' Reading that immediately made me think of Paul Broué and his family on their bicycles on the summer's day when they bumped into the gendarmes mustering for the round-up of Jews at Aulus-les-Bains.

In January 1943 Fritz Sauckel demanded that another quarter of a million workers should be sent to Germany, and in response the Vichy regime introduced the system which dealt the final blow to its claim to be a guardian of the interest of the French people. The STO, or Service du Travail Obligatoire, came into force in February 1943. The new law required all men born between 1920 and 1922 to register for compulsory labour at their local town hall. Some categories of workers were exempt (agricultural workers and miners among them), some were able to defer their service (students, for example), but most were liable for deportation to work in Germany.

The French historian Fabrice Grenard has described the STO as 'the moment when Vichy plunged into the most extreme form of collaboration'. The law touched almost everyone, because almost every family had a young man liable for the transports. Within a month the government's internal intelligence service, the Renseignements Généraux, was reporting that 'even those who until now have shown an irreproachable respect for the government and sincerely admire its policies seem to be shaken in their convictions. Huge numbers of parents of children who will be liable have publicly stated their view that the government has gone too far and that things will go badly wrong.' And opposition to the new law spread like wildfire. The reports coming into Vichy from departments all over France bore testimony to an almost universally hostile reaction; the *préfets* referred to 'discontent growing all the time', 'general anxiety which becomes more and more acute', and a 'fierce opposition to the hated deportations to Germany'.

Thousands of young men tried to escape the deportations and became what were known as *réfractaires*. The word, which means 'a refractory or rebellious person', was originally used by the Vichy authorities to indicate the gravity of the crime these men were committing, but it soon became a badge of honour (it was especially resonant for some Catholics, because it was the term used to describe priests who resisted the anti-clerical legislation at the time of the French Revolution). People at every level in French society became involved in helping the *réfractaires*: doctors wrote false sick notes, mayors and their staff handed out false papers and ration cards, employers took on *réfractaires* under false identities, farmers fed them and hid them in their barns. And as a result a huge proportion of the French population became accustomed to law-breaking; 'under the pressure of the STO', Fabrice Grenard writes, 'ordinary men and women discovered in themselves a talent for living as outlaws'.

As well as these clandestine acts of defiance the STO provoked public demonstrations against the regime, something almost unprecedented since the fall of France. Women sometimes formed human chains to stop the trains leaving for Germany, and in one small town in the Tarn two thousand parents and friends turned out to protest when a train carrying 116 young men left for the east; they sang the Marseillaise and the Internationale and chanted 'Down with Laval' until the police broke up the meeting. In March 1943 one of France's most senior church leaders, Cardinal Liénart of Lille, declared that it was not a Christian duty to obey the STO, and parish priests in many areas routinely helped *réfractaires*. Even many otherwise loyal gendarmes sympathized with these so-called criminals and were less than enthusiastic about pursuing them. The cumulative impact was a general corrosion of Vichy's authority, which eventually went well beyond discontent with the STO; the social compact which even an authoritarian regime needs to govern began to fall apart.

The STO also led directly to the Resistance phenomenon we now know as the *maquis* – those glamorous groups of tommy-gun-toting beret wearers which loom so large in our imaginations when we think of the French Resistance.

At the end of 1943 the German authorities put the number of *réfractaires* at 400,000. That figure may well have been exaggerated to put pressure on the French administration, but even the lowest estimates (Fabrice Grenard puts the true figure at between 100,000 and 200,000) represent an outlaw society on a massive scale. Many *réfractaires* followed Paul Broué and his friends over the mountains into Spain; 1943 was the high point of traffic across the Pyrenees. Others moved away from home and sought employment in 'protected' industries – usually in mining. Still others sought refuge with friends and relatives living in remote areas. But thousands of *réfractaires* simply melted away into the countryside.

They could only stay hidden and survive with the complicity of the rural population. It has sometimes been argued that the French Resistance began as a primarily urban phenomenon, and that the socially conservative French peasantry were more in tune than city dwellers with the conservative values of 'Work, Family, Fatherland' which the Vichy regime claimed to represent. But agriculture was desperately short of manpower by 1943, and when, in the spring of that year, Vichy removed agricultural workers born in 1922 from the list of those exempt from the STO they provoked outrage throughout the countryside. The final piece of the jigsaw had slipped into place; the sometimes huge bands of refugees from the STO living rough in the countryside found themselves in a welcoming environment, supported by a rural population. The *maquis* was born.

It is not quite clear when or why the term '*maquis*' came to be used in the way we now understand it. The word is from Corsica rather than the French mainland, and is still used today to describe the island's wild countryside. But in the spring of 1943 it very quickly became established throughout rural France as a way of describing the bands of outlaws who had rejected Vichy as well as the areas they inhabited. 'The concept did not exist in January 1943; it was everywhere by June,' writes H. R. Kedward. The terms '*prendre le maquis*' and '*maquisards*' entered the language. By no means all the *réfractaires* wanted to fight (indeed some modern estimates suggest that only 10 per cent of *réfractaires* actually took up arms) but they formed a natural pool of potential recruits for the Armée Secrète established by Jean Moulin and the MUR.

Henri Frenay, the leader of the group Combat, said at a meeting of the MUR in April 1943 that the 'official' Resistance had been caught unawares by the explosion of the *maquis*. 'Individual initiatives have come into play beyond our influence,' he said. 'Groups have established themselves and taken to the mountains.' The MUR quickly set up a nationwide *'service de maquis'* to co-ordinate assistance to the camps in the countryside and to formalize the system for providing help to those who were simply refugees from the STO and training to those who wanted to fight.

As the *maquis* became more established and better run, that in turn encouraged more *réfractaires*. In the first three months of 1943 a quarter of a million men left France for Germany; in the following two months the figure was just 37,000. In Ariège, Paul Broué's department, for example, only 13 per cent of those liable for STO were *réfractaires* in April 1943, but the figure had risen to 81 per cent by July. The MUR estimated that by the autumn of 1943 there were between 20,000 and 30,000 *maquisards* in the southern zone of France (concentrated in the more mountainous areas) and a further 5,000 to 10,000 in the northern zone (concentrated in rural regions like Brittany and Normandy). The numbers fell back a little during the following winter (living *en plein air* in the mountains is one thing in the summer, but rather different in the winter) but by the beginning of 1944 the *maquis* as a whole was certainly big enough to be considered a potentially significant fighting force.

The emergence of the *maquis* was of course encouraged by BBC propaganda, and its organization was increasingly assisted by British supplies and British officers – and the Resistance structures created by Jean Moulin certainly helped to coordinate the way the many different *maquis* groups up and down France operated. But it was Vichy, not London, General de Gaulle or the

Resistance leaders of the MUR that really made the *maquis*; without the hated STO the *maquis* might never have come into existence. It is a remarkable example of a repressive regime helping to create the conditions for its own destruction. The STO also ensured that Marshal Pétain's regime would be forever damned in French memory – not just for what it did to Jews, but for what it tried to do to the French as a whole.

The increase in the level of traffic over the Pyrenees after the introduction of the STO was dramatic. Scott Goodall has written a guide to the Chemin de la Liberté and argues that it was the STO and the fear of deportation to Germany which really established the route that today's trek follows. 'Husbands were separated from their wives and children from their parents,' he writes, 'all rounded up by force and shipped out in railway wagons . . . Conditions in the labour camps were appalling . . . It was against this backdrop of hate, misery and despair that *Le Chemin de La Liberté* was born.'

Most British and American writing on wartime escapes through the Pyrenees has focused – perhaps unsurprisingly – on the Allied servicemen and the escape lines that helped them, but they were really only a very small part of the story. The numbers game in this area is extremely tricky; nailing down accurate figures for a clandestine activity is bound to be difficult. But all the estimates of the traffic across the Pyrenees reflect the fact that the number of French who escaped that way was far greater than the number of soldiers and airmen from the United States or from Britain and its empire.

Keith Janes puts the latter figure at some 1,500, including 600 American airmen. In his guide to the Chemin, Scott Goodall quotes a figure of 33,000 for French escapers along the length of the Pyrenees. Emilienne Eychenne puts the total number of escapers at 30,000, while the historian Michael Marrus estimates

100,000. A study of the records at Sort prison has shown that only 10 per cent of those detained there after crossing the mountains were military personnel. All we can really say with certainty is that the number of French trying to escape the Occupation far outweighed the number of British and Allied fighting men trying to get home.

A very high proportion of them left after the introduction of the STO. In the Ariège department where the Chemin begins, for example, the traffic was heaviest in the summer of 1943, with 113 successful escapes in the month of June alone. Obviously it is impossible to be sure about the motives of all those who fled during that period, but Emilienne Eychenne, in her definitive history of escapes from Ariège and its neighbour, Haute-Garonne, estimates that more than 70 per cent of those who left via those two departments were in the age group eligible for deportation to Germany under the STO.

Eychenne also records the poignant facts that the oldest escaper from Ariège during this period was seventy-five, and that among the Jews who crossed the mountains in the same region there were a small number of babies and children who had only just reached the age when they could walk. It is far from impossible that one of these *petits juifs* – or *petites juives* – was Joan Salter, whose story is recorded in Chapters Five and Fourteen.

The flow of serving French soldiers and disenchanted Vichy officials across the Pyrenees increased during 1943 too. When the Germans occupied the whole of France in November 1942, some of those who had been loyal to Vichy judged that the Nazis had unilaterally breached the terms of the Armistice, and so considered themselves free of any obligations which the Armistice dictated. Paul Broué, with his almost uncanny ability to catch a glimpse of history as it passed, was a chance witness to an event which reflected that trend – though not in itself hugely significant it is an intriguing historical footnote.

On the evening of 20 December 1942, Paul saw a party of four men being escorted off the mountain under German guard; one of them, who was remarkably tall, was singing the Marseillaise in a loud voice.

The party had arrived a few days earlier and spent a night at a hotel in Foix before transferring to one in St Girons. From there they were picked up by a *passeur* at half past nine in the evening and escorted up the river Salat to an isolated mountain cabin at 4,500 feet, where they slept. During the night it snowed, and as they prepared to set out the following morning they saw a German patrol moving along the pass above them. They hid behind some rocks until they saw another German patrol heading up towards them. They tried to escape by heading to another cabin below them – they reached the cabin but the Germans followed their footprints in the snow. One of the party popped out of their hiding place for a pee and saw the Germans approaching – he warned their *passeur*, who escaped, but the rest of the party were taken into custody.

The party included a certain Captain Blanchard of the Foreign Legion, a young man better known as Prince Louis Napoleon, the Bonaparte pretender to the French imperial throne. After failing in his attempts to join the French army at the outbreak of war (at the time heirs to the French throne were forbidden by law from living in France) he joined the Foreign Legion instead, served in North Africa before being demobilized, and at the time of his arrest was on his way to join de Gaulle in London.

Even more significant – in terms of what it said about the way opinion in France was changing – was the presence in the party of Roger de Saivre, who had served as a senior official in Marshal Pétain's office since the previous summer. Though a vocal anti-

Nazi, de Saivre had also been a prominent anti-communist polemicist before the war and was fervently committed to the socially and morally conservative political ideals of the Vichy regime. He lost his Vichy job because he objected to the German invasion of the Vichy zone – he went public with his views and the Germans demanded his dismissal. After his arrest in the Pyrenees he was sent to Dachau, which he survived.

11

Guides, Smugglers and Spaniards

Florentino with RAF evader George Duffee

G UIDING ALL THIS TRAFFIC ACROSS the Pyrenees was – like feeding and housing the *réfractaires* of the *maquis* – a considerable logistical challenge, and was only possible because of the general willingness to break the law in the face of the STO. Pretty much every social class and profession were involved. Emilienne Eychenne found that in the Haute-Garonne department the helpers included a prison guard, the public prosecutor in

Toulouse, a police inspector, hoteliers, doctors, insurance agents, aristocratic ladies, business people, those working in the Toulouse theatre, members of the clergy, lawyers, vets and teachers. In Ariège she identified 15 smugglers, 38 workers on rural industrial sites, 4 foresters, 5 tram drivers, 51 peasants (in France the word simply means 'small-scale agricultural workers', and it carries none of the pejorative weight we give it in English), 10 members of the 'liberal professions' (anyone with a professional qualification at degree level or above, such as doctors, lawyers, engineers or architects), 31 civil servants, 11 teachers, 12 tradesmen, 41 people working as artisans or in small businesses, 3 priests and 11 members of the armed forces.

The railways and the hotel business were – for obvious reasons – especially important to the escape lines. Scott Goodall has recorded a local tradition that when trains reached the iron bridge across the river Salat on the outskirts of St Girons the guard would blow the whistle as a signal to escapers to jump (both the railway lines and the bridge have long since gone, but the modern road bridge which replaced them is now the starting point for the Chemin). In many places along the line from Toulouse towards the mountains the stationmasters were in on the game, arranging for escapers to be spirited away as soon as they reached the platform, and the signalling system was used to warn drivers whether or not the coast was clear as they pulled into a station. Francis Aguila, in his book *Passeurs d'Hommes et Femmes de l'Ombre*, has identified a number of hotels and restaurants in the Foix area which were used as safe houses, and describes an arrangement between railway workers and the hotelier who ran the Restaurant de la Charmille at the junction of the Foix, Lavalanet and Tarascon roads; escapers were hidden in the boiler rooms of trains, disguised as stokers with blue uniforms and coal-streaked faces, and then told to jump just as the train approached a tunnel near the restaurant. They would be picked up and taken off to the Charmille to be cleaned up and fed before beginning their journeys across the Pyrenees. (The restaurant is still there, but there is now a motorway which bypasses the crossroads where it stands and it looks as if it has fallen on hard times.)

Today everyone involved would probably be described as members of 'the Resistance'. Whether they would all have seen themselves as *résistants* at the time is open to question. Apart from anything else there was a huge variation in the level of involvement – from someone like Françoise, masterminding a highly complex network from her headquarters in Toulouse, down to the village priest who is recorded as having successfully poisoned a patrol dog by tempting it with a fried sponge.

The relationship between the Resistance, the *maquis* and the groups organizing escapes across the Pyrenees was complex, and understanding it is made that bit more difficult by a difference between the ways the British and the French describe those involved. In the summer of 2012 the British Escape Lines Memorial Society, which is dedicated to raising public consciousness about this whole area of the Second World War, unveiled a monument in the National Memorial Arboretum in Staffordshire. It is a large lump of Pyrenean rock brought over from a quarry near St Girons, and it is inscribed with a dedication to Allied escapers and evaders and their 'helpers'; British accounts tend to sweep everyone involved in the escaping business under that title.

But the French make a distinction between two different kinds of 'helper': the *agents de passage* (people like Paul Broué who helped escapers on their way to the mountains) and the *passeurs*, a very specific term for those who actually guided people over the mountains to the border (it was also used to cover guides who smuggled people over the demarcation line between the Occupied and Free Zones of France).

Today *passeurs* are celebrated for their skill and bravery, and they are generally spoken of with the reverence due to all those who risked their lives in the struggle against Nazism; there is a fine monument to them at the Col de la Core, the lunchtime picnic spot on the second day of the Chemin de la Liberté (it is the last point on the walk you can reach by road, and worth visiting for the spectacular views). But attitudes to the *passeurs* during the war were altogether more ambiguous, and Kedward has written of a '*mythe noir de passeur*', which arose largely from the fact that most of them insisted on being paid. Being a *passeur* was extraordinarily dangerous, and people undertook the role for all sorts of reasons. Some were undoubtedly driven by idealism, but some were also in it for the money and little else – today we would call them people traffickers.

The Pyrenean experience of José de la Barre, the aristocratic young Belgian underground operative we met in Chapter Seven, illustrates what a frightening place the world of the *passeurs* could be. After her cover was blown in Belgium she made her way through France and finally reached the Pyrenees in December 1942, just after the German occupation of the whole country. She and her companion, Guillaume, planned to escape via Andorra, the tiny independent mountain state which is sandwiched between France and Spain. After a night in Toulouse and another in Foix, they made their way to L'Hospitalet, the last village before the border, where they had been told to make contact with the parish priest, a certain Abbé Roo.

The *abbé* told them that the Germans had just completed a sweep through the area, arresting several of the *passeurs* he usually recommended. Leaving José and Guillaume to warm up in his vestry, he paid a visit to the madame of the local brothel in the hope that she might know of someone else who could do the job. She was indeed able to help; she put the *abbé* in touch with three smugglers who were planning to leave for Andorra early the following morning.

This trio turned up at the vestry at midnight. 'Sturdy men, clad in rough but serviceable clothing and each carrying a rucksack,' José de la Barre wrote in her memoir *Granny Was a Spy*. 'I thought it was well that they were our friends: they would have been formidable enemies . . . We had a silent supper, during which, no doubt, they were as busy summing us up as we were them. On them Guillaume and I now depended; it would be no exaggeration to say that we were putting our lives in their hands. Up there in the mountains, in areas remote from any human settlement, we could easily be robbed or abandoned – if not worse – and in such a case our chances of survival would be slim indeed.'

It took them the rest of the night and most of the following day to reach Andorra. 'The smugglers were all fit men,' José wrote, 'and accustomed to such exertions; they made their living by crossing frequently between France and Spain. We, however, had experienced the hardships of over two years of severe food rationing and so were by no means fit . . . We found it extremely difficult to keep up with our guides, although the loads which they were carrying were far heavier than the few belongings to which we still clung. As the mountain slopes became steeper, we had to use our hands to prevent ourselves from slipping back, and these soon became bruised and cut; we had to summon up every last reserve of physical strength and tenacity of purpose to keep going.' After the war José de la Barre married an Englishman and became Lady Villiers (her husband was the boss of British Steel) and I visited her at her home in Windsor Great Park while researching this book. She was of a venerable age and cheerfully admitted that her memory of these events had become somewhat hazy with the years, but when I asked her whether she had ever considered giving up during her climb across the mountains the steel glinted: 'In my experience one does not get very far with such a way of thinking,' she said.

The smugglers proved to be honest thieves, and duly delivered José and Guillaume to Andorra, but arranging the next stage of their mountain journey was trickier still. The pair spent two days negotiating with *passeurs* who could take them on to Spain. 'A stout man, who did not give his name, offered to exchange our dollars for pesetas at what seemed to us, gullible as we were, a good rate,' José remembered, 'but the daughter of the house where we were staying pointed out that his "pesetas" were worthless notes, issued by the former Republican government. We turned down the deal, whereupon the stout man became very nasty and hinted that he might well turn us over to the local police.'

The pair eventually found two Spanish guides who were willing to take them on for an acceptable price. Gonzales and Ribero were both former Republicans who had been condemned to death in absentia by the Franco regime, and were supporting themselves by acting as *passeurs*. The party set out at nine in the evening – it was midwinter, so it was dark – and the journey began with a traverse along 'a narrow goat path hanging, it seemed, in mid-air halfway down a canyon'. Suddenly the two guides came to a halt. 'Before Guillaume and I quite realized what was happening,' José wrote, 'we found ourselves staring into the barrels of two pistols, held by our guides. Ribero said, coldly and dispassionately, "Give us the money you are hiding or else."'

José's account of what followed suggests the steel I glimpsed was true. She somehow persuaded 'these desperadoes' that she and her companion had no money beyond the fee they had agreed to pay. The moment of danger passed. 'I heard Guillaume make a rather poor joke,' she recalled, 'the muzzles of the guns dropped, and with a grin the Spaniards returned them to their holsters. Then they wanted to shake hands in token that there was no ill feeling.' Gonzales and Ribero then proved such good guides for the gruelling remainder of the journey that when they all parted company José gave them her father's gold watch. (Years later she received a letter from them asking whether she would like to buy it back.)

Of course not all *passeurs* were smugglers, and not all smuggler *passeurs* were unscrupulous. The Comet Line's Florentino Goicoechea, after all, was famous for his loyalty as well as his skill in negotiating the mountain passes. But there was a rich smuggling culture in the Pyrenees, much of it concentrated in the area around Andorra, and smuggling experience was a natural training for a job as a *passeur*. Claude Benet writes that in Andorra 'Almost every family had its smuggler, who knew the mountains well and was familiar with the hidden mountain roads, and many of them quite naturally became guides or *passeurs*.' The shepherds of Ariège were equally adept at moving across unguarded borders at the high passes. And there was really quite a lot of money swilling around the Pyrenees at this period – some of it provided by the British in the form of fees for bringing servicemen home, but much of it brought down to the mountains by the steady stream of refugees looking for a way out.

There are all sorts of stories about the way the smuggler *passeurs* preyed upon their clients. Sometimes they would lead them deep into the mountains and then demand additional money to complete the journey; they would, it seems, take more or less anything in lieu of cash – watches, signet rings, wedding rings, pens. Emilienne Eychenne records an incident in which a *passeur* insisted on being allowed to extract his clients' gold teeth before delivering them to the border. *Passeurs* in the Ariège were often armed, and straightforward hold-ups of the kind José de la Barre and her companion faced were not uncommon.

The smuggler *passeurs* had a reputation for moving at a punishing speed and – just to make things that bit tougher – would sometimes ask their clients to carry some of their contraband. They spoke a local dialect which was neither Spanish nor French and was impenetrable to outsiders, and they favoured clothes of dark purple corduroy in a style which dated back to pre-Civil War days in Spain. Eychenne refers to them as 'nimble ragamuffins' and 'picturesque rogues'.

In earlier chapters I have described the development of two of the best-known escape lines, Pat O'Leary and Comet. In the final stages of the war, as the traffic over the Pyrenees grew, the number of different escape lines and networks multiplied in the most dizzying manner. Claude Benet, in his book *Passeurs, Fugitifs, et Espions*, lists the following groups which operated escape lines through Andorra alone: O'Leary, Françoise, Marie-Claire (run by the aristocratic English nurse Mary Lindell), EWA or EVA (which stood for 'EVA-cuation', and was used mostly by Poles), Bourgogne (founded by Gaullist intelligence in partnership with MI9 and run mostly by French soldiers), Brandy (so called because its founder's alias was Martell), Sabot (like Comet, a Belgian line), Organisation Juive de Combat (OJC), F2 Polonais, Dutch-Paris (founded by a Dutch Jewish businessman living in the French capital), Paris-Brussels (about which little seems to be known), Bret Morton, the mainstream MUR resistance movement, Buckmaster, Combat, the exotically named Visigoth-Lorraine, Jeannine Vocabule, AKAK (for the Americans), the Spanish POUM (Partido Obrero de Unificación Marxista, or Workers' Party of Marxist Unity) and Le Groupe Martin (which appears to have been an offshoot of POUM and dealt mostly with Spanish refugees). Emilienne Eychenne identifies several other lines working in

Ariège including Andalousia, Beryl, Gallia, Prunus and Charette (all working for the Free French in London) and YAYA and NANA (which, like AKAK, were American lines).

The divisions between all these groups were not always clearly drawn; a *passeur* or an *agent de passage* could certainly work for more than one of them. However, those who ran the lines might have very different priorities.

For some of them, working on an escape line was a way of resisting and might lead to full-time involvement with the *maquis*. François Rouan, for example, was an army captain who deserted in North Africa to join the Free French but was captured and sent to prison in Marseilles. He escaped and made his way back to his home department of Ariège, where he soon became involved in a network. 'We smuggled Poles, Czechs, and men from the RAF across the border, for which I later received the DSO,' he recalled in an interview. 'It became a movement of anti-fascist resistance, grouping together immigrant miners, construction and forestry workers – all very ordinary men.' Rouan went on to command a *maquis* unit, training new recruits and leading sabotage and ambush operations against the Germans.

But there were also Spanish networks run by Republican refugees who were much more interested in developing the means to resume the fight with Franco than they were in kicking the Germans out of France. They would sometimes ask to be paid in weapons rather than money, and Eychenne describes an incident in Ariège when a couple of Spanish guides refused to accept anything but machine guns as payment for taking a party across the border. The most important and best-known leader of a Spanish network was a young teacher and anarchist called Francisco Ponzán Vidal, and the way he operated illustrates what a tangled web of politics and alliances of convenience there was in the Pyrenees.

Ponzán Vidal, nicknamed 'Specs' because of his short-sightedness, was an intellectual whose appearance suggested he was better suited to the library than the battlefield. He became involved in far-left politics early in the 1930s, and in 1932 he was gaoled for supporting a group of striking chemical workers who had tried to blow up the home of their company's director. He had a colourful civil war; after serving in various jobs in the Republican administration he resigned and fought as a guerrilla, operating behind the lines of Franco's forces. With Franco's victory he fled to France – leaving a stash of weapons hidden in Andorra on his way north – and was interned in Le Vernet concentration camp.

Almost immediately, operating from within the camp, Ponzán Vidal began setting up a network of anti-fascist forces along the Pyrenees. During the six months of his internment he slipped out of Le Vernet on at least sixteen occasions, including several trips to Toulouse and one to dig up his weapons cache in the mountains, and in August 1939 a local communist who ran a garage 'employed' him as a mechanic, thus securing his release. Ponzán Vidal set up his headquarters in the Ariège town of Varilhes, and devoted himself full time to his clandestine activities. He was wounded in a battle with Franco's troops in 1940 (he was trying to spring a couple of anarcho-syndicalist militants from gaol) and arrested by the French again in 1942. He was returned to Le Vernet but again got out (this time he had to escape).

Ponzán Vidal's politics put him well to the left of most British political leaders (it is intriguing to speculate on the views of the then Labour leader Clement Attlee on anarcho-syndicalism) but he made a marriage of convenience with the British intelligence services. He hooked up with the Ian Garrow/Pat O'Leary organization very early on, and his Spanish Republicans proved to be spectacularly successful mountain guides.

Ponzán Vidal's objective was not simply to help prosecute the war against the Nazis; he wanted money to prepare for a new assault on Franco's forces, and MI9 became concerned about the way his men were 'constantly demanding higher tariffs'. Pat O'Leary is reported to have said of the Spanish anarchist, 'Vidal had no particular liking for the British. He regarded them, just as he regarded the French or the Germans, as "pawns on a chess-board". The board was Spain, beyond the mountains. Spain under the thrall of Franco. A rebel against fate, eager for action, always true to his anarchist ideals, Vidal was forever demanding arms. "Handguns – I need handguns – and rifles."'

But Ponzán Vidal proved himself extremely useful to Britain – indeed he was involved in extracting undercover operatives from France as well as the more run-of-the-mill traffic of aircrews. In early December 1942 a dozen Royal Marines staged an especially daring raid on German shipping in the French port of Bordeaux. The 'Cockleshell Heroes', as they later became known, slipped into the harbour in canoes and successfully attached limpet mines to six German ships. Most of the party were subsequently caught and executed by the Germans, but two marines survived the operation. Major Blondie Hasler (the commanding officer) and Marine Bill Sparks managed to make contact with Mary Lindell – she of the Marie-Claire Line mentioned above. They were passed on to Pat O'Leary in Toulouse and he sent them over the Pyrenees in the company of two of Ponzán Vidal's guides, who escorted them safely to the British consulate in Barcelona. O'Leary was caught while they were in the mountains, so Hasler and Sparks could perhaps claim to be the last of the Pat Line escapers.

Ponzán Vidal was arrested in 1943 and imprisoned in Toulouse. Just before the city was liberated by the Resistance in 1944 the Germans took him into the woods on the road near the village of Buzet-sur-Tarn along with some fifty other anti-fascists. They were all shot and the bodies were burnt, their remains piled into two barns in a crude attempt to cover up the crime – the massacre was one of those instances of pointless and almost casual brutality which marked the Germans' withdrawal from France and so greatly increased the resentment they left behind. The French awarded Ponzán Vidal the posthumous rank of captain in the French army and the British gave him a royal commendation for bravery in 1948. There is strong evidence that he was responsible for organizing the Pyrenean escape of Airey Neave, who of course went on to be Margaret Thatcher's campaign manager when she successfully stood for the leadership of the Conservative Party in 1975. You do rather wonder what Vidal's anarchist soul would have made of all that.

I have already described the impact of the Spanish Civil War along the Pyrenees in the months before the Second World War began; its legacy was to have an important influence on the way the war ended in the region too.

By 1942 there were still some 120,000–150,000 Spanish Republican refugees living in south-west France. Vichy conscripted many of them to work in remote rural factories and immigrant labour camps, and had also sent large numbers to Germany – 8,000 Spaniards were deported to the notorious Mauthausen labour camp in Austria. They were regarded with deep suspicion by Vichy and routinely harassed by the regime's police. All of this – together, of course, with their political views – made them natural candidates for the *maquis*. 'For them,' Claude Benet writes, 'the struggle against fascism in France was a logical follow-up to their struggle against the fascism that was now established in Spain, with Franco at its head, and it was therefore a necessary precursor to the re-conquest of their country. They knew that if Nazism were to triumph in France Franco would be strengthened, and they reasoned that if Nazism was beaten the Allies would help them to bring down their dictator.'

The Spaniards had the combat experience which most *maquis* lacked, and in the course of 1942 they began to organize themselves into fighting units. In November that year the Spanish Communist Party, which had been riven with the bewildering and impenetrable factionalism that so often plagued far-left politics, managed to unite in a single movement and formed a guerrilla army – according to Julian Jackson it numbered some 3,500 men by June 1944. By the same date the 2nd Brigade of the Guérilleros Espagnols in Toulouse was in a position to deploy a couple of hundred fighters (commanded by former inmates of Le Vernet), and there were brigades of a similar size in the neighbouring departments.

Indeed the influence of the Guérilleros spread right across southern France; a company of some fifty Spaniards were involved in the Battle of the Glières Plateau (one of the most famous open battles between the Germans and their Milice allies and the *maquisards*) in the Savoie region near the Swiss border. When Nancy Wake, the Pat Line helper known as the White Mouse, was parachuted back into central France as an SOE operative in the Montluçon area she found herself working alongside a large contingent of Spanish *maquisards*. They provided her with a bodyguard after an assassination attempt on her by a drunken Frenchman (he was so drunk he forgot to throw his grenade, and blew himself up). Her close protection team accompanied her whenever she travelled by car. They were all veterans of the Spanish Civil War and in her memoirs Nancy Wake wrote of them with great affection: 'These six Spaniards became devoted to me and I never had any worries when I was with them … If we stopped in a village for a meal and anyone dared to look sideways at me they would stand there looking fierce with their Sten guns at the ready. They would inspect the kitchens and one day they forced two men to show their identity cards simply because they were staring at me during lunch.'

The French countryside had become a dangerous place by the time Nancy Wake was tearing through the lanes with her gun-toting Spaniards in 1944. In May 1943 the official Resistance leader with responsibility for the *maquis* issued a directive on the way *maquisards* should conduct themselves. 'The *maquisard* will respect private property and the life of French, Allied and neutral citizens,' he wrote, 'not just because the existence of the *maquis* depends on the good will of the population, but because members of the *maquis* are the nation's elite and should show the world by example that in good Frenchmen bravery and decency come together.' This idealistic call for restraint was not heard every-where. The emergence of the *maquis* as a force for the liberation of France was accompanied by the emergence of what were known as *maquis noirs*.

Some members of the *maquis noirs* were simply young men who desperately needed to feed themselves and turned to what we might today call 'juvenile crime'. Others were serious gangsters for whom the general collapse of the state's authority offered the sort of opportunities they could only have dreamt of in more settled times. The widespread availability of weapons gave them their means, and the general identification of the *maquis* with the Resistance gave them their cover. In parts of *la France profonde* the bands of marauding '*voleurs maquisards*' became a serious threat to life and livelihood. Villages began to organize all-night guards and the old practice of 'ringing the tocsin' to warn of approaching danger was revived.

There was another, sinister echo of one of the bloodier passages of France's past. During the late eighteenth century, in the aftermath of the French Revolution, parts of the countryside were tyrannized by groups known as *chauffeurs*, or stokers, a reference to their habit of torturing their victims by applying a burning-hot poker to the soles of their feet. In the final months of the German occupation gangs of *maquis noirs* began using the same technique to force isolated country dwellers to reveal where they kept their money and valuables. Sometimes – in a modern twist to this tried and trusted method of torture – they shot their victims once they had the information they wanted.

12

Death in the Mountains

'Piston' and family at his garage

THE CEREMONY AT THE BARRAU BARN takes place just before lunch on the first day of the Chemin. It is usually attended by the last surviving member of the wartime dynasty of Barrau *passeurs*, and the year I did the walk a local guitarist joined the group too and sang a lament she had composed in honour of the young man who died at the spot in September 1943. 'In and around the Ariège villages of Seix and Sentenac-d'Oust,' writes Scott Goodall, 'the family name of Barrau is not only well known, it is treated with respect bordering on reverence.'

The older generation of Barrau brothers, Jean and Norbert, worked as *passeurs* until they were arrested in April 1943 and deported to a labour camp in Germany, where they both died. Norbert's sons, Paul, aged twenty and Louis, aged nineteen, took on the mantle, escorting parties of thirty or more across the mountains.

On the night of 12 September 1943 Louis Barrau was waiting alone in a barn above St Girons, expecting a party of refugees; they were to be led up from the town by one of his friends. But a German patrol and a contingent of Vichy police turned up instead; Louis had been betrayed.

They surrounded the barn and demanded that Louis surrender. When he refused they set light to the building; Louis made a run for it but was shot and killed almost immediately. The Germans came for Paul Barrau too, but he used his knowledge of the mountains to outwit them, and after five nights on the run he escaped to Spain.

The possibility of sudden death was an ever-present reality in the world of the *passeurs*. It might come from a bullet; it might equally well come (more often to their clients than to them) from exhaustion or cold, or indeed a fall. Sometimes, in the loneliness of the mountains, people expired in circumstances that were never known. In his book *Passeurs, Fugitifs, et Espions*, Claude Benet records a conversation with an elderly *passeur* who was haunted by his memories of the dead. The old man conjured up this startling image: 'On one of his trips, when he arrived at the Cabane de Peyregrand, he was met by a dead man frozen into something close to an upright position, gazing at him with a fixed stare.' He also 'recalled people who were lost when they fell from the slippery slopes with their mortally dangerous hazards. He remembered that you could not stop to help them – they were probably dead anyway and you had to push on without delay.'

The Andorran writer Francesc Viadiu has left a striking account of the death of a mysterious and beautiful woman *passeur* called Eloise; it is imaginatively written – it had to be, since neither of the Canadian pilots she was escorting survived either. It suggests something close to a 'cult' of death, or at least an attempt to romanticize the reality.

'All three of them [Eloise and the two pilots] disappeared into a much deeper snowdrift than any they had so far encountered. Only Eloise, calling on all her strength, managed to break to the surface again. The effort exhausted all her physical reserves and she had to stop to allow the beating of her heart to subside. She stretched out on the snow. How good it was to lie on this bed of soft snow! ... A sweet sleep took possession of her body and closed her eyelids ... The Giant [which I take to be a personification of the mountain] had finished his hunt and stilled the anger of the squalls. As the wind died down the mist returned to the gorge from which it had been driven and the moon shone once again, casting its rays everywhere. The mountain again donned its coat of diamonds, sapphires, rubies and emeralds which, in the light of the moon, rivalled the stars in the heavens in their brilliance. The Giant dressed in his finest attire to receive the body of this heroine, lying peacefully in a shroud of snow studded with precious stones.'

One story that recurs repeatedly in the mythology which surrounds the *passeurs* is that when their clients became too exhausted to walk it was the practice to execute them; they were going to die anyway – so the logic runs – and it was kinder to make it quick. And of course the consequence of a weak and exhausted but still living fugitive falling into the hands of the Germans could be catastrophic. However, the memoirs I've read suggest it was much more common for *passeurs* to use extreme methods – sometimes including violence – to goad people onwards.

In October 1943 two *passeurs* embarked on an ill-fated trip to guide a party of six American airmen and six French soldiers to Spain via Andorra. To avoid German patrols the party had to make a long detour, walking for thirty hours in heavy snow. When three of the Americans reached a point of complete collapse one of the *passeurs* drew his revolver and threatened to shoot them if they did not keep walking. When that failed, he fired a bullet close to the head of one of them. Even that did not move the exhausted men. The *passeur* did not, however, follow through with this threat; the three were left behind. They died anyway (presumably from cold and exhaustion) and their bodies were found a year later.

The British soldier and journalist George Millar tells a similar story in his escaping epic *Horned Pigeon*. Millar was captured in North Africa and his astonishing journey took him through Italian and German prison camps and right across France before he reached the Pyrenees. He set out to cross the mountains from Perpignan, but he and his party had to give up the attempt when their *passeur* disappeared (the man's body was later discovered in the river Tech, but the circumstances of his death were never established). Millar's second attempt on the mountains had to be abandoned because the guide lost his way. He made the third effort in the company of a group of American airmen and one of them – whom Millar had nicknamed 'Gable', after the dashing film actor Clark – became exhausted in the final stages of the climb to the Spanish border. Gable asked Millar (who had good French) to plead with their guide for a rest.

'"Rest?" yelled the guide . . . "I'll give him rest, the pig."

'He danced down the slope and slapped Gable sharply several

times on the face. This roused the poor man, and, supported by Fritz and me, he did another fifty yards.

'Then he collapsed finally. Fritz and I tried everything we could think of, praise, vilification, encouragement, massage, wine from the Spaniard's skin, alcohol from Fritz's little bottle. The big man would not move. Tears oozed from his eyes.'

They did get Gable a little further, but when he collapsed again the Spanish *passeur* lost patience altogether. '"Enough of this foolery," screamed the guide. "I have been taking men across all this winter and I never saw such women. This is the worst part. Sooner or later the Germans will pass here. Are you going to throw your chance away for one weakling?"

'He suddenly darted on Gable.

'"I will *make* you go on," he shouted. Before we could stop him he seized two handfuls of Gable's black hair and began to bash his big head against a tree-trunk. Gable only moaned gently.

'"I don't care what you do to me. I can't go on."'

In his memoirs Millar recalled asking himself where his duty lay at this point. There was obviously a moral obligation to Gable, who would be at great risk if he was left behind and was clearly beyond the point at which he was capable of a rational judgement. On the other hand Millar also felt a strong sense of obligation to all the people who had helped him on his journey thus far. 'Was my duty to this man, or to all that lay behind me and all that lay ahead?' he asked himself. The Americans naturally felt equally torn about leaving behind a brother-in-arms and compatriot, and there was some debate about the best thing to do. In the end most of the group decided to push on; they covered Gable's body with leaves in the hope of providing him with a little warmth, and one other airman – who had become close to Gable while the two of them had been in hiding together and was himself exhausted – elected to stay behind too.

It is worth reflecting for a moment or two on the circumstances in which judgements of this kind had to be made. Millar's case was exceptional – as a POW he had been moved from North Africa to Italy and then Germany, and he had been helped by dozens of people during his three months on the run as an escaper. But almost everyone who reached the Pyrenees had been through a great deal to get there. Exhaustion often set in during the final stages of the mountain journey, with the prize of the border and freedom tantalizingly close. Even those who had not reached the point of collapse would in all likelihood be themselves close to the limits of their endurance. And the sort of dilemma which Millar and his American companions faced almost always arose in extreme mountain conditions, with the risk of detection by a German patrol ever present.

As it turned out, Millar's story had a happy ending: he heard later that the two Americans had managed to get to Spain on their own. But the factors I've listed above sometimes led to judgements which can look callous in retrospect, even if they seemed – and indeed almost certainly were – logical at the time. Many of them played a part in the one instance I have encountered of a *passeur* who really did carry out a summary execution of one of his clients.

The *passeur* in question was called Lazare Cabrero-Monclus, and was also known (presumably in recognition of his great skill, since he was a man of neat mountain build) as 'El Magno'. He worked as part of a network set up by Ponzán Vidal, and in November 1942 he was engaged to take five Jewish refugees to Spain. They included an MP and Jacques Grumbach, the editor of an underground newspaper called *Populaire*, who had found things too hot for comfort in Marseilles since the arrival of the Germans earlier in the month (as a Jew and an underground newspaper man he was doubly in danger). At the last minute the group was joined by an Englishman called Thornton, a former chauffeur at the Rolls-Royce offices in Paris – Pyrenean escaping often made strange bedfellows.

Cabrero-Monclus must have had some idea of the sort of journey he could expect when his party presented themselves with heavy luggage containing quantities of old books. Most of them were unfit and they all made heavy weather of the walk. Grumbach, six foot tall, overweight and suffering from a weak heart, found the going especially tough. Before long he was dangerously short of breath; he fell and broke his ankle.

The guides – El Magno had brought two assistants – told him to tighten the ankle support on his boots and keep going while his muscles were still warm, but by the time they reached the first shelter – two hours later than planned – it was clear that Grumbach would need to rest. It was equally apparent that the other members of the party were too exhausted to carry their injured companion, so El Magno decided to leave him in the shelter while he escorted the others to a cabin higher in the mountains.

By the time he returned forty-five minutes later the temperature had dropped to minus ten degrees. He found Grumbach unable to move or to speak; he had used his penknife to cut away the ankle supports on his boot, and the resulting pain from his broken ankle had rendered him almost unconscious. The *passeur* judged him beyond hope, and was concerned about the fate that would befall his other five clients if he left them for too long; although it was only November the conditions were getting steadily worse, and there was a serious risk that they would succumb to hypothermia.

El Magno took a momentous decision. 'The poor man could go no further,' he said later, 'so I shot him in the head with my revolver.' He then removed Grumbach's identity papers to avoid any possibility that the body might lead to the escape network, took his money and his watch (to make it look like a robbery) and tipped the body over a ridge.

He returned to the rest of the party and escorted them into neutral Andorra – at some point the other two guides seem to have melted away, leaving him to manage things on his own. He told Grumbach's friends that the injured man had been spotted making his own way back down the mountain, but he did confess to Ponzán Vidal what had happened, explaining to him that '*il a du piquer le type aux lunettes*' – which roughly translates as 'he had had to sting the bloke with the glasses'.

After this incident El Magno continued guiding parties over the mountains for several escape line leaders including Ponzán Vidal and Françoise Dissard, but at the end of the war he chose to remove himself to Andorra for a while. We know the detail of the story because in 1950 Grumbach's body was discovered in the mountains (mutilated boot and all). Cabrero-Monclus, back in France by this stage, was charged with murder. But he succeeded in convincing a court in Toulouse that what he did had been justified, and he was acquitted in 1953.

The risks the *passeurs* faced of being captured or killed greatly increased after November 1942. The way the demarcation line was drawn between the Free and Occupied Zones meant that there had been a German presence at the Atlantic end of the Pyrenees (including the crossing favoured by Dédée de Jongh and the Comet Line) since the Armistice, but along the rest of the mountain range the French operated their own patchier and often more tolerant security regime. With the German occupation of the whole country things became altogether tighter all the way from the Atlantic to the Mediterranean.

In Ariège, for example, the Germans decreed a wide *zone interdite* along the border; living in towns like St Girons and moving about the neighbourhood involved carrying around a bewilderingly complex collection of passes and work permits. The main security force – the men who actually went up into the mountains to chase parties of escapers – were the Grenzschutz, or Border Guards. They sported an edelweiss on their caps, which may help explain why today local people will sometimes tell you that the Nazi troops in the region were Austrians, chosen for their affinity with mountain life.

In Ariège the weather was still fine when the Border Guards arrived in the late autumn of 1942 and they were able to make several trips to reconnoitre the frontier before the winter set in. One of their local headquarters was the Château de Beauregard on the outskirts of St Girons; it is now an extremely nice holiday hotel with a swimming pool, a spa and rooms named after great French poets. In July 1943 the overall commander-in-chief of the Grenzschutz paid a visit there to oversee the establishment of an elite group dedicated to hunting down *passeurs* and escapers.

In the early months after the occupation of the whole of France the regular troops of the Wehrmacht, the German Armed Forces, were not much involved in chasing refugees or indeed in fighting the emerging *maquis*. For a German soldier in the spring of 1943 a posting to sunny south-west France must have been con-sidered something of a cushy number – especially when contrasted with the slaughter and misery so many of their compatriots had recently endured at Stalingrad. But the full panoply of different security services which the Nazi state could deploy was represented in the region.

When the Vichy prime minister, Pierre Laval, was told that Nazi Germany was an authoritarian state he is said to have remarked yes, 'but what a lot of authorities'. Nazi power in Berlin was administered by a tangle of interlocking and often competing agencies, and the Nazis brought the system with them wherever they went. In France the Sicherheitspolizei, or Security Police (sometimes known as the SIPO), had primary responsibility for the protection of German troops. In theory – under the terms of the Armistice – that was the only police function the Germans were allowed to exercise (the Vichy authorities were supposed to take care of everything else), but in reality the SIPO became increasingly involved in policing more generally. The SIPO in France was run from Paris by Helmut Knochen, a committed Nazi ideologue and an enthusiast for the Final Solution. In Ariège they set themselves up at another château just outside the departmental capital of Foix.

The Gestapo (the Geheime Staatspolizei, or Secret State Police, as they were more properly known) established themselves in Toulouse (their office there was the organization's regional headquarters for the whole of southern France). There is a tendency to use the term 'Gestapo' to cover the German police generally, but they were in fact a relatively small presence in France. They were part of the SIPO but had maintained their own identity, and spent much of their energy keeping an eye on their fellow Germans to ensure they went about their business with appropriate zeal. The Feldgendarmerie (Field Police) also had a presence in the region, as did the Sicherheitsdienst. This last organization – more commonly known as the SD – was originally founded as the Nazi Party's own security force, and had been formally incorporated into the state security apparatus in 1939. Its job was intelligence gathering, and it ran networks of informers throughout the Reich and its occupied territories.

The Germans achieved some significant results in their campaign to stop the flow of refugees into Spain. Emilienne Eychenne has meticulously documented the tally of their successes in the Ariège and Haute-Garonne departments. In the

Ariège department German patrols killed eight *passeurs* and imprisoned around a hundred *passeurs* and *agents de passage*. The Germans also arrested 160 escapers (as against a mere 49 arrested by the French before the Germans arrived). In the neighbouring department of Haute-Garonnne the figures were similar: 150 guides and 127 would-be escapers were arrested after November 1942, while the French had managed to pick up only around a dozen before then. And the overwhelming majority of those who were caught by the Germans were deported to concentration camps in the Reich, where many of them died.

But the German authorities were covering an impossibly large area with resources that were inevitably limited by the exigencies of war; while walking the Chemin I found myself reflecting how easy it is to disappear in the mountains if you want to, especially if you know the terrain well. The mountain conditions may some-times have been a serious obstacle to the fugitives, but their German hunters had to deal with those conditions too, and in the remoter reaches local knowledge was a huge advantage. There are examples of *passeurs* who – unlike Louis Barrau – did manage to escape after being cornered.

Jean Bénazet, also known as 'Piston', was a *passeur* of legendary standing in the central Pyrenees in rather the way Florentino Goicoechea was at the eastern end of the mountains. 'He is "the" *passeur ariégeois*,' according to Francis Aguila, 'with-out doubt the best of the best.'

He and his wife ran the town garage in Varilhes, which is not far from Le Vernet, and in 1939 he came into contact with Ponzán Vidal through the offices of the local bakers, two Spanish refugees who used to make bread runs to the camp to help their interned compatriots. It was Bénazet who gave the Spanish anarchist the 'job' as a mechanic which allowed him to leave the camp. Bénazet was himself very much a man of the left – he had been shocked by the treatment of the Republican refugees during the Retirada, and recorded the haunting diary entry I quoted in Chapter Three – and became a pivotal figure in Ponzán Vidal's anti-fascist network. When Ponzán Vidal left Le Vernet in the autumn of 1939 he set up his headquarters at Bénazet's home in Varilhes, and Bénazet himself became one of his most trusted *passeurs*.

Bénazet was a keen sportsman – a rugby player in his youth and a skier until the age of seventy-five – and enjoyed fishing in the mountain lakes. He recorded the number of escapers he successfully helped as 'trout' in his log book; thus in 1943 it read '18 April, 9; 27 April, 7; 1 May, 6' and so on. On 13 June he was escorting a party of no fewer than eighteen young Frenchmen trying to reach North Africa when they were surprised by a patrol of two Germans just above Aulus-les-Bains, almost certainly as a result of a tip-off by someone local.

Six members of the party were a little higher than the rest and managed to hide, but Bénazet and twelve others were forced to stop when the Germans fired warning shots and climbed down towards them. Bénazet, knowing that as a guide he faced, as he put it later, 'a trip to the concentration camps or summary execution', waited until he was hidden from the view of one of the men by a rock and made a run for it, but the second member of the patrol spotted him and opened fire, so he was forced to put his hands up again.

He tried to fall behind the rest of the group, gradually slipping to the back of the line and stopping from time to time to do up his laces, but one of the Germans stopped each time he did. So Bénazet made his way back into the centre of the group and waited until – after four hours' march – they were on a bend in thickly wooded terrain before making another break for freedom. The Germans fired at him but missed (a bullet went through his trouser leg), and although he suffered a serious groin injury from slipping on a rock (for which he underwent surgery the following month), he managed to get away, along with an eighteen-year-old from Pamiers who followed him when he threw himself into the trees.

After this near miss Bénazet gave up working as a *passeur*, but continued to provide supplies for a *maquis* group near the mountain village of Massat. In the autumn of 1943 he was denounced to the Germans and had to go underground; he was smuggled up to Toulouse by railway workers and spent the rest of the war living on false papers as an active *résistant* until the liberation of the city. Most of the young men captured with him on his last trip as a *passeur* were deported to Germany, and when Jean Bénazet died in 1991 his last wish was to be buried without flowers as a way of showing solidarity with those who had died in the camps.

The way the Germans took the lead in security operations in the mountains in the course of 1943 reflected a more general trend across what had once been called the 'Free Zone'; the occupiers were becoming increasingly disenchanted with the effectiveness of the French security services. The peace agreement between Vichy and Germany allowed for the establishment of a so-called Armée de l'Armistice of around 95,000 men, but it was disbanded not long after the German occupation of the whole of France at the end of 1942. And the Vichy police were themselves infected by the general lack of respect for the regime's laws which followed the introduction of the STO.

The evidence that many police were actively helping *réfractaires* to escape had become so strong in the summer of 1943 that the Vichy prime minister, Pierre Laval, sent out a round-robin letter warning that anyone who failed to enforce the STO with full rigour would themselves face deportation to Germany. In her account of the perils facing *réfractaires* who tried to escape over the Pyrenees, Emilienne Eychenne writes that 'There were gendarmes who would arrest you, give you a good burst of Vichy propaganda, and then leave the ground-floor window very obviously open as they shut the door.' She gives the example of a group of Breton *réfractaires* who were arrested in Seix on their way across the mountains in June 1943. The officers gave them a talking-to about the dangers of trying to get to Spain – and then left them alone in the gendarmerie for the night with the door unlocked; 'at four in the morning,' Eychenne writes, 'the gendarmerie was discreetly abandoned by its unwilling guests'.

Because the Vichy authorities found it more and more difficult to enforce the law by using the regular police, they had to rely heavily on two security organizations they had created themselves to root out *maquisards* and track down *réfractaires*: the quasi-military force Groupes Mobiles de Réserve, or GMR, which had been established in 1941, and the body known as the Milice.

The Milice Français (which simply means the French Militia) was not founded until January 1943, two and a half years after the fall of France and the establishment of Marshal Pétain's Vichy government, but it was responsible for much of the fratricidal violence which characterized the final months of Germany's occupation of France, and its actions contributed mightily to the bitterness with which Vichy is remembered by so many French.

It was the child of a meeting between Pierre Laval and Adolf Hitler in December 1942. The French prime minister sought and was granted (so much for the idea that Vichy was independent of the Germans) permission to establish his own security force. Laval handed the task of organizing the new body to Joseph Darnand, a hero of the Great War who had spent the inter-war years running a garage business in Nice and indulging in resentful far-right politics; he was a prominent figure among the right-wing thugs known as Cagoulards – which literally translates as 'the hoodies', a reference to their habit of wearing dark red hoods over their faces when they made their violent forays on to the streets.

The core of the Milice was drawn from the Service d'Ordre Légionnaire, or SOL, a far-right group created by Darnand in the aftermath of the fall of France, which had already established a reputation for violence and enthusiastic collaboration with the Germans. Darnand saw the new organization as a French version of the Nazi Party's Brown Shirts. There were several levels of membership (the mad minds which organized the Milice drew on medieval orders of chivalry for their inspiration) and the Franc-Garde section lived in barracks and were, to all intents and purposes, full-time paramilitaries. They took an oath vowing to defend Christian civilization and rejecting – among other things – democracy, individualism, international capitalism, bolshevism, Freemasonry and 'Jewish leprosy'.

The membership of the Milice was modest when set against the official law enforcement agencies of the French state, even in its truncated form; under the terms of the Armistice Vichy was allowed sixty thousand gendarmes while the Milice attracted a membership of no more than between twenty-five and thirty thousand volunteers. Often they were not especially well armed; photographs of Milice members show them equipped with captured Allied machine guns, rifles and pistols. But what they lacked in numbers and equipment they made up for in their ruthlessness – they regularly tortured other French men and women – and, often, their ideological enthusiasm.

Some joined the Milice because it offered good rations and pay; members were exempt from the STO and petty criminals could secure an amnesty by volunteering. But most of them signed up because they were fascist ideologues, and many would certainly have been members of the Nazi Party if they had been born German instead of French. There was one significant point of difference between them and their Nazi allies: French right-wing extremism (like its Spanish cousin) was deeply rooted in traditionalist Catholicism. But the *miliciens* collaborated because they admired what the Nazis were trying to achieve, not just because they felt they had to go along with the realities of the Occupation.

Indeed in August 1943 Darnand swore a personal oath of loyalty to Hitler and was formally recognized by the Reich as a Sturmbannfuhrer in the Waffen-SS. Several hundred of his Milice members also joined the Waffen-SS and actually fought on the Eastern Front. In *The Storm of War* the historian Andrew Roberts notes that one of Darnand's officers, Joseph Lecussan, carried a Star of David made from the skin of a Jew in his wallet, and was responsible for burying a group of Jewish men alive by ordering his militiamen to push them down a well and drop bags of cement on top of them. The Milice marched to the song of the Service d'Ordre Legionnaire which came before it:

> *Miliciens,* let us purify France,
> Bolcheviks, free-masons, all these enemies,
> The shameful rot of Israel,
> France tears you from its heart and vomits you out.

> For the men behind our defeat
> No punishment is too severe
> We want their heads
> We want them at the pillory.

Relations between the Germans and the Vichy regime became increasingly difficult towards the end of 1943, and in December

René Bousquet, who had by that stage arrested and handed over more than sixty thousand Jews, lost his job as head of the police at Berlin's insistence. Joseph Darnand was subsequently appointed to fulfil his functions and was named Secretary General for the Maintenance of Order. That meant that by the beginning of 1944 Vichy had effectively handed over the duty of law enforcement to a man whose organization routinely operated outside the law. The Milice was an ideological movement driven by a crusading fascist spirit rather than a conventional security body with a loyalty to the state and its political masters. Many of its commanders were willing to prosecute their campaigns by methods which took no account of the legal norms to which Vichy theoretically subscribed, there was no real judicial oversight of its activities, and as Vichy's authority collapsed the Milice acted more and more as an extra-judicial force driven by the warped convictions of its leaders and members.

During my visit to Ariège to walk the Chemin I interviewed Olivier Naduce, a local historian, and he gave me a copy of his pamphlet about the wartime history of Jean Bénazet's home village of Varilhes. The story of the great *passeur* occupies pride of place, but the booklet also includes an intriguing insight into the divisions and violence that haunted France in the final months of the war.

At the beginning of 1944 some twenty inhabitants of the village were *miliciens*, including the mayor. The Resistance planted bombs at some of their homes, and eighteen inhabitants were detained in reprisal. Many of them had nothing to do with the Resistance – a record of left-wing political activism was quite enough to get you picked up in such circumstances.

Some of them were tortured at the German security headquarters in Foix, then all the men were sent to Mauthausen or Buchenwald and the women to Ravensbrück. There were two more rounds of arrests in neighbouring villages in May (just before D-Day). Twenty-five people from these tiny communities were deported to the camps, and only ten came back. In total 450 *ariégeois* were deported – one for every 330 members of the population, the highest proportion for any department in France.

– 13 –

Endings

Rimont, a martyred village

IF YOU TAKE THE ROAD FROM St Girons towards Foix you will see the village of Rimont on your left some ten kilometres after leaving the town. The main street is built along a ridge and dominated by the hexagonal tower of the church – which, like many in the region, seems bigger and swankier than the jumble of modest houses around its skirts could really justify.

There is nothing in the scene to mark it as in any way

exceptional. If you have spent a little time in the neighbourhood the name Rimont may ring a bell or two because the village makes a very good hard *chèvre* cheese which is served in some of the local restaurants, but even if you are minded to take a detour at this point on the D117 you are much more likely to turn right than left – just as you pass the exit to Rimont there are signs to the pretty old monastery of Combelongue which nestles in a hollow a couple of kilometres in the other direction.

Rimont is coy about its history – or at least about some bits of its history. After the dreadful events that unfolded here in 1944 it was declared a *village martyr*, and a distinguished local historian, writing on the fiftieth anniversary of the Battle of Rimont, described it as a 'double symbol, of the horrors of Nazi barbarism and the victory of Resistance Fighters over Hitler's army'. But there is a part of the story which is more difficult to remember, much less celebrate.

The monument in the square outside the church includes a panel in remembrance of 'The Civilian Dead [*victimes civiles* is the phrase used in the French] of the Liberation, 1944'. There are eleven names on the list, but nothing to indicate how they died. In fact nine of them were victims of a Nazi war crime, while two of them were murdered by their own compatriots.

By the early months of 1944 the escapers and evaders who went over the Pyrenees were heading for a world where the darkness seemed to be lifting; everyone was expecting an Allied landing in France soon (indeed many had expected it at the end of 1943) and the days when Britain stood alone and faced an uncertain future were long gone. As things turned out there were of course many months of tough fighting still to come, but the pilots crowding into Françoise Dissard's villa in Toulouse on their way south would surely have felt confident of ultimate victory by this stage of the war.

And yet dark shadows were falling over the French country-side through which they passed. In many areas of France the most savage acts were carried out at the very last. Some of the most brutal atrocities by the Nazis and by their Vichy allies took place after D-Day, when the ultimate outcome of the war was beyond any real doubt. Regions like the south-west had of course seen no fighting at all at the time of the fall of France, and even as the level of sabotage and terrorism against the occupiers grew in 1943 it would have been possible to live a relatively peaceful life in the countryside. Yet in the final months leading up to the liberation of France there was so much fighting between the French them-selves that many historians now refer to a *guerre franco-français*, a French civil war which was played out as a kind of sub-plot to the world war which was reaching its climax.

Carmen Callil argues that 'Much about the defeat of France and its suffering during the Occupation becomes clearer when those years are viewed as a French civil war, a variant of that of its Spanish neighbour . . . certain aspects of the Vichy State become more comprehensible when viewed from a Spanish rather than a German perspective.' The historian Henry Rousso has suggested that the origins of the fratricidal violence of 1944 go right back to 1936, the year both France and Spain elected governments of the left known as 'Popular Fronts', and he described the Vichy regime as 'in many respects . . . a form of revenge' against France's Popular Front – in just the way Franco's insurrection was a form of revenge against Spain's. Marshal Pétain was the French ambassador to Franco's Spain in 1939, and praised the 'wise leadership of General Franco'. Callil calls the two of them 'kissing cousins, not a relationship Pétain and his fellows had with Hitler, or Mussolini'.

I have found researching events in France during the summer of 1944 the most unsettling experience of writing this book because it is so difficult to understand the motivation of those involved. Two parallel themes stand out: the determination of many German troops to remain true to the very worst aspects of Nazi repression even as their control over the population dissolved, and a similar descent into ever greater cruelty by the Milice and its allies, a process which accelerated as the end of Vichy drew closer.

Claude Delpla, a local historian who has produced a meticulous account of the events leading up to the Battle of Rimont, wrote that 'Certain *Ariégeois*, blinded by their political prejudices or their alliances, lost their sense of reality and forgot that there are lines one should not cross. It was a strange kind of blindness which, at the moment when Allied troops and the first contingents of Free French set foot in Normandy, led some obstinate spirits to wager everything on a victory for Hitler! At the moment when almost everyone realized that Germany really had lost the war, some swam against the tide, unable to see beyond the boundaries of their own neighbourhood or community, and wedded to the derisory power they enjoyed.'

Towns and villages all over southern France have their stories of horror from this period. Here are two from the part of France I've come to know while writing this book. One of these dramas was played out almost entirely in Ariège, while the other began there but, in a dark mirror image of some of the escapes I have written about, involved a journey right across France and beyond its borders – a journey not to freedom but to captivity and, in many cases, to death. I shall describe them in some detail because I think that soaking oneself completely in the events of the time is the only way to understand the blindness that Claude Delpla describes; the individual traumas many endured during the final chapter of the German occupation of France were so all-absorbing that it is perhaps not really so strange that people sometimes missed the bigger picture.

Francesco Nitti was a detainee in Le Vernet at the time of D-Day. 'The Allies have landed in Northern France,' he recorded in his diary. 'Here everything is calm. We wait anxiously for news.'

Nitti was a veteran Italian anti-fascist with an adventurous past. He had been imprisoned by Mussolini and escaped to fight in Spain. Exiled to France after the Spanish Civil War, he joined the French Resistance early on and was arrested along with the writer and *résistant* Jean Cassou in 1942. By June 1944 he had been imprisoned in Le Vernet for nearly a year.

When he arrived at the camp in the summer of 1943 there were around a thousand inmates, and at one point during his time there the figure rose as high as one thousand five hundred. The last Jews from Le Vernet were handed over to the Germans in May 1944, and most of the non-Jews who were fit enough to work had been deported by the end of that month. At the time of D-Day there were around four hundred detainees left in the camp, most of them old or sick. This rump included a large number of wounded veterans of the Spanish Civil War, including many amputees. The camp routine had eased up a good deal since Arthur Koestler's days there. Nitti noticed that many of the guards were as pleased as the inmates to hear about the Allied landings (although the presence of members of the Milice among them made it unwise to express such sentiments).

Four days after D-Day Nitti was woken by a shout outside his barracks: 'Wake up . . . the Germans have taken over the camp.' Early that morning German army units had arrived, disarmed the French gendarmes and locked up almost all the French staff in the section reserved for political prisoners. The only Frenchman spared this indignity was the deputy commander of the camp, who was called, by a curious coincidence, Monsieur Vernet. Vernet spoke German and always moved with an armed escort because the *maquis* in Ariège had vowed to kill him. Most of the new arrivals were too old to fight at the front but had been passed fit for light duties. The officers and NCOs, however, were veterans of the Eastern Front and bullied their men.

The day after the Germans took over Le Vernet they mounted an operation against the *maquis* in the area around St Girons and Rimont.

Rimont had been a centre of Resistance activity for some time by this stage. The village was one of the headquarters of a company called Carborex which produced charcoal – a highly valued commodity as most civilian cars and lorries had been converted to run off charcoal-burning engines because of the acute petrol shortages. Carborex had been founded by a prominent member of the pre-war Communist Party and became a front organization for Resistance activity, employing both Spanish Republicans and French communists. By late 1943 Rimont was well known as a place where aspiring *maquisards* would receive a sympathetic reception, and a *maquis* group set up shop in an abandoned farm near the village. In the autumn of 1943 they mounted a series of small-scale operations, attacking a factory in Pamiers, stealing a tonne of explosives from a local power station and attacking a Milice bus (it turned out to be nearly empty, but they managed to wound the driver).

The attack on the *maquis* on 10 June 1944 was carried out by units from the Milice and German troops, including some from the SS Das Reich division (Das Reich soldiers were, on that same day, responsible for the massacre of Oradour-sur-Glane, during which almost the entire population of a village near Limoges was wiped out and four hundred and fifty of its women and children were murdered and burnt in the church). To avoid being surrounded the *maquis* – a mixture of French communists and Spanish *guérilleros* – scattered in different directions, and a group of them made their way to a mountain pass called the Col de la Crouzette just south of today's D117 road between St Girons and Foix. The Maquis de la Crouzette was to play an important part in the liberation of the Ariège department.

At Le Vernet, events moved quickly.

A week after the German takeover a further sixty men – 'the last in a state to wield a shovel' in the judgement of Francesco Nitti – were deported to the work camps. Nitti assumed the rest of them would be forgotten as the Germans turned their attention to more important priorities. 'We imagined that we could no longer be a prey of interest to the Germans,' he wrote. 'Old men, the disabled, the one-legged, could we possibly be deported? We could not believe it, especially when all available transport would be committed to the German war machine, at the moment when the Allies had established a foothold in Europe. How could we seem "units" worth moving or deporting? Our logic gave us reason to hope, but the German logic had nothing to do with ours.'

On 30 June Le Vernet's remaining detainees were woken at dawn and the evacuation of the camp began. M. Vernet read out a roll call. The inmates were divided into three groups: those considered most dangerous, those who had been interned for offences which had simply been forgotten, and those guilty of minor infractions. The purpose of this piece of bureaucracy remains obscure; all of them were to be deported to Germany. They were forced on to lorries, each one guarded by an escort of a German soldier and several French *miliciens*. Nitti took particular note of a *milicien* in his truck who kept fiddling with his machine gun in a threatening manner. 'An all too familiar fascist specimen,' he wrote, 'full of arrogance, thoughtlessness and cowardice.'

The detainees were taken to a barracks in Toulouse, where they were joined by several dozen other prisoners from the region. Word of their whereabouts got around, and the following afternoon some of the men were able to speak to wives and daughters who gathered in the street outside their cells. On the morning of 2 July they were loaded on to trains at Toulouse station. Nitti noted that many of their new guards, especially the younger ones, carried Nazi Party insignia on their uniforms.

Some six hundred detainees, including around forty women, were crammed into trucks designed for animals. The accommodation gave Nitti the title for the short (and compelling) account he wrote of the journey; it is called '8 horses, 70 men'. It was a boiling hot summer and the escort nailed planks of wood over the windows on the carriages. The detainees spent their first night on the train sitting at Toulouse station, and on 3 July they left for Bordeaux. When they arrived they were given some water and allowed off the carriages in groups of four or five to defecate. Nitti's carriage was so crowded that they had to sleep in shifts – there was only room for a third of those on board to lie down at any one time.

From Bordeaux the train headed north again, and just outside Angoulême the prisoners and their escort got their first real taste of what it meant to run a transport like this through a war zone. While they were being shunted into a siding at a small rural station some Allied planes passed overhead. The Germans immediately abandoned the train and headed into the surrounding countryside, leaving the prisoners locked up in their cattle trucks. Nitti wrote later, 'to be machine-gunned in open countryside by a plane is extremely unpleasant. I had had the experience during the Spanish war on several occasions. But you can at least run where you want, throw yourself onto the ground, lie in a ditch or behind a bush or under the branches of a tree; you have the illusion and the hope that the pilot will not see you. But being shut into a wooden carriage, in the middle of an abandoned station,

knowing that your carriage and those around it are the chosen
target for the bullets of a plane which can take as much time as it
likes to get you in its sights, to be forced to sit still waiting for the
fatal bullet which will deliver you from the nightmare . . . that is
real anguish.'

The attacking planes were Lockheed Lightnings – American
fighters used for dive bombing and ground attacks. As the first
one strafed the line of the train Christian de Roquemaurel, another
prisoner, slid over to the window of his truck; he watched the
plane rising steeply into the sky at the end of its run, 'spinning
with the mad jumpiness of a giant insect'. Next to him another
man was using bits of clothing to put together a makeshift
tricolour to wave at the pilots. De Roquemaurel described the air
'shaken by the din of bursts of gunfire and the scream of engines
pushed to the limit' as one fighter after another raked the train
with bullets. Holes opened in the wooden roof of the truck as they
hit home, and he heard the groan of a wounded man.

The attack ended just as suddenly as it had begun – perhaps
the pilots had seen the tricolours and white handkerchiefs which
de Roquemaurel's neighbour and some others had managed to
poke through the sides of the trucks. The dead and wounded –
including several Germans – were laid out on the station platform
to be transported to Angoulême. In the confusion three detainees
tried to escape; they were caught by the guards and another
prisoner watched them being lined up against the wall of the
station and executed by firing squad.

For the next three days the train wandered around the lines in
an apparently aimless fashion. Nitti compared it to 'a ship without
a captain, at one moment pushed towards the shore by the waves,
at the next leaving the coast behind as it heads towards some
distant port under full sail'. The prisoners picked up hints that
their escort were terrified of being attacked by the *maquis*, for

whom trains were an attractive target. At dawn on 8 July, the transport finally reached Angoulême. The station had just been bombed, and Nitti described the scene as an 'unforgettable spectacle'. 'By the early light of the day,' he wrote, 'we saw locomotives and carriages which had been destroyed, broken to bits, tipped on top of one another. The broken rails stretched upwards like gaunt arms reaching for the sky. The buildings were ruined, broken, deserted.'

There were parties of workmen on the platforms trying to clean the place up, and when they saw the trainload of prisoners emerge from the tunnel leading into the station they gazed at it in amazement, as if it was a 'strange vision'. Nitti's convoy has gone down in history as *le train fantôme*, the ghost train.

It was obvious as soon as they reached Angoulême that they could go no further north by this route, and the train headed back in the direction of Bordeaux. For three days and nights they remained on the train at Bordeaux station – they had been locked up in their trucks for almost two weeks by this stage – and on 12 July they were taken off the train and marched to the city's synagogue, which had been commandeered as a temporary prison.

On the following day, 13 July, back in Ariège, a group of French fascists assassinated two prominent Rimont residents.

Paul Laffont had a distinguished career in national politics behind him when the war broke out; he served as a minister (secretary of state for post and telecommunications) in two governments in the early 1920s, and in 1939 he was a senator and president of the Ariège General Council – the most senior political position in the department. He was a member of the Gauche Démocratique group in the Senate and, like many others on the centre left, he voted to grant full powers to Marshal Pétain during the crisis of 1940. But he soon became disenchanted with the direction taken by Vichy and gradually distanced himself from the regime and indeed from politics. Laffont left the Senate in 1940 and withdrew to his country house at La Vignasse, on the eastern edge of Rimont. In the summer of 1944 he was in his sixtieth year.

The Germans and the Milice strongly suspected that Laffont had links with the Resistance. The former senator had in fact approached the mainstream Gaullist resistance movement, MUR, the previous year, but they rejected him because of his past support for Pétain. When the Maquis de la Crouzette was established he made another attempt to re-engage with the politics of the day, and on three occasions he gave the new *maquis* significant sums of money. A couple of strangers turned up at La Vignasse one day and tried to persuade him to sign up to a Resistance group they claimed to represent; suspicious, he explained that he had left politics and asked them to leave. Paul Laffont then used his contacts with the local police to check the plates on their car; the vehicle turned out to be registered to the German security services.

The event that led to his murder was well beyond his control, and took place many hundreds of miles away: in late June 1944 the Resistance succeeded in assassinating Philippe Henriot, the much-hated Vichy propaganda minister, in his Paris flat. The collaborationists down in Ariège decided that a tit-for-tat assassination of a former minister from the pre-war Third Republic would be a suitable response.

Early on the morning of 13 July a group from the far-right organization Le Parti Populaire Français, or PPF, turned up at the former senator's country house. The PPF was even more enthusiastically pro-Nazi than the Milice – its leader, Jacques Doriot, served in a German uniform on the Eastern Front. Paul Laffont was bundled into a van and driven away, but some of the PPF thugs stayed on to ransack the house. They made so much noise that the alarm was raised in Rimont, and the local doctor, Léon-Charles Labro, who was close to Laffont, came out to investigate – only to be dragged off himself. The bodies of the two men were found in separate locations some days later. Both had been beaten and tortured before execution.

In the aftermath of the assassinations the *maquis* showed that they could sometimes be as ruthless as their opponents. Lists of suspected collaborators in Rimont and the nearby village of La Bastide-de-Sérou were drawn up, and on 15 July two *maquis* groups – one drawn from the mainstream resistance movement, the Armée Secrète, and another, a mixture of French communists and Spanish *guérilleros*, from the Maquis de la Crouzette – moved round the area picking people up.

In his account of events leading up to the Battle of Rimont Claude Delpla observed drily that 'The rush that was inevitable in such circumstances involved certain mistakes which are explained by the power of rumour at a time when the only information available went by word of mouth.' Mistakes in such turbulent times could have fatal consequences. In one village the *maquis* unit got an address wrong and shot another member of the Resistance by mistake. Of the twenty people arrested, eleven were taken into the hills near the Col de la Crouzette, tried and summarily executed. There were some 'clear mistakes', Delpla wrote, and 'cases of malicious denunciation'. One of the dead was, like his killers, a communist.

It was around this time that the passengers of the *train fantôme*, settling into life at the Bordeaux synagogue with no immediate prospect of continuing their journey, began to detect signs of alarm – if not yet despondency – among their guards. They discovered that the escort had been sent down from Paris with the assurance that their assignment would last no more than three or four days – which was the usual journey time for convoys of deportees heading north. Instead they had spent days travelling the French countryside and had been strafed by Allied planes. Now they were holed up in a strange and uncomfortable place without any idea how or when they would be able to continue their journey, and the news from the front line was less than encouraging. 'We hardly needed a newspaper to tell us that things were going well for our side,' Nitti wrote, 'the worried look of the Germans was enough to give us confidence.'

The days dragged on. The synagogue was overcrowded and desperately hot. The prisoners were plagued by fleas and had nothing to do but play chess and read the few books they found about the place. One of Nitti's friends had managed to bring along his Bible and lent it to the Italian writer for agreed hours each day – Nitti recalled devouring the Gospels and the Acts of the Apostles with real pleasure. The prisoners did manage to find out a little about what was going on in the outside world themselves. A woman who lived across the road from the synagogue used to hold up a slate at her window with news of the Allied advances in Normandy. They were also able to pinch occasional copies of the army newspaper which was distributed among their guards – it was in the pages of *Soldaten am Atlantik* that they read details of the bomb plot against Hitler on 20 July.

The day after the abortive attempt to blow up the Führer, German troops in Ariège made a major assault on the Maquis de la Crouzette. They were supported by a large detachment of *miliciens* under the Milice commander for Ariège and the neighbouring department of Haute-Garonne. Paramilitaries from the PPF – the organization responsible for the assassination of Paul Laffont and Doctor Labro – were also involved. The fighting in the hills south of today's D117 lasted from eight in the morning until six in the evening.

Two refugees – a Polish-Jewish lawyer and a Spanish

Republican who had been hiding in an empty barn just below the Col de la Crouzette – were killed trying to reach the main body of *maquisards*, but the attack was kept at bay. Nightfall brought a summer mist, and the *maquisards* melted away into the hills, again avoiding encirclement. The *miliciens*, enraged by the failure of the operation, sacked two hamlets, burning down six houses and ten farm buildings. The Germans also put several farms to the torch and slaughtered their cattle.

On 31 July in the Bordeaux synagogue, Francesco Nitti noted in his diary, 'The fleas were very active last night.' At four that afternoon one of the senior officers of the escort called for silence and read out the names of ten prisoners. They were told to collect their things. No one knew where they were being taken or why, but everyone had a strong sense of foreboding. The next morning the prisoners saw that the baggage belonging to the ten men had been left by the wall of the synagogue. It later emerged that they had been taken to a nearby military prison and in the days following they were twice led out for execution, but twice returned to their cells because the firing squad failed to turn up. They were finally shot at the third attempt in early August, standing along a ditch that had been dug to receive their bodies. Because of the administrative confusion about the executions the Germans announced they had been carried out two days before the men were actually killed.

In Ariège at eight in the morning on 2 August the Milice arrested Clovis Dedieu at his home in Castelnau-Durban, four kilometres from Rimont. Dedieu had been a rugby player of legendary skill and since hanging up his boots had worked as a restaurateur and butcher. Rugby and food are the two passions of the south-west, and Dedieu was a figure of some local standing. He was heavily involved in clandestine activity, feeding and hiding STO *réfractaires*, helping Resistance groups to receive parachute drops of equipment and providing intelligence to the Maquis de la Crouzette.

Clovis Dedieu was taken to the Milice barracks in Foix and tortured for fourteen hours before dying on the afternoon of 4 August – without, it seems, having given anything away. His body was buried in a field during the night and identified some days later. Today a street in Castelnau-Durban and the local rugby ground bear his name.

On 6 August Marshal Pétain finally complained about what he called the 'baneful' (*néfaste*) activities of the Milice. In a letter to his prime minister, Pierre Laval, he accused the organization of undermining the authority of the official representatives of the state, torturing, murdering and terrorizing the population. He said they had become 'Frenchmen delivering their compatriots to the Gestapo'. Joseph Darnand's reply is much quoted: 'In the course of these four years I have received your compliments and your felicitations. You encouraged me . . . and today, because the Americans are at the gates of Paris, you start to tell me that I shall be a stain on the honour of France? It is something you might have thought of a little earlier.'

The *train fantôme* finally left Bordeaux on 10 August. The original deportees – who by this stage had spent nearly a month in the city's synagogue – were joined by around a hundred men and seventy women from the main Bordeaux prison. There were recently arrested young *résistants* among them, and, Nitti noticed, a priest and two French gendarmes in uniform. They set off south, first retracing their journey to Toulouse and then continuing east via Carcassonne, Béziers and Montpellier.

The August heat of the Midi again turned the wooden trucks into furnaces. 'It was difficult to breathe, and we never stopped sweating, day or night,' Nitti wrote. 'The space was so tight that we could not avoid touching one another and our sweat and smells mingled. It was impossible to sleep; our arms and legs were stiffened by the preposterous positions we were forced to adopt.' There were four or five prisoners with tuberculosis in Nitti's car who found the lack of air especially difficult to cope with – they frequently passed out. At Remoulins – between Nîmes and Avignon – they watched as the body of a man who had died of asphyxiation was carried out of the next carriage.

Marie Bartette, one of the women prisoners, described seeing a whole group of men laid out unconscious on the verge at the same stop; a Spanish doctor and a priest, both prisoners, were ministering to them. She later established that a group of men had escaped from their truck near Toulouse; and the Germans had sealed the wagon and denied the detainees food and water by way of reprisal.

The train remained at Remoulins station for five days (while they were there a French railway worker managed to unlock one of the trucks, allowing another small group to escape). On 15 August the Allies and the Free French forces landed in southern France along the Côte d'Azur, and the *train fantôme* was once again close to the front line.

The Allies quickly began to push their way up the Rhône valley, and it soon became evident to the escort of the *train fantôme* that they would no longer be able to use the line north; the Allies were bombing the railways and the bridges across the river and the *maquisards* were blowing up the lines wherever they could. So at Roquemaure the deportees were told to get off the train and walk instead. They set off through the vineyards of the Rhône valley in full sun, the women at the head of the column. The main railway bridge across the Rhône had been destroyed, so the column of prisoners picked their way over a wooden bridge pockmarked with holes from the bombing. Whenever an Allied plane passed overhead the German guards forced the deportees on to the ground – a few managed to escape in the confusion.

Almost all those who left accounts of this epic trek remembered agonizing thirst. The Germans gave the prisoners nothing to drink and beat anyone who broke ranks when they passed a drinking fountain. When they reached the celebrated wine-making village of Châteauneuf-du-Pape on the east bank of the Rhône the deportees broke into the Marseillaise as a way of showing their defiance. The local people brought out wine and water and gave them to the prisoners whenever they saw an opportunity – the German guards tried to fend off anyone who approached the column.

After nine hours in the broiling heat the column reached the station in the town of Sorgues. They were such a pitiful sight by this stage that dozens of people simply poured into the station precinct in defiance of the Germans. They carried food and drink – some of them even brought clothes and shoes too. The railway workers helped more deportees to escape whenever they saw a chance. The rest were piled back into a new set of cattle trucks and the journey north began again. In the course of the trek some prisoners managed to drop notes in the hope that they would be picked up and passed on to their families. One of them is displayed at the Le Vernet museum in Ariège: 'To whoever finds this letter: please contact Madame Bosca at Saint Antoine-de-Filcar, Lot-et-Garonne, and tell her that her husband passed through Agen on 10 August. He is leaving for Germany and is in good health. He sends kisses to all his family.'

Not long after the train left Sorgues there was another machine-gun attack by Allied aircraft. This time many of the prisoners had their makeshift tricolours ready – in Nitti's truck they used an old sweater for the blue, a shirt for the white and a scarf for the red – and the shooting stopped quickly, but several prisoners were killed and injured. At the next stop, Montélimar, the dead and wounded were unloaded from the train. Nitti watched a group of railway workers gather round the bodies but recorded that 'the Germans, faithful to their instructions to the end, chased them away violently'. The Allied forces were now very close indeed; the Battle of Montélimar, one of the decisive engagements of the campaign in southern France, began just a day or two after the latest incarnation of the *train fantôme* left the city's station. When they arrived at Valence on 20 August Nitti saw a blonde woman in the stationmaster's office holding up a piece of cardboard; it read, 'Paris is surrounded. Have courage.'

The Allied landing in Provence was the signal for a general uprising by the Resistance in southern France. In Ariège the departmental capital, Foix, was liberated on 19 August after fierce fighting (with Spanish *guérilleros* taking the lead against the Germans). The following day, a Sunday, the Maquis de la Crouzette made their way down from their mountain fastness to liberate St Girons. The Germans retreated to the town's college and to the Château de Beauregard (the Border Guards' headquarters which is now such a nice hotel), and by midday their defences were wavering and it began to look as if the battle was close to being won.

But at this point a column of reinforcements arrived from the town of Boussens, on the river Garonne to the north-west of St Girons. A small group of *maquisards* (French communists from the Maquis de la Crouzette) were dug in between St Girons station and the beautiful old hill village of St Lizier, and managed to keep the column at a standstill for most of the afternoon, but eventually, at around six in the evening, the new arrivals forced their way through and made contact with the German garrison. The fighters of the Maquis de la Crouzette had to concede defeat, and withdrew back into the hills.

We have met all sorts of people in this book who reached the Pyrenees after long journeys and many adventures, but none of the visitors to the region I have described before had come quite as far as the troops of the relief column which arrived in St Girons on the evening of 20 August 1944. The French nicknamed them 'the Mongols', but they were more properly called soldiers of the Legion of Turkestan. The senior officers were German, but most of the ordinary soldiers were Muslims from the 'Stans' of the Soviet Union – Uzbeks, Kyrgyz, Kazaks and Tajiks.

The Germans raised several such 'legions' by encouraging anti-Soviet nationalism among the peoples of the Soviet Union – so there were also, for example, a Georgian Legion, an Armenian Legion and an Azerbaijan Legion. In theory those who joined were volunteers, but many of them had been captured on the Eastern Front and given the choice between prison camp (where many of them would probably have died of hunger) and service in the German army. The Legion of Turkestan was based and trained in Poland and units were transferred to France in late 1943 to help fight the *maquis*. The fear the legion inspired probably owed as much to the alien appearance of its soldiers as it did to their actions; the legion suffered a high desertion rate, which suggests that its reputation for ferocious fanaticism was unjustified (it must have been difficult to persuade yourself that killing French men and women in the Pyrenees would contribute very much to the struggle for an independent homeland in Central Asia). But when 'the Mongols' arrived in the south-west in the autumn of 1944 a 'Great Terror' took hold of the countryside. 'The same phrase echoed from one village to the next,' according to Claude Delpla, '"The Mongols have arrived."' The column which relieved the German garrison in St Girons was around two thousand strong.

The fighters of the Maquis de la Crouzette had withdrawn without any idea that there were so many of them, and on the morning of 21 August everyone seems to have assumed the battle for the town was as good as won. The people of Rimont were so confident that they actually hoisted the tricolour from the church tower, and a local farmer was asked to bring a cow into the village to provide food for the expected liberation party. The only defenders of the village were a group of some twenty badly armed local *résistants* and a Spanish machine-gun party deployed along the main road.

At 9 a.m. the local mechanic, who had been posted as a look-out, spotted the German column moving out of St Girons towards Rimont. He counted forty-four trucks heading along the road and could not even see the end of the line. When he raised the alarm Jean Farras, the leader of the Rimont *résistants*, gave the order to evacuate the village, but some older residents preferred to lock themselves in their homes. The situation was further confused by the village police, who had asked people to stay in their houses because they were expecting a visit from a party of Germans (who presumably did not know that the area had turned into a battlefield).

The small detachment of defenders managed to hold up the column on the road, but they soon ran out of ammunition. The German commander, Major Schopplein, ordered his troops to surround Rimont, and by 11.30 they had secured control of most of the village.

Major Schopplein gave his troops the chilling instruction to 'burn the village and force a way through by any means'. One of his officers, a Lieutenant Harms, a Lutheran pastor in civilian life, refused to obey: 'Act like Christians,' he told his troops (an odd instruction to the largely Muslim Central Asians, perhaps); 'I loathe this way of making war.' The lieutenant also warned that anyone caught looting would be shot, and his section passed through the village without incident.

However, Lieutenant Scherhag, the next officer who came through, took up the major's orders all too enthusiastically, and one of the most shameful episodes of the German withdrawal from France began. Groups of German and Central Asian soldiers began breaking into houses and raping women. Claude Delpla quotes the following witness statement from one of the victims:

'The German troops and the Mongols (there is no distinction to be made, in my opinion at least, between the conduct of one or the other) arrived in the village and forced their way into the house, and after it had been searched by several groups my husband was taken away and other members of the family were put under guard in the street. I meanwhile, holding my three-year-old little girl by the hand, was invited by a German (in the company of Mongols and other Germans) to go up to the first floor. Thinking they wanted to undertake a thorough search, and not wanting to provoke them, I followed.

'When we reached the bedroom they used gestures to tell me that they wanted me to satisfy them. I shouted in protest, and the child shouted and cried when she heard me; a huge Mongol tore her away from me and her tears redoubled. She was in a panic when I took her back into my arms. There were several of them and they bent me across the bed. I held back my cries and tried to reassure the child by gasping out a few words. I remember repeating distractedly "Once upon a time there was a little girl . . ." My clothes were torn and they raped me [Mongols and Germans], two of them holding me down by the arms to help a third. How many times? 5? 6? I no longer know.'

One man, a teacher called Jean-Baptiste Alio, managed to get hold of a gun and shot a 'Mongol' soldier through the neck in an attempt to protect his wife. He was caught and taken before Major Schopplein, who ordered that he be executed. Several of his soldiers refused to carry out the order, so Schopplein did the job himself. There is a small marble cross marking the spot on the left-hand side of the road heading into Rimont.

The Germans systematically torched the village, throwing incendiary grenades through the doorways and forcing everyone on to the streets. Several groups of hostages were taken, interrogated and threatened with execution – one group was lined up along a wall by Paul Laffont's house at the end of the village. Another group was forced into a meadow in the line of fire from a Resistance unit which was engaging the Germans from a hillside; they spent the day lying down as the bullets passed over their heads. Twenty-five children (and some priests who were looking after them) were pinned down by the battle in the Combelongue monastery, where they were attending a holiday camp. Claude Delpla suggests they only escaped the full rage of the legion's troops because a Protestant German NCO refused to fire on a building which displayed a crucifix.

The legion's troops shot the 65-year-old farmer who had brought a cow into the village for the expected liberation celebration. Most of the eleven civilian casualties were in their sixties and seventies – the oldest was a 78-year-old man who was shot dead while he was hoeing potatoes outside his back door. A 77-year-old woman was hit and killed by a stray bullet in her wheelchair, and a 71-year-old man was found dead in his house, where he had tried to hide. The village and several neighbouring farms and hamlets were almost completely destroyed – 236 buildings were burnt down in all, including the Mairie and the village school.

Somehow the village postmistress managed to keep her head through all this; she put a telephone call through to Foix, now of course in the hands of the *maquisards* and Spanish *guérilleros*. Reinforcements from the Maquis de la Crouzette headed towards Rimont, and as the word spread *maquis* groups from all over the area converged on the battle. Major Schopplein's decision to put Rimont to the torch turned out to be a strategic mistake as well as a war crime: his men had gone about the business of burning the village with some thoroughness, and it took time; the delay allowed *maquis* fighters to establish themselves along both sides of the road leading out of the village. As the column tried to press on towards Foix, it took fire on both flanks. By the evening of 21 August the Germans had managed to get no further than the village of Castelnau-Durban – just a few kilometres beyond Rimont and little more than fifteen kilometres from St Girons itself.

On the morning of 22 August the fighting resumed, with a steady stream of reinforcements joining the attack on the increasingly embattled German column. A *maquisard* was taken prisoner in the course of the morning and when he was threatened with execution he had the wit to tell Major Schopplein that his men were surrounded by a force of four thousand – including British and American troops – who would kill a hundred Germans for each *maquisard* who was shot. The actual size of the forces facing the Germans was a little more than a tenth of that figure – they did include a British major and a Canadian lieutenant who had been parachuted into the area as liaison officers a couple of weeks earlier, but they were otherwise all irregular troops of one kind and another. But Schopplein was so demoralized by this stage that he believed the story. Towards the evening a German staff car appeared flying a white flag. Major Schopplein surrendered along with some fifteen hundred troops.

The victorious *maquisards* drove back to Foix with their haul. They arrived in the middle of the night and in an interview years later 'Commandant Robert' – the 25-year-old Spaniard whose *guérilleros* had liberated Foix a couple of days earlier – described being mobbed by men in pyjamas and women in their nightdresses. It was the final act in the liberation of the Ariège department.

Thirteen Central Asians and two Germans who had been captured at Rimont itself were summarily executed by the villagers amid the embers of their homes. Other members of the Legion of Turkestan were picked up in the countryside in the days that followed, as were several French collaborators. Those responsible for killing Charles Labro and Paul Laffont were executed at St Lizier the following month.

The bulk of the prisoners were taken to the place which had, until the previous month, been such a powerful symbol of the malign alliance between the Vichy regime and Nazi Germany – the Le Vernet concentration camp. On the way to the camp Major Schopplein realized how badly he had misread things and tried to kill himself. His captors controlled him but he was later – according to the official record – shot while trying to escape. Lieutenant Scherhag was also taken to Le Vernet; he was tried as a war criminal and executed by firing squad.

While the Battle of Rimont was being fought out in Ariège, the Le Vernet veteran Francesco Nitti was steeling himself for a terrifying escape attempt from the *train fantôme*. In his memoir he quotes Dostoyevsky's first instruction to himself in his notes on *The Brothers Karamazov*: '1. To find out whether it is possible to lie between the tracks while a train moves over you at full speed.' Nitti declares, 'Yes, Dostoyevsky, not only can one lie between the tracks while the train moves over you, one can leave the train by a hole in the floor and lie on the track under moving carriages.' It was possible, but it was also extremely dangerous. There was a railway worker in Nitti's carriage, a mechanic who had worked in the Pyrenean town of Ustaritz, and he warned the escaping party that there would be a steel hook at the end of the convoy which could kill them.

On the night of 23/24 August – at about the time Major Schopplein was beginning to discover what life in Le Vernet was like – Nitti and his friends levered up the floor of their cattle truck. Like those who crossed the Pyrenees, he saw the promise of liberty in stones: 'At that moment,' he wrote, 'freedom was represented by the ribbon of pebbly earth that ran before our eyes.' Nitti and thirty other men in his wagon dropped from the train as it approached the German border. As instructed, he lay face down with his arms tight to his sides, and listened to the sound of the train receding in the sleeping countryside. Some of his companions had not listened closely enough to the mechanic's warning about the steel hook; five or six of them were found crushed on the line a few days later.

Once it crossed the border into Germany the train began to move more quickly. Conchita Ramos, a Spanish refugee who had grown up in the Ariège village of Varilhes, remembered the train's first stop on German territory: 'through the windows we could read the word "Saarbrück"; it was the end of our hopes. We were in Germany! Goodbye France!' She remembered a group of prisoners being taken off the train at this point, including fourteen German sailors convicted of insubordination and a French woman who was due to be beheaded (she in fact survived, and Conchita Ramos later met her at Ravensbrück).

On 28 August the *train fantôme* reached Dachau. Of those still on board, 291 had begun their journey nearly two months earlier at Le Vernet. It was three days after the liberation of Paris and a week after the liberation of Ariège, but there was still plenty of time for many of them to die before the war was over: 112 deportees from the *train fantôme* were moved on to Mauthausen; 87 of them were dead by the time the camp was liberated by the Americans in May 1945.

The Chemin de la Liberté walk is an act of remembrance, and

part of the process of remembrance is an attempt to make sense of the past. It is relatively easy to do that with the story of the escapers and their helpers – you can see the point of it all, and the moral lines are, for the most part, cleanly drawn. It is much more difficult to make any kind of sense of the violence and cruelty at Rimont or the epic determination of the *train fantôme*'s escort to deliver their sad cargo to the camps. The bitterness left by pointless horror lingers longer.

– 14 –

Fanny/Joan's Tale 2

Fanny/Joan reunited with her father

Aₛ ᴀ ᴠᴇʀʏ ʏᴏᴜɴɢ ᴄʜɪʟᴅ Joan Salter – or Fanny Zimetbaum, as she was then – spoke fluent French. She knows this because she has dug out an American social worker's report which records the fact; it describes her as 'a very winsome girl . . . well developed physically and mentally who speaks flawless French'. As an adult she made several attempts to relearn her French but found herself quite unable to do so. It is surely not too fanciful to see a connection between this baffling language block and the fact that from the ages of three to seven Fanny/Joan was forced to go through a complete change of identity.

When the female members of the Zimetbaum family – Fanny, her mother Bronia and her half-sister Liliane – arrived in neutral territory after their Pyrenean journey in the winter of 1942, they were interned by the Spanish authorities. 'Although history puts Spain in the Fascist camp,' she wrote later, 'everyone I know who was a refugee there – my mother included – spoke highly of the Spanish people and their kindness.' Liliane, who was seven, was placed in a convent while Fanny and their mother were given over to the care of American Quakers.

The American Friends Service Committee or AFSC – as the Quaker refugee organization was officially known – had operated in Vichy France from the Armistice in 1940 until the German occupation of the whole country in November 1942. Working under the auspices of the United States Committee for the Care of European Children, it had succeeded in getting some eight hundred young Jews out of the country and away to the United States via Lisbon (including, intriguingly, a small number from the Château de la Hille).

There's a moving news-wire photograph of a group of these young refugees smiling happily as their ship arrives in New York in September 1941. The caption reads: 'Refugee children here on *Serpa Pinto*: New York. Sorrowful story was told of these children, some of the 56 who arrived September 21 on the *Serpa Pinto* from Lisbon under the auspices of the U.S. Committee for the Care of European Children. Before their train left Marseilles for Lisbon, many of the parents, already imprisoned in concentration camps for two years, were allowed exactly six minutes to see their children. Though starving to see their children, the parents were starving physically and spent part of the six minutes eating food given to them by the children.' The dates do not quite work – if the parents had been in concentration camps for two years they would have been interned well before the defeat of France, let alone the Vichy round-ups. But the story is confirmed in a letter from an American refugee organizer in Lisbon to Eleanor Roosevelt; he told the First Lady that 'these kiddies, knowing that they were to see their parents, refused to eat their breakfasts . . . that morning but wrapped up bread and rolls and bits of sugar and handed them to their parents when they met.'

After the German takeover of the Free Zone the AFSC moved to Spain and Portugal, where it worked in cooperation with a group called the American-Jewish Joint Distribution Committee. The JDC was originally established in 1914 to help Jews in Ottoman Palestine who were cut off from European support by the outbreak of the First World War. During the 1920s and 1930s it established itself as an important source of aid to Jews in trouble all over the world – a function it still fulfils today – and with the German invasion of France in 1940 its European headquarters was transferred from Paris to Lisbon. It was through the good offices of the JDC and the Quakers that Fanny embarked on the next stage of her journey.

The story – as the adult Joan has pieced it together – goes something like this. In November 1942 a ship set sail for Europe with space and visas for five hundred French Jewish children. The Vichy regime had agreed to let them go, but by the time the ship made land in Portugal the Germans had occupied the whole of France and it had become impossible to extract the children from the clutches of the Nazis.

It was decided that the visas should be given instead to Jewish refugee children who had reached Spain and Portugal. Many of them were orphans – or at least children who had been separated from their parents – but a few places were offered to children still in parental care. Bronia Zimetbaum feared that Spain might soon fall to the Nazis – an entirely reasonable anxiety given her experiences in Belgium and France – and decided to send Liliane and Fanny.

Fanny's paperwork proved problematic. The visas were intended for French-born children and she had of course been born in Belgium; one of the documents she has found in the course of researching her life is a telegram from Lisbon to the State Department in Washington asking for advice on whether she should be allowed to travel. But eventually she and Liliane set sail for the New World aboard the *Serpa Pinto* like hundreds of other Jewish children before them. Her file in the archives of the Joint Distribution Committee records that 'Zimetbaum, Fanny, daughter of Bronja', registered with the number 1702 at the Hotel Navarra in Barcelona, 'left with a children's convoy for the United States, 29/5/43'. There was no question of Bronia being allowed to travel with her children. Quaker and Jewish groups in the United States were lobbying hard (with the support of the First Lady, Eleanor Roosevelt) for an easing of immigration quotas, but Congress would not have it.

When Fanny reached Philadelphia her physical and mental health were checked – this is where the social worker's report quoted above was written up – and with Liliane she was taken on by foster parents, Dr and Mrs Farell. Though they were not able to adopt her formally they changed her name to Joan Farell and brought her up as their own, speaking English, of course, instead of the Polish and French she was used to. Joan has found an official report on her progress which reads, 'This little girl walked into the arms of her foster parents and has a very secure place in their affections. The foster parents are middle class people living in a suburban community and have fine standards of living. Fanny fits into such a home, whereas Liliane has to strive very hard to meet their standards.' Liliane was moved to an orphanage and then a series of foster homes, while Joan settled into her new life.

She had no idea of what had happened to her parents, but a document she found later proves that her mother, who remained in Spain until 1945, did get news of the children. A report of an interview with Bronia in Barcelona includes this unbearably poignant observation: 'Mrs Z makes an excellent impression. Although obviously very much moved by news of her children, she was restrained and intelligent in speaking of them.'

Joan's stay in the United States was supposed to be temporary, but it was not until 1947 that the refugee agencies, struggling with the millions of people who had been displaced by the war, were able to reunite the family. Miraculously, they had all survived. Joan's father Jakob had, she later learnt, reached Britain thanks to one of those extraordinary pieces of luck which could be decisive in such chaotic times.

After crossing the mountains to Spain, Jakob had managed to make his way to Lisbon. For several weeks he 'hopped on and off trains, hiding in bushes and stealing what food he could' (Joan's words) and persuaded a fisherman to smuggle him down the Spanish coast and past the border with Portugal. In the Portuguese capital he presented himself at the British embassy as a candidate for the Free Polish Forces (which were based in London), but the British told him he needed an exit visa from his country of origin first, and sent him round to the Polish embassy instead.

He was physically exhausted by this stage, and acutely anxious about Bronia and the children – he had of course had no word of whether they had been able to follow him across the mountains. The prospect of having to overcome yet another obstacle proved almost too much, and Jakob was so demoralized by the time he reached the Polish embassy that he scarcely looked up when an official entered the interview room. After giving his name and his home city (Tarnow, in south-east Poland), he was astonished to hear a familiar voice saying, 'You are Jerzy Zimetbaum's brother, aren't you?' The official interviewing him was a schoolfriend from happier days. Jakob's papers were duly put in order and on 1 January 1943 he was on a ship to Gibraltar. He remained in London for the rest of the war and Bronia joined him in 1945.

Joan Salter wrote of the Zimetbaums' reunion in 1947, 'This might seem like a fairy tale ending,' and listening to the family's extraordinary story when I interviewed her in her north London home I found myself desperately hoping that they would indeed live happily ever after. But it was not to be.

For Joan the most complicated problem was that they were no longer 'the Zimetbaums'. She was seven when she was reunited with her parents, and she was deeply conflicted about her real identity. Having settled comfortably into middle-class American life as Joan Farell, she had no desire at all to turn back into 'Fanny Zimetbaum, Stateless Person', as she was described on the document her foster father pressed into her hand as she boarded the plane. And she found her biological parents 'broken in health, spirit and mind. They were working all hours of the day and night to try and pick up the pieces of their lives, and were ill-equipped to deal with the return of their angry and alienated children.'

For the next decade – so through most of her teens – she moved between her two families in Britain and the United States, trying to preserve both her lives but instead becoming 'more and more confused' about who she really was. 'Nobody's adolescence is easy,' she wrote. 'Mine was a nightmare. I would stand for hours by the window watching passers-by. All I wanted was to be "normal" like them.'

Eventually her relationship with her American foster mother broke down, although she kept her American name. But her British family was never a close one either, despite – or perhaps because of – all they had been through; 'you can't stick people back together', she told me. On top of everything else there was the terrible burden of grief left by the Holocaust. Bronia was the only member of her wider family to survive the war; her parents, her seven siblings, their spouses and their children, every one of them had died.

Joan Salter married a British man and had two children here, and now thinks of herself as fully British. It was not until 1982 – four decades after that journey across the Pyrenees – that she really began exploring her family's past. When her American foster father died she met a woman at the funeral who had been a fellow passenger on the *Serpa Pinto*. The two of them began to talk about what had happened to them and Joan suddenly felt that she must – as she put it to me – 'get on top of' what she had until then regarded as 'a sort of secret'.

She went to Philadelphia to see the Quakers and to New York to see the JDC, and in both places she combed the archives for traces of her younger self. She went to France to retrace the journeys her parents had made in those fraught and dangerous years before they escaped to Spain, and she went to Tarnow in Poland in search of her roots. In the course of her research she discovered that many of the stories her father told her as a child – which had seemed too wild to be believed – were almost certainly true. Joan Salter now gives talks on her life and has recorded her story in a book called *We Remember*, a collection of memoirs and reflections by child survivors of the Holocaust. But perhaps the greatest blessing which flowed from her exploration of the past was that 'my father and I were at last able to find some peace in our relationship, in our travels back through his memories'.

Her mother, however, still 'found the past too painful to revisit voluntarily', although she was not above using it as a form of moral blackmail from time to time. Joan has one very funny story about this which will strike a chord with anyone who has had to deal with an elderly and difficult parent. When one of Joan's cousins died in Belgium her father – who was in hospital and nearing the end of his life – instructed her that she must attend the funeral as the family's representative. Since her mother was too frail to be left alone she arranged for Bronia to go into a care home for the three days she would be away. As she pushed her mother through the front door of her flat in her wheelchair Bronia grabbed hold of the door frame and turned on her: 'I carried you over the Pyrenees in my own arms! I stopped the guide from killing you when he said you must be suffocated! And now you reward me by putting me in a home!'

– 15 –

Remembering

A young François Mitterand with Marshall Pétain

IT HAS BECOME A COMMONPLACE that remembering – and its more formal sibling remembrance – is a way of making peace with a painful past. In Britain official remembrance is a relatively recent concept; it sprang out of the First World War and the appalling carnage of the Western Front. In 1937 the poet Edmund Blunden wrote that 'Those who experienced the horror of the trenches on the Western Front lived from day to day, and those who stopped to reflect often felt that their death would be nothing short of a complete and final disappearance.' The building of the Cenotaph, the silence at the eleventh hour of the eleventh day of the eleventh month, the wearing of poppies and indeed the founding of the Royal British Legion which sells them, all these things were part of a national determination to demonstrate that death on an industrial scale did not automatically mean the annihilation of the individual.

And it proved an extraordinarily popular and successful phenomenon, growing through the Second World War and Britain's many modern wars, and reflected most recently in the way the people of Wootton Bassett welcomed home the dead of Afghanistan. More than that, remembrance is linked more and more with the idea of reconciliation, and internationally it has become a hugely important part of conflict resolution. For example, the success of South Africa's Truth and Reconciliation Commission – which forced those guilty of torture and murder in the name of the state to confront the reality of what they had done – has demonstrated that clear-eyed remembering can be a way of healing deep divisions, a powerful political tool in fractured societies.

But it is easy to forget what a difficult process remembering can be. I once moderated a debate on the subject in which Archbishop Desmond Tutu, who chaired the Truth and Reconciliation Commission, argued with characteristic eloquence that confronting the past is the only way to forgiveness. Mary Kayitesi Blewitt, a Rwandan who lost fifty members of her family in her country's genocide, countered that forgiveness could also be seen as an injustice to those who had been killed. The bishop was of course right – at least I think he was – but Mary Blewitt's passion and logic were unforgettable, and I have found sentiments very close to hers in French writing about the Occupation.

Jean Cassou, for example, who so eloquently articulates the emotions the Resistance inspired and was himself a very early *résistant*, wrote in his post-war reflection *La Mémoire Courte* that 'the only possible reaction' to what he called the 'Germanic-sadistic regime' of the Nazis in France was hatred. He recalled borrowing a Bible from a fellow prisoner at a Vichy camp. 'My eyes fell on these words from the psalmist,' he wrote, '"I hate them with a perfect hate" (Ps. CXXXIX). Yes, I said to myself, hatred can be and must be a perfect thing, like a thought or a shape. Something achieved, accomplished and pure.' He says such hatred must be 'unchangeable' because it is founded on reason, and he calls it 'holy hatred'.

Individual lives were bent and broken by the Second World War in a way and on a scale it is difficult for us to grasp today, and Joan Salter's story is by no means the only one to demonstrate how difficult it has been to come to terms with what this great hammer of history did to frail humans.

In telling the story of the Château de la Hille in Chapter Six, I have drawn heavily on the memoir left by one of the children there, Inge Joseph Bleier, which was turned into a book by her nephew, an American journalist called David Gumpert. The saddest passages relate to her descent towards death from a drug overdose in the late 1970s, long after she had established a new life in the United States.

Her daughter Julie asked her about early boyfriends, and Inge told her about Walter, the young man she had fallen in love with at the Château de la Hille and who later died in a labour camp. When Julie reached her teenage years it triggered anguished memories: 'As she began doing the things that teenagers do,' Inge wrote, '. . . I began having dreams and flashbacks. I'd have night-mares about Walter and Mutti [her mother] in concentration camps, trying to get out. I'd dream about myself at Le Vernet, trying to reach them through the barbed wire.' She began to suffer from the skin and stomach problems she had endured when she and the other children were living in the barn in Seyre, near Toulouse, before moving to the Château, and she took drugs to deal with the symptoms. 'I began taking various pain relievers to dull the stomach pains,' she wrote. 'I was sure it all had something to do with my malnutrition during the war years. When I put on even a few pounds, I was certain I was becoming overweight, so I began taking diet pills to curb my appetite and improve my mood. And on and on it went, until I lost track of what pills I was supposed to take. As in Seyre, when I indulged in red wine, I once again felt my connection to Papa – we were both drug addicts.'

Inge Bleier was found dead at her house in Chicago in 1983. Ten years later her daughter Julie gave David Gumpert the manuscript of Inge's memories of the Château de la Hille, which came as a revelation to him. In his afterword to the book, he wrote, 'Someone who has not grown up surrounded by Holocaust survivors, as I did, may find it strange that I learned so little about Inge's experience when she was alive. While today the Holocaust is openly discussed by most survivors, in my growing-up years such discussion was forbidden. Survivors didn't want to talk about it, and nephews and nieces knew not to pry. I knew Inge had been in hiding in Europe during the Holocaust, but I knew none of the details.' David Gumpert began to research Inge's life in very much the way Joan Salter has researched hers. At the end of this odyssey of discovery he concluded that the Château de la Hille story was a 'reaffirmation of the strength of the human spirit under the most trying conditions' – which it certainly was – but also accepted that 'there are nearly endless questions and only partial answers for a historical period which will never be fully understood'.

Nearly ten years after Inge Bleier's death a new edition of

Denise Dufournier's Ravensbrück memoir, *La Maison des Mortes*, was published in Paris, and she added a chapter called 'Later . . . a reflection'. It was nearly half a century since her deportation and internment, and she was a wife and a mother of grown-up children, but the anger burned as fiercely as ever. Indeed, she writes of her determination to keep her experiences alive and vivid, pleading with the 'small flame that I still feel within me' that it should never allow itself to be extinguished. 'If ever I wander in those cold roads bordered by hedgerows of prejudice and lies,' she writes, 'light in my heart the memory of that poor dying face which had already lost sight of me.' The thought of watching one of her friends die prompts a cascade of painful memories: 'Terrible death amid a terrible stench! Faces swollen with boils, legs and arms without flesh, bodies without strength, hideous tatters of humanity, that was suffering. And so too was the "sheet" which was never changed, the neighbour who endlessly coughed up phlegm, spat, and swore, the glass of water you were not allowed to touch, the nurse who did not stop when you called her in the corridor – and all you wanted to know was whether death was really coming – and above all the stench, the stench, the stench.'

Denise Dufournier's daughter Caroline McAdam Clark told me that her mother stayed close to the friends she had made at Ravensbrück in the way most of us keep up friendships made at school or at university. 'Later . . . a reflection' is written in the form of an imagined conversation with her fellow Ravensbrück graduates, and it is a meditation on the gulf that separates them all from those who did not go through the same experiences. 'How can one explain it to them, and what good would it do?' she asks. Simple words and concepts – suffering, work, friendship, washing – have a different meaning for her and her friends because of what they have endured. The rest of the world must, Dufournier declares, 'understand once and for all that it is useless to persecute us [with questions], that we cannot explain, because we would need to forge a new language to express ideas, sensations and feelings that they will never experience'.

Her younger daughter, Alexandra McAdam Clark, another south Londoner, told me her mother regretted not attending the Ravensbrück war crimes trials at Hamburg in the 1940s because that might have helped her deal with what happened. But the passing of the years had evidently made some difference to her, because there are insights in this later piece of writing that are not in the original book (which was written immediately after her liberation). The most striking is her reflection on what it was like to be completely stripped of the customs and conventions which form our lives in day-to-day society. 'Was it not in the camp that we really understood our lives?' she wrote. 'We were always in the presence of nothingness, of the void, of death. We were deprived of – or should that be freed from? – our families, of social conventions and the inequalities which those create. This stripping away of things went well beyond the absence of clothes, make-up and such like. What really mattered was the stripping back of our inner selves, to the core, so that in the end, and for the first time, we came to know ourselves.'

But 'Later . . . a reflection' is informed by a very strong sense of unfinished business. When the camp became overcrowded in 1944 the authorities built a vast tent to accommodate those who could not be found places in huts, and some of the very worst of Ravensbrück's horrors unfolded there. Right at the end of her essay Denise Dufournier addresses a friend called Antoinette who died in the tent: 'In London today is the day of the official victory celebrations. I have tried to associate the memory of you with this glorious military parade. In vain! It made me feel that you did not share in this victory even though you struggled so hard for it.' And she returns to the impossibility of finding the words to express the reality of the camp: 'Antoinette, you know all too well the words I need to explain to "them", but you took them with you, and I do not know them.'

Both Denise Dufournier's daughters told me their mother was a witty woman with a dark sense of humour. Alexandra says she could be very funny about the experience of re-entering ordinary society when she came back from Ravensbrück; she and the other prisoners were still dressed in clothes they had found in the huge hoard which had been confiscated from the inmates by the camp authorities, and she arrived back in Paris dressed incongruously in a ball gown. Caroline McAdam Clark remembers her mother making mordant jokes at her own expense when she saw her own death approaching in old age. But Caroline also says that Denise was always somewhat intolerant of frivolity, especially among young people. And she judged things through the prism of those early experiences. She was, for example, angered and distressed by the crimes committed during the Bosnian war – which she feared negated everything she had fought for – and she loathed *'Allo 'Allo!*, the facetious BBC television comedy about the French Resistance which was broadcast in the 1980s.

Nations can be traumatized by the past just as individuals can. There is a common perception in Britain that France has never really faced up to the truth about the Occupation and that the dark years of 1940–44 have in some way been 'buried'. This is manifest nonsense – and greatly irritates many French. But it is certainly true that the search for a way of remembering that period which is both accurate and adequate has been a powerful undercurrent in the French nation's life ever since the liberation, and the periodic eruptions of public debate about the truth and its mean-ing continued for half a century and more.

In 1990 the French historian Henry Rousso published a brilliant account of this struggle called *The Vichy Syndrome: From*

1944 until today. Four years later he followed it up with *Vichy, an ever-present past* (the original French title, *Le Passé qui ne passe pas*, is even more suggestive) which he wrote in collaboration with a journalist called Eric Conan. The two books have together had a profound impact on the way the French view their 'memory wars'.

The Vichy Syndrome divided the saga into three phases. Rousso called the first 'Unfinished Mourning'. In the last chapter I recorded some of the reprisals taken by the Resistance against collaborators and captured Nazi troops after the Battle of Rimont and the liberation of Ariège. The pattern of summary execution was repeated across much of France. Estimates of the number of people who were killed without due process of law vary wildly; some sources have put it at over a hundred thousand, some at thirty to forty thousand. The official French government estimates are that around ten thousand people were executed without a properly constituted trial before or after the liberation of France. That lower figure is almost certainly closer to the truth, but it still amounts to mass murder, and the purge or *épuration sauvage* as it was known (as opposed to the *épuration légale* which followed it once de Gaulle had established his control) greatly compromised the way the Resistance was regarded in the years immediately after the war.

The *épuration* clouded waters that were already murky, and it proved quite impossible for the country to unite in the kind of collective mourning that is so familiar to us in Britain. As the American historian Robert Paxton put it, 'Opinions differed too radically about which heroes could legitimately be celebrated: Was it those who had rashly fought on, with de Gaulle and the Resistance, or those who had prudently sought some accommodation with the apparently victorious Nazis, alongside Marshal Pétain and his French State at Vichy? Nor was there agreement about which of the many dead could legitimately be mourned: the soldiers who lost the war in 1940, the resisters hunted down by the Vichy police or the Gestapo, the collaborators summarily executed in the heat of liberation, the victims of Allied bombings, the anti-Communist volunteers who died in Nazi uniform on the Russian front, or the Free French forces who arrived in 1944 as part of the Allied Liberation armies.'

There was no adequate answer to these questions, and the result of that was monuments like the one at Rimont, where the names of those who were killed by their compatriots are mixed without explanation with those who fell at the hands of the Nazi occupiers. There is a famous one in the Fontainebleau forest to Georges Mandel, a pre-war government minister who bravely (he was Jewish) refused a place on de Gaulle's plane to London in 1940, and was described by Churchill as 'the first resister'. Mandel was captured by the Milice in the orgy of reprisals that followed the assassination of the Vichy propaganda minister and Milice member Philippe Henriot and executed by them on 7 July 1944. Two years later a monument was erected at the spot, sculpted by one of France's most prominent public artists, and thousands of people, including a clutch of former prime ministers, turned out to see it unveiled. But the inscription is, to put it mildly, reticent. 'Here died Georges Mandel,' it reads, 'murdered by the enemies of France on 7 July 1946.' There is no mention of the fact that those 'enemies of France' were themselves French.

Rousso contrasts this coyness with the thousands of heroic statues of *poilus* (the French equivalent of tommies) erected in villages all over France at the end of the First World War. That war claimed more than a million and a half French lives. Far fewer French men and women died in the Second World War, but behind the raw figures the picture is infinitely more complex. 'Of the 600,000 dead [in the Second World War], only a third had died weapon in hand,' Rousso writes. 'The rest had vanished in bombardments, executions, massacres and deportations or had fallen victim to internal combat in France or its colonies.'

The next 'phase' in the memory wars he calls 'Repressions' and 'Invented Honour'. Charles de Gaulle, he argues, conjured up a brilliantly useful national myth which allowed the French to forget the realities of Vichy and collaboration. According to this version of history, resistance began with his *appel* to the French people on the BBC on 18 June 1940 and never wavered. Vichy was, as Robert Paxton put it, 'limited to a marginal handful of traitors'. De Gaulle and the Resistance (with a capital R) were represented as the only true faces of France during the Second World War.

The climax of Gaullist myth-making came with the transfer of Jean Moulin's ashes to the Panthéon in December 1964. The Panthéon was originally designed as a church dedicated to St Geneviève, the patron saint of Paris, but during the French Revolution it was converted into a mausoleum for the burial of great figures in French life – a kind of secular Westminster Abbey. The transfer of Moulin's remains was decided upon as a way of marking the twentieth anniversary of France's liberation, and they were brought to the Panthéon on a freezing cold winter's day in a ceremony of great solemnity. Buglers of the Gardes Républicaines led nine companies of marchers – three from each branch of the services – past the catafalque as it stood outside the shrine. Charles de Gaulle, who was then serving as the first president of the newly established Fifth Republic, and his senior ministers took the salute and then bowed to the casket before it was moved into the shrine. That great anthem of the Resistance, the 'Song of the Partisans', was sung.

The eulogy was delivered by the novelist and Resistance veteran André Malraux, de Gaulle's minister for culture. Malraux praised Moulin as the man who managed to unite the many different groups of resisters – whom he strikingly described as 'the people of the night' – into a fighting force, and this of course was a way of casting reflected glory on the man who sent Moulin back to France with that mission, General de Gaulle himself. It was a highly political speech designed to praise the president as much as the man who was being honoured by the reinterment – indeed you could argue that the whole ceremony was a dramatic and elaborately choreographed piece of political spin-doctoring.

But there was a deeper alchemy at work as well. Henry Rousso described the speech as 'an ideological tour de force, a proof of the fundamental axiom of Gaullian resistancialism in a series of equations; the Resistance equals de Gaulle, de Gaulle equals France, hence the Resistance equals France'. The last of those equations – the idea that France and the Resistance were essentially the same thing – was every bit as important as the crude Gaullist politics. In Malraux's interpretation the Resistance became much more than a military or political organization; he called it a 'profound, organic centuries-old sentiment that has taken on the aura of a legend'.

In a shimmering piece of rhetoric Malraux described the moment he first encountered this phenomenon. In 1944 he had been part of a *maquis* unit fighting in a rural and deeply traditional area of western France. 'In a village in the Corrèze,' he told the crowds outside the Panthéon, 'the Germans had killed members of a *maquis* group, and ordered the mayor to have the bodies buried in secret, at dawn. It is the custom in this region for all the women of the village to attend the funeral of anyone from the village, and for each woman to stand on the tomb of her own family during the ceremony. No one in the village knew these *maquis* fighters, who were from Alsace. When the bodies reached the cemetery, borne by the local villagers under the menacing guard of German machine guns, the night, which fell back like the outgoing tide, revealed the black-clad forms of the women of

Corrèze, from top to bottom of the mountainside, motionless and silent, each standing on the tomb of her own family, waiting for the French dead to be buried.' There is no room for the story of collaboration in Malraux's version of history. Like de Gaulle's own *appel* on 18 June 1940, Malraux's eulogy to Jean Moulin gave France a new way of understanding its past.

But it could not, of course, last for ever. Rousso describes the third phase he identified in his history of memory as 'The Broken Mirror'. In the early 1970s, he argued, France began almost obsessively raking over the history of collaboration as the generation defined by the political protests of 1968 (the *soixante-huitards*, as the French call them) judged their parents. The sense that the Resistance no longer had to be treated as something sacred even filtered across the Channel in the shape of that British television comedy which Denise Dufournier disliked so much: the adventures of René and his friends in *'Allo 'Allo!* represent the slapstick version of André Malraux's heroic vision of history.

In 1989, well into the 'Broken Mirror' phase and while I was based in Paris as the BBC's television correspondent, the French police arrested a former *milicien* called Paul Touvier at a convent in Nice. Touvier had been appointed as the organization's regional head of intelligence in January 1944 and served in the job until the liberation of Lyons in September that year, so he had an important role during those very bloody months. But he could scarcely have been described as a high-ranking Vichy official. It was what happened *after* the war that really made his case stand out; for forty-five years Paul Touvier had lived almost continuously in hiding in France itself, and for much of that time he had been under the protection of members of the Roman Catholic clergy.

When Lyons fell to Free French forces and Resistance fighters, Touvier avoided arrest with the help of a priest called Abbé Vautherin, who had acted as an informal chaplain to the

Milice in the city and had been authorized by the archbishop to say mass for its members at their barracks on Sundays. Touvier was condemned to death in absentia for treason and sharing intelligence with the enemy. He was arrested in July 1947 but escaped (in circumstances that have never been fully explained) a few days later, and then disappeared into an extraordinarily wide-ranging Catholic network which included priests and monks of the Benedictines, the Cistercians, the Dominicans, the Carmelites, the Jesuits, the Carthusians and the Capucins.

For much of the time Touvier lived in monasteries – notably in the magnificent mountain fastness of the Grande Chartreuse above Lyons – but he was able to enjoy a surprisingly 'normal' life during his time on the run. In 1947 one of the priests looking after him secretly celebrated his marriage to Monique Berthet (there was no civil registration of the union, for obvious reasons, so they were married only in the eyes of the Church) and the couple went on to have several children. Through the good offices of his priestly friends Touvier even managed to find work as a typist, producing clean copies of university theses for medical students in Lyons.

Some of the priests who helped him had senior positions in the Church hierarchy, and in the late 1960s two of them, Monsignors Charles Duquaire and Julien Gouet, mounted a campaign to have Touvier pardoned. They managed to secure the support of no less a figure than Cardinal Jean Villot, who was in Rome serving as secretary of state (the Vatican equivalent of a prime minister) to Pope Paul VI. Villot – whom Duquaire had known during the cardinal's time as Archbishop of Lyons – expressed the view that 'Whatever the mistakes of the past, I believe that the amount of time that has passed – nearly a quarter of a century – the exemplary conduct of M. Touvier during this long and tragic period of his existence, the passionate desire of his wife and children to lead a normal family life, all this in my eyes justifies the broadest benevolence' towards the former *milicien*. A cascade of ecclesiastical supplication poured into President Pompidou's in-tray at the Elysée Palace; it included letters from a cardinal, a bishop, and assorted abbots and priors from the religious orders which had been hiding the fugitive from justice. The monsignors also managed to enlist several prominent former *résistants* for their campaign; Colonel Rémy, the Resistance leader who wrote the early history of the Comet Line, was among the six who sent their own pleas for clemency to the president.

In November 1971 Georges Pompidou quietly granted Touvier a presidential pardon. The reasons he later gave for his decision are typical of the views of many of his generation. 'Our country,' he declared at a press conference the following year, 'has for thirty years gone from one national drama to another . . . Will we keep the wounds of national divisions open for ever? Hasn't the time come to throw a veil over the past, to forget those days when the French did not love one another, when they tore one another apart and even killed one another? In saying this I am not trying a political gambit . . . I am saying it out of respect for France.' Pompidou had stood next to de Gaulle on the reviewing stand at the Panthéon as André Malraux delivered that remarkable eulogy to Jean Moulin eight years earlier.

But the national mood had changed significantly in the years since 1964. The news that Touvier had been pardoned was broken by the magazine *L'Express* in the summer of 1972, and the story provoked an uproar. Until then many people had scarcely heard of him – he may have been a monster, but in 1944 he was a monster on a local rather than the national stage. The public outcry provoked by the presidential pardon set in train a process which eventually turned him into a symbol of the Vichy regime as a whole. And people began to look a little more closely at what he had actually done during his time in the Milice; in November 1973 the son of one of his victims initiated legal proceedings which would eventually lead to his conviction for crimes against humanity.

After the debacle of the presidential pardon Touvier disappeared back into hiding. He was still able to call on some of his faithful Catholic friends, especially in traditionalist monasteries, but the number of priests willing to help him was diminishing steadily. Touvier was eventually reduced to relying on the loonier right-wing fringes of the Church. The Nice convent where he was finally caught in 1989 was part of the schismatic Society of Pius X – the fundamentalist group led by Archbishop Marcel Lefebvre, which split with Rome over the reforms of the Second Vatican Council in the 1960s.

The late 1980s was a time of plenty at the BBC. My producer in the Paris Bureau and I were both gripped by the sheer weirdness of the Touvier story, and we persuaded the editor of *Newsnight* to spring us from the daily news grind so that we could spend a week or so retracing his extraordinary peregrinations around the monasteries of France. In Lyons we interviewed one of the public prosecutors working on the case, and as we were packing up our equipment afterwards he asked whether we were planning to talk to a man called Louis Goudard. 'You really should go and see him,' he said. 'He has only just come forward as a witness, and his evidence could be critical.' He gave us the address.

We found M. Goudard at home in his slightly scruffy farmhouse in the countryside outside Lyons, and our hearts sank when he asked whether we were in a hurry; we had in fact shoehorned the interview into an already packed schedule. He looked crestfallen when I began to explain this, and my journalistic guardian angel kicked me in the shins and told me to mind my manners.

Thank goodness; we were rewarded with one of the most moving interviews I have ever conducted. M. Goudard explained that he had never told his story to anyone, not even his children. He wished to unburden himself to us.

The assassination of the Vichy propaganda minister, Philippe Henriot, in June 1944 was considered especially provocative by the Milice and its allies, not least because Henriot was himself a *milicien*. As we have already seen, it led to the revenge killing of former senator Paul Laffont, living in retirement in far-away Ariège, and to the execution of Georges Mandel in the forest of Fontainebleau. Louis Goudard was to have been another victim; he was among eight men rounded up in the Lyons area by Paul Touvier and his *miliciens* to be executed in reprisal for the Henriot assassination. Goudard was a communist *résistant* and the other seven condemned men were Jews; Touvier spared Goudard at the eleventh hour, but the seven Jews went to their deaths, shot against a wall at Rillieux-la-Pape on 29 June 1944.

Goudard explained to us that it was a custom for condemned men to sing on the night before their execution: if you were a Gaullist you kept your spirits up with the Marseillaise; if you were a communist it was the Internationale. But one of the seven men picked up with him turned out to have a trained voice, and instead of bellowing a defiant anthem, this condemned singer performed a passage from Puccini's *Tosca*: the aria sung by the painter-revolutionary Cavaradossi in his cell before he faced the firing squad at the Castel Sant'Angelo in Rome.

'Even the guards,' Goudard told us, 'listened in silence' as the young man's voice rang through the Fort Montluc prison; '*E muoio disperato/E non ho amato mai tanto la vita*,' he sang ('I die in despair, never have I loved life so dearly'). Puccini's music at this point in the opera can bring a tear or two to the eye when you hear it in the opera house at Covent Garden; its impact on men in a real prison facing the prospect of a real firing squad is beyond imagination. And there was yet another twist to the story's pathos. The singer went to his death the following morning with the rest of the group, but no one knew who he was; six of the dead are remembered by name on the plaque which now marks the spot where they died, but the singer is recorded there simply as X INCONNU.

At the end of this spell-binding interview – there was much more and I wish now that I had kept a copy – the need to bustle on so that we could keep up with our schedule somehow seemed less compelling. We accepted a glass of wine, then lunch, then another glass of wine. At some point (I think around the cheese stage) M. Goudard put *Tosca* on the gramophone (it was a long time ago). The afternoon ended in a haze of sentiment. I have wondered since whether M. Goudard talked so freely partly because of the BBC's association with the Resistance and, by extension, with his long-suppressed memories of what must surely have been one of the most intense experiences of his life. I cherish my memory of the day – it was one of those moments when being a journalist, especially a BBC journalist, felt like a privilege.

But the full significance of M. Goudard's evidence – and the way it underlined the uncomfortable oddness of the whole Touvier story – only really came home to me when I was researching this book.

Putting together a case against Touvier that would stick proved extremely difficult. By the time he was arrested his main convictions (from the 1940s) had been exhausted by the statute of limitations, and the presidential pardon of 1971 had muddied the legal position further. He was therefore prosecuted for the rare and ill-defined offence of 'crimes against humanity'.

The legal standing of crimes against humanity was based on the statutes of the International Military Tribunal which tried Nazi leaders at Nuremberg. The provisional French government which was in place in 1945 had signed up to them along with Britain, the United States and the Soviet Union, but applying the principle which guided the Nuremberg trials in the 1940s to French domestic law nearly half a century later posed all sorts of legal difficulties. In 1992, three years after Touvier's arrest, the Paris Court of Criminal Appeals ruled that the charges could not be made to work; despite all those decades as a fugitive from justice, the court declared, Paul Touvier had no case to answer.

In delivering their ruling the judges made some highly contentious historical statements which said much more about their understanding – or perhaps one should say misunderstanding – of their country's past than they did about the details of the case in hand. The judges described the Vichy regime as 'a constellation of "good intentions" and of political animosities' which was not a 'state practising ideological hegemony' (in the way Hitler's regime had been, for example) and did not regard Jews as 'enemies of the state'. What, then, about the statute against the Jews of October 1940? The mass deportations? Henry Rousso described the ruling as 'enough to make one shudder with its pseudo-historical reasoning' and says it 'would have caused any university student to fail on a history exam'.

There was an appeal against the appeal. The final ruling by the Criminal Court of Appeal upheld some aspects of the earlier judgement, but overturned others. The upshot of all this was that the question of Touvier's guilt or innocence of crimes against humanity turned almost entirely on the way he conducted himself in the events leading up to the seven executions at Rillieux-la-Pape.

And therein lay multiple ironies; ironies which vividly illustrate the pitfalls of using the law – which concerns itself with questions of individual guilt or innocence – to settle questions of history, and which also help to explain why it has been so difficult for France to find peace with her past.

The first irony was that Paul Touvier had long ago admitted his part in the Rillieux killings – indeed he was himself responsible for bringing attention to them. They did not feature at all in the 1940s charges which led to him being condemned to death in absentia, but in the early stages of his campaign for a pardon Touvier brought the incident up of his own accord, and tried to argue that his actions should be considered a mitigating factor. According to his account (which he repeated at his trial), the Gestapo in Lyons had demanded a hundred Jewish hostages in reprisal for Henriot's assassination. The figure had, Touvier claimed, been talked down to thirty by his boss, the regional head of the Milice, Victor de Bourmont, who also – so the story went – managed to secure agreement that the matter should be dealt with by the Milice and not the Germans, since the killing of Henriot was a 'strictly French matter'. The number was then negotiated down further by Touvier himself. He even succeeded in reducing the figure again at the last minute by sparing the French communist Louis Goudard. Yes, he had sent seven men to their death, and yes, he had made a distinction between Jewish and Gentile lives (this is where Louis Goudard's testimony was so important) but all this was in the pursuit of the greater good. Far from being crimes against humanity, the executions at Rillieux-la-Pape should be regarded as an illustration of his good intentions.

The fact that Touvier advanced this extraordinary piece of logic in his own defence speaks volumes about his mindset. But the argument also damaged his case for legal reasons he could not possibly have imagined at the time he originally raised the issue. The ruling that emerged from the final Appeal Court hearing of 1992 limited the definition of crimes against humanity to actions taken in support of the fascist regimes in Berlin and Rome;

'According to Article 6 of the statutes of the International Military Tribunal at Nuremberg,' it said, 'the authors and accomplices of crimes against humanity are punished only if they acted for a European country of the Axis.' By insisting that the executions at Rillieux were initially instigated by the Gestapo Touvier very neatly made the prosecution case. He was duly convicted and spent the remaining years of his life behind bars (he died in 1996).

But Touvier's account of deals being done behind the scenes between the Milice and the Germans before the Rillieux-la-Pape executions was almost certainly a fiction. There is no documentary evidence at all to support his assertion that the Gestapo in Lyons had demanded a hundred Jewish hostages, and an earlier investigation into the case had concluded that this line of argument was 'completely unconvincing'. 'There is no reason why the Germans would have involved the Milice in this operation,' an examining magistrate had stated in 1991, '. . . in view of the fact that they held at the Fort Montluc prison a very large number of Jewish prisoners, whose immediate execution would have been much simpler and just as symbolic in the eyes of the public.' The final irony of the Touvier affair is that the offence for which he was convicted probably did not in fact qualify for the legal definition of a 'crime against humanity', and it was his own lies which made it appear that it did. And because Touvier's conviction depended on establishing that the executions had been instigated by the Germans, there could be no question of the Touvier trial becoming a broader trial of the Vichy regime. Many people hoped that Touvier's appearance in the dock would be a grand cathartic settling of scores with the past, but the whole thing proved much too messy and murky for that.

The Touvier Affair did, however, prompt one important piece of historical house-cleaning. Cardinal Decourtray, the Archbishop of Lyons and also president of the French Bishops' Conference at the time of Touvier's arrest, commissioned a group of distinguished historians to investigate the Church's role, and he gave them free access to his archiepiscopal archives. Launching the commission's work at a press conference, the cardinal declared that he hoped the project would contribute to 'the healthy and necessary efforts of those who are trying to shed light, after fifty years, on events which shook both the country and the Church, in the hope that some lessons for the future can be drawn from them'. The commission's report, published as a book in 1992, is a model of clarity, and it is an infinitely more satisfying account of the Touvier Affair and its meaning than the trial.

The authors suggest a complex set of reasons why so many priests had been willing to help the fugitive – ranging from the monastic tradition of asylum to the broader Christian belief in compassion and forgiveness. The final section of their essay of explanation is called 'Religion and Politics', and here they conclude that Touvier's ideas reflected a particular strand of French Catholicism, one shared by many of those who gave him sanctuary. They describe it as 'an intransigent and counter-revolutionary Catholicism which sees the modern world as a challenge to the divine plan, and which struggles against democracy and freedom'. They write that 'Those who adopt this vision not only do not blame Touvier for the part he played, do not look for excuses, they actually vindicate him and honour in him a man who has been wronged and a martyr in a just cause. Paul Touvier has never expressed the slightest regret for his role; he has defended himself for having spilt blood, but he has never repented his membership of the Milice, or of holding a position of command there. Some of his defenders see in him a victim of a plot by the eternal enemies of the true faith; free-masons, Jews, communists, democrats, all those whom Touvier swore to fight . . .' Touvier, in other words, and, by implication, the organization to which he belonged, were part of the fabric of French society.

Touvier certainly deserved his punishment, but he was unlucky to face trial at a time when the whole question of Vichy was especially raw in French public life. In the year of Touvier's arrest the distinguished historian and Nazi hunter Serge Klarsfeld filed charges against René Bousquet, the former Vichy police chief, for his part in the deportation of children following the episode known as the Vél d'Hiver, the round-up of Jewish men, women and children from which Joan Salter and her family so narrowly escaped thanks to the kindness of a French police officer. Bousquet was indicted for crimes against humanity in 1991, and would have been a much better focus for a trial which exposed the broader culpability of the Vichy regime. His collusion with the Nazis in the deportation of Jews to the camps is now a matter of public record, and his post-war rehabilitation was an outrageous offence to history. Bousquet was given his Légion d'Honneur back in 1957 and received an amnesty in 1958. He then pursued a successful second career as a banker and media executive, and played an influential part in public life as a prominent supporter of François Mitterrand's campaign for the presidency in 1981. But a few weeks before his trial Bousquet was murdered by a publicity-seeker called Christian Didier, who had a history of pursuing former Vichy officials and held a press conference to reveal what he had done (he received a ten-year gaol sentence).

François Mitterrand's friendship with René Bousquet continued well into his first term as president of the republic, and there was a widespread perception that the president used his influence to delay legal proceedings against his old friend (Mitterrand later admitted that this was true). François

Mitterrand's final years in office were dogged by questions about his attitude to Vichy and collaboration.

In 1992 he became embroiled in an ugly row over the commemoration of the fiftieth anniversary of the Vél d'Hiver. The president came under considerable public pressure to use the occasion to acknowledge that the Vichy French state had been responsible for the persecution of Jews. Mitterrand refused to do this on the Gaullist grounds that the Vichy regime had never been the real 'French state', and certainly should not be confused with the French Republic. He was booed at the commemoration ceremony in Paris. That same year it emerged that the president had for the previous five years been arranging for a wreath to be laid at Marshal Pétain's grave on each Armistice Day; this provoked another public uproar and he eventually had to discontinue the practice.

Nineteen ninety-four, the year of the Touvier trial and Mitterrand's last in office, saw the publication of two important books which sent yet more storms of controversy swirling round the Elysée Palace. In the spring the historian Olivier Wieviorka published a series of interviews with former *résistants* who had gone on to occupy prominent positions in public life. In the course of his interview with Mitterrand, Wieviorka asked the president whether he supported the idea of bringing former Vichy officials like Bousquet to trial. The president replied, 'My own instinct is that it should not be done, except in really exceptional circumstances.' He dismissed Touvier with characteristic hauteur as *'une sorte de pègre politique'*, an almost untranslatable phrase meaning something along the lines of 'a kind of political lowlife' or 'a member of the political equivalent of the criminal classes'. The president put Bousquet – who was still alive when the interview took place – in an altogether different category; Mitterrand described him as 'the very prototype of those high officials who were compromised or allowed themselves to be compromised. To what degree? . . . that is what must be judged. And it was judged, after all, after the war. Forty-five years later they are old men. There aren't many witnesses left and it no longer makes much sense. In French history, it is rare that deep social divisions are not wiped away within twenty years by amnesties or a willingness to forget . . . One cannot live always on memory and bitterness.' If you reflect as you read those words that Bousquet was responsible for sending some sixty thousand Jews to the camps, and that he personally cancelled the orders protecting children and the parents of young children from deportation, it is easy to understand why Mitterrand's remarks caused such outrage.

Then, in September 1994, came Pierre Péan's book *Une Jeunesse Française*, its cover adorned with one of the nuggets of historical gold the author had managed to dig up: a photograph of an earnest-looking young François Mitterrand listening respectfully to the Vichy leader Marshal Pétain. The reason for the president's reluctance to condemn those involved in Vichy suddenly seemed clear: he had himself been involved to a far greater extent than anyone had realized. The fact that Mitterrand had served in the Vichy regime as an official responsible for prisoners of war was widely known, but his supporters had always dismissed this as a brief and inconsequential prelude to his time as a leader in the Resistance. Péan's book showed that Mitterrand joined the regime earlier than had been thought, and stayed loyal to it when others left because of its increasingly collaborationist policies. And it drew a convincing portrait of a young Mitterrand who shared many of the far-right, traditionalist Catholic and xenophobic ideals which underpinned Vichy policy – and were so elegantly condemned in the report of the commission on Touvier and the Church.

A few months after the publication of *Une Jeunesse Française* François Mitterrand's second term of office ended and this remarkable and – whatever you think of his morality or his ideas – brilliant politician withdrew from the public stage. Jacques Chirac, his successor, was the first French president from a generation untouched by the controversies of the years of the Occupation; Chirac was seven at the time of the fall of France in 1940. He was also known as 'Le Bulldozer' because of his less than subtle political style, and he took on France's obsession with its memory wars with characteristic directness.

On 16 July 1995 the new president delivered a speech to mark the fifty-third anniversary of the Vél d'Hiver round-up. He plunged immediately into the meat of the matter. 'There are times in the life of a nation,' he began, 'that are painful for memory and for the idea that we have of our country. It is hard to speak of these times, because we are not always capable of finding the right words to recall the horror and to express our sorrow for those who experienced this tragedy: they are forever marked in their soul and in their flesh by the memory of these days of fear and shame.' Le Bulldozer simply drove over the agonized hair-splitting which characterized his predecessor's pronouncements on France's culpability. 'Yes, it is true that the criminal insanity of the occupying forces was backed up by French people and by the French State,' he said. 'France, land of Enlightenment and of Human Rights, land of hospitality and asylum, France, on that day [of the Vél d'Hiv round-up] committed an irreparable act. It failed to keep its word and delivered those it was protecting to their executioners.' Chirac even used the phrase 'collective sin', and cited the Bosnian crisis – then high on the international agenda – to ram home why all this mattered; the real values championed by France, he argued, 'are presently being flouted right under our noses here in Europe, by the practitioners of "ethnic cleansing".

Let us know how to learn the lessons of History. Let us refuse to be passive observers, or accomplices, of the unacceptable.'

It is of course dangerous to make too much of one speech. Charles de Gaulle's *appel* is only remembered because subsequent events proved it to be so far-sighted, and André Malraux's eulogy to Jean Moulin, though it is a remarkable piece of rhetoric in itself, would never have had the impact it did had it not chimed with the mood of the day. But President Chirac's address at the Vél d'Hiver anniversary does seem to have marked the opening of a new chapter in French attitudes, and in retrospect the great public convulsions of the mid-1990s look like the last campaign in the memory wars that had been fought out for so long. The last big Vichy trial – of Maurice Papon, a senior wartime official in the Bordeaux region – took place in 1998. It was another messy affair, but there was no question about where the head of state stood; Chirac three times refused Papon's petition for release from gaol on the grounds of ill health (although Papon was eventually released by the courts at the age of ninety-two).

And perhaps by confronting the worst of the past, President Chirac helped make it easier for people to celebrate the best of it. There were of course happy endings too, although some of them were a long time coming.

Jeanne Rogalle, the shepherd's daughter who helped her father escort Jews across the mountains from Aulus-les-Bains in the winter of 1942, never stopped worrying about the baby boy she had carried into Spain. 'To our regret,' she said in an interview published in 2000, 'since the end of the war we have not heard any news from those whom we helped cross into Spain. Even today, I sometimes wonder what happened to the baby I carried to a new life.' When the piece came out a group of local people decided to try to track down the Belgian family whom she and her father had helped. Michel Roquejoffre, a retired general in the French army, who had commanded the French forces in the first Gulf War and lived in the Ariège town of Pamiers, took up the cause.

The prison records at the Spanish town of Sort, where the family were held after being picked up by the Spanish police, provided the first clues. Word went out on the internet among researchers who specialized in tracking down the families of Jewish refugees, and one morning a Canadian businessman called Claude Henle found an email in his inbox from someone in Amsterdam: did he recognize the name Weiler? It was his mother's maiden name; the crucial connection was made. The Weiler/Henle family had reached the United States in 1944 (aboard the *Serpa Pinto*, the same ship which took Joan Salter across the Atlantic) and made their way to Canada, where they had prospered.

Claude Henle says his father had always wanted to return to the Pyrenees, and would often talk about the family's adventures there. Henle senior was dead by the time the new connection with Jeanne Rogalle was made, but in 2004 Claude travelled back to Aulus-les-Bains. He watched General Roquejoffre pin the Légion d'Honneur to Mme Rogalle's chest, and told her proudly about his marriage, his four children and eleven grandchildren, the riches of a life made possible by her actions. The two are still in touch, and Mme Rogalle showed me her photographs of them together, and the Christmas cards from Montreal.

To tie up the story for our BBC series, we interviewed Mr Henle from Canada. 'She took a chance with her life to help us,' he told me. 'How can you describe in words something like that? There are no words to describe the risks these people took.'

Postscript

I<small>N EARLY</small> 2011 <small>MY WIFE AND</small> I bought a run-down farmhouse in the Ariège department, the setting for so many of the stories in this book. It was a complete coincidence that I began work on this project a few months later, but what I have learnt has given holiday life there a peculiar quality. Coming from the airport, we turn off the A64 motorway just after Noé, where Vichy set up a concentration camp in 1941, and after heading down the Route des Pyrénées we turn right at the T-junction in Pailhès, the site of the station (long since closed) used by Swiss staff arriving to work at the Château de la Hille. We sometimes eat in the Auberge d'Autan, the restaurant attached to the Château de Beauregard, which the occupying Germans made their local headquarters in 1942. If we go to the Saturday market in St Girons (some twenty minutes' drive away) we pass the turnoff to Rimont, the *village martyr* which was burnt so comprehensively by the soldiers of the Legion of Turkestan in 1944. The walk to the Cascade d'Ars, where Jeanne Rogalle and her party stopped to eat on their trek to Spain from Aulus-les-Bains, is a favourite outing. I sometimes have to shake myself to escape from the 1940s.

The area has been completely left behind by the modern world. Ariège has been a place of consequence, but not for a very long time. Archaeological finds in the Grotte du Mas d'Azil, the huge cave where Betty Bloom remembers being taken on an excursion from the Château de la Hille, suggest that for a period in prehistory it was a gathering place for people from all over what is now south-west France, a prehistoric hub for trade, gossip and politics. There is nothing remotely cosmopolitan about this wonderfully sleepy place today.

And it seems to have an odd ability to compost away its history. Our nearest village is Le Mas d'Azil, close to the cave, and this was once a walled town boasting a huge and immensely power-ful Benedictine monastery. The only traces are bits of monastic masonry which have been reused in later buildings, like the ecclesiastical coat of arms inset in the wall just across the road from our local pizzeria. I am told the monastery once occupied the site of the big square by the river which is now used for games of *pétanque*, but there is nothing left to show that that was so. The tranquillity of the place is essential to its charm – indeed, the sense that it lives by the rhythms of an earlier age is one of the reasons we bought the house. But the way it seems to absorb the past into the somnolent beauty of the landscape is slightly unsettling.

In the early thirteenth century the region was the scene of terrible atrocities committed in the name of religion. The Albigensian Crusade was launched by Pope Innocent III to suppress a heresy called Catharism. The full theology of the Cathars has been lost, but they were 'dualists' in the sense that they saw life as a continual struggle between good and evil, and believed that everything material and fleshly was evil by nature. They held vegetarianism to be the ideal way of life, they were opposed to marriage and indeed to sexual reproduction of any kind, and they were anti-clerical, rejecting what they saw as the corruption of the Roman Church's priestly class.

The campaign to suppress these dangerous ideas was prosecuted with brutal zeal. At the siege of Béziers the abbot commanding the crusaders, Arnaud-Amaury of Cîteaux, is said to have been asked by his men how they should tell the difference between Cathars and good Christians. '*Caedite eos. Novit enim Dominus qui sunt eius,*' came the reply – 'Kill them all. The Lord will recognize His own.' In a letter to Pope Innocent after taking the city Arnaud boasted, 'Today, your Holiness, twenty thousand heretics were put to the sword' (the figure was almost certainly an exaggeration, but still . . .).

The final act in the Cathar drama took place at Montségur in Ariège, a fortress on a rocky outcrop that rises dramatically to nearly four thousand feet above sea level. Montségur was defended by around a hundred soldiers – the higher-ranking Cathar men, known as Perfecti, were pacifists and could not fight – and in 1243 they were besieged by a force of ten thousand crusaders. They held out for more than nine months. When the siege ended more than two hundred Cathars were burnt to death on a vast pyre at the foot of the hill. The gaunt castle ruins that stand there today are from a later date, but it is still a haunting place.

Will the memory of what happened in this region during the dark years of Occupation one day seem as remote as the Cathars and their castles? I am not so sure. There seems to be something different about the way the Second World War is being remembered.

Traditional forms of remembrance belong to the state. Events like the memorial ceremony at the Cenotaph are the way the state – and through the state the nation as a whole – thanks and recognizes those who have sacrificed themselves on our behalf. But there is an increasing appetite for what Charles Bagot Jewitt calls, in his introduction to the collection of essays *Lest We Forget*, 'comradeship memorials', memorials erected more spontaneously by individuals or small groups in honour of other individuals or groups.

Sometimes these can be designed to rescue the dead from being unjustly forgotten; Bagot Jewitt cites the example of the Polish Armed Forces Memorial at the National Memorial Arboretum, which was initiated by the children of Poles who fought for the Allies and 'tells the story of their parents' contribution to the British and Allied war effort in an attempt to "right the wrong" when Polish servicemen were not allowed to take part in victory parades for fear of antagonizing Stalin's Soviet Union'. And sometimes this kind of memorial can be a direct challenge to the spirit of state remembrance; there is a very moving monument at the arboretum to those shot at dawn for cowardice during the First World War.

Comradeship remembrance is more intimate than state remembrance; it is an expression of affection and respect for individuals because of who they were and what they did, not a collective endorsement of the cause in which they were caught up. And it is the spirit behind events like walking the Chemin de la Liberté.

The stories the Chemin celebrates were not decisive in determining the outcome of the Second World War. Yes, whenever an airman who had been shot down over occupied Europe made it home to Britain it boosted the morale of his fellow flyers immeasurably. Yes, the thousands of Frenchmen like Paul Broué who escaped over the Pyrenees and returned to France as trained soldiers made a real military contribution to the defeat of Germany. And yes, the Pyrenees offered a back door to safety to

Jews like the Zimetbaums and the Dreyfus family, and for secret warriors like Airey Neave, Nancy Wake, Hugh Dormer and the Cockleshell Heroes who got away. But no one would claim that what you might call the 'Pyrenean Front' of the war made a difference in the way that, say, Stalingrad or the Normandy landings did, and you are unlikely to find any of this reflected in big-picture histories of the Second World War.

But my sense is that for most Chemin walkers, many of whom have a connection with people who, as it were, 'did it for real', that is not the point; they are commemorating the personal stories of those who walked to freedom and those who helped them.

The number of veterans of those cruel crossings during the war years is of course steadily declining, but that does not seem to be reducing interest in what happened. Indeed, the next generation is often more devoted to keeping the past alive. Keith Janes's father kept his diary secret, and Joan Salter's family were so traumatized by the impact of the war years that they fought shy of their memories. Yet both Keith and Joan have devoted huge amounts of energy to researching their past.

Denise Dufournier's daughter Alexandra and her partner were inspired to buy a flat in the Bayonne area because of Denise's role in the Comet Line; the view includes the farmhouse at Urrugne where this book began, and where Andrée de Jongh was arrested in January 1943.

Alexandra gave me a detail about her mother's arrest which is inconsequential but touching. It must have been a warm day, because she had taken off her jacket. The Germans left it behind when they took her away, and the family who owned the apartment where she was picked up looked after it until the end of the war. They returned it to its rightful owner when she got back to Paris after her time in Ravensbrück, and Alexandra now has it at her home in south London. It is a well-cut tweed number, so unmistakably 1940s in its style that it takes you straight back, like time's arrow . . . to the heat of a Parisian June in wartime, the knock on the door, the excitement of a secret life of resistance suddenly dissolving into the shock of arrest and an ominous sense of what was to come. Alexandra has sometimes worn the jacket herself 'in memoriam'.

I said in my introduction that I wanted to get a real sense of what it was like to be part of the escaping story of the 1940s because it must have been 'fun'. I now realize that that is not the right word. The right language has, as Denise Dufournier wrote in 'Later . . . a reflection', gone with the dead.

But remembering is as important as ever, and personal remembrance matters even more in the context of today's morally ambiguous wars.

One of my companions when I walked the Chemin was a Liverpool lad called Adam Hornby. I do not think he knew very much about the history of the escape lines or their significance in the Second World War. He was doing the walk for a much more important personal reason: it was a tribute to his brother Simon, who had been killed in Afghanistan in 2009 while serving with the Duke of Lancaster's Regiment. Adam was carrying his brother's rucksack and listened to Simon's songs on his iPod as he swung along with the rest of us. He found the going tough, and said that he imagined Simon walking with him to keep himself going.

Appendix

Itinerary of the 2011 Chemin de la Liberté,
reprinted with the permission of Scott Goodall

LE CHEMIN DE LA LIBERTÉ

*Retracing the WW2 Escape Route from Saint-Girons, Ariège,
France, across the Central Pyrenees to Esterri d'Aneu, Spain*

Le Chemin de la Liberté or Freedom Trail, France, is based on
the town of Saint-Girons in the *département* of Ariège, 100 kilometres south of Toulouse. The trail retraces one of the hardest
wartime escape routes over the central Pyrenees into Northern
Spain.

Useful French maps are IGN (Institut Géographique National)
No. 2047OT-TOP 25 ST-GIRONS Couserans; 2048OT-TOP 25-
AULUS-LES-BAINS Mont Valier, and IGN Carte de Randonnées
... PYRENEES CARTE No. 6 COUSERANS Valier-Maubermé.
These are available in Britain if you seek out a decent map shop!

The event follows the route taken by mountain guides and
their escaping groups through the Pyrenean foothills southwards
and upwards to the Spanish frontier via the soaring massif of

Mont Valier (2838 metres). During WW2 this route was established originally for Frenchmen fleeing from their Nazi oppressors in an attempt to reach North Africa via Spain and join the Free French Forces of General de Gaulle. As the war progressed, the trail was used by many shot-down Allied airmen who were being filtered south on a regular basis along the Pat O'Leary, Dutch-Paris and Marie-Claire escape lines.

During the second week of July each year, a four-day hike takes place to commemorate all those guides, couriers and safe-house keepers who kept this route open during the last war and in several cases sacrificed their own lives while doing so.

DAY ONE . . . *Thursday 7 July, 2011*

The first day of the hike starts at 0645 on the bridge over the River Salat in Saint-Girons. Once an arched, impressive railway bridge of soaring girders, it formed part of the main line between Foix and Saint-Girons. In the 1950s the line was closed and became the local ring road. The bridge itself was demolished in 1991 and replaced by a much more modest and modern construction of concrete and steel with a few fish-bowl street-lamps thrown in for bad measure. Inaugurated in 1995 as *Le Pont Chemin de la Liberté*, it commemorates the many wartime French and Allied evaders who leapt from the train at this point – warned by two blasts on the steam whistle from the driver – and were collected by waiting guides to be formed into groups in isolated barns ready for their final night ascent to the Spanish frontier.

All hikers need to be awake and alert at the Parc de Palétès by 0500.

Arrangements will have been made earlier to leave spare kit and equipment in a room which will be securely locked during your four days in the mountains. Full details concerning this will be given to team leaders on arrival. Breakfast will not be available at 0500 in the restaurant but the Parc proprietor has very kindly agreed to leave thermos flasks of coffee and a supply of rolls, bread and croissants on the tables so that participants can help themselves to a dawn snack.

At 0630 a coach will arrive to transport all hikers to the Chemin bridge and the start of the hike proper. Please note that the coach will NOT climb the several z-bends which lead from the main road to the leisure centre itself, so all participants must walk down to the flat area below (five minutes), with their rucksacks and catch the coach from there.

On the bridge itself there is a short ceremony, a few words of encouragement from Monsieur Murillo the recently-elected Mayor, the playing of the Marseillaise, the Hymn of Resistance (the famous *Chant des Partisans* which you'll hear several times over the four days) and then at 0700 . . . WE'RE OFF!

It's advisable to carry two litres of water for this first stage, plus a few energy bars, etc. The first two hours are up and down, mainly through beech woods in the hills above Saint-Girons. We will have one 15-minute break at approximately 0930 hours before a longish descent then tackle a tough stretch up through the village of Alos (where water bottles can be refilled at the ice-cold local fountain).

We're now into the fourth hour of walking, time approximately 1130.

We then climb VERY STEEPLY up through another beech wood to the highest point of the day, the Col de Plantach at 1000 metres (3300 feet). Time now 1230. Another 30 minutes' descent takes us to the Col de l'Artigue and a barn where 19-year-old *passeur* Louis Barrau was betrayed by a Spanish 'friend' and shot by the Germans in September 1943 while waiting to guide a mixed group of Allied airmen and French *évadés* on their final ascent to the Spanish frontier. Transport to the Col from Saint-Girons will be organised for supporters and veterans.

It will take us six hours walking from Saint-Girons to the Col de l'Artigue. There will be a ceremony and laying of wreaths, followed by a very filling, merry and enjoyable outdoor lunch provided free by the Barrau family and the municipality of Saint-Girons. This is an exceptional chance to meet the local people (especially the Barrau family), and if the weather is good, you'll have stunning views of the Pyrenees and . . . the problems to come!

Assuming we arrive on schedule at the Col de l'Artigue at 1300 hours, we'll then start the final stage to Aunac at 1500 hours. There is a gratifying descent followed by another steep climb and we arrive at the memorial to the Evadés de France at Aunac at approximately 1800. Again, supporters and veterans are given transport from the Col de l'Artigue to Aunac.

Height now 700 metres (2310 feet). The third ceremony of the day is held here and then transport is again provided to shuttle all hikers and supporters down to the town of Seix, where the hikers spend the night. There is a brief *vin d'honneur* offered by the local Mayor, Monsieur Laffont, and then we'll move to the offered accommodation in the local gymnasium. In other words we all (usually about 50 people) sleep on the floor of the gymnasium which is – as most French floors usually are – beautifully and immaculately tiled. Toilets are available plus seven or eight fairly lukewarm showers (for girls and boys) and sometimes, if we're very lucky, we can borrow judo mats from the local club next door. This has happened only once in the last three years, so please be prepared to sleep on your own karrimat on your own section of French tiled floor and do your best to ignore the snoring and other animal sounds which will pervade the atmosphere during the hours of darkness. This is a FREEDOM TRAIL after all, and you're not looking for a comfortable bed, just an escape from injustice and tyranny!

BUT . . . to offset the night-time misery, aching limbs and weeping blisters, a very good meal (with wine included) is served at 2000 hours in *La Maison du Haut Salat*, a restaurant and holiday centre directly opposite the aforesaid gym. The cost of this meal is included in the overall price of the four-day hike but individual veterans and supporters will have to pay (usually 16 euros).

Total distance from Saint-Girons to Aunac is 21 kilometres (13 miles) but my advice on this first day is to forget distance and think of difficulty of terrain, stumbling through head-high ferns, bushes, mossy ravines, etc, etc . . . all of which slows a group up. Believe you me, it will take 8 hours of walking to cover this fairly modest distance. So go easy on all the free booze at lunchtime. A few years ago an eager young Royal Signals apprentice soldier from Harrogate reached the Col de l'Artigue in fine fettle, met two former French evaders, was offered a glass or two . . . or four . . . and then . . . well, it's all history now, anyway!

Bonne nuit!

DAY TWO . . . *Friday 8 July, 2011*

A very good continental breakfast is served at *La Maison du Haut Salat* from 0600 hours. Again, this is included in the overall price. We start day two's hike at 0800 hours. For the first hour we'll be walking on a minor road which climbs steadily up the Esbints valley. The tarmac ends at the gîte d'étape d'Esbints and a well-marked trail leads on through woods ending in a steep climb up to the Col de la Core at 1395 metres (4603 feet).

It will take nearly four hours to reach the Col, where another memorial has been erected in memory of all the local wartime *passeurs*. There will be a short ceremony here followed by a snack lunch which walkers must provide for themselves. At this point we meet up again with local people and veteran evaders. Water replenishment is provided here as well. PLEASE NOTE . . . ANYONE IN ANY DOUBT ABOUT HIS OR HER ABILITY TO COMPLETE THE TREK MUST ABANDON AT THIS POINT WHILE ROAD TRANSPORT BACK TO BASE IS STILL AVAILABLE.

At approximately 1430 we set off on the final stage to La Cabane de Subera, a two-hour hike into the mountains proper. No more roads, just soaring mountain peaks. The height now is 1499 metres (4946 feet). One half of the cabin is occupied by a French shepherd during the summer months and the other half is reserved for a party of French officials who arrive to join us at Subera on Friday evening.

The terrain is mountain pasture encircled by high cliffs, so there is plenty of space for walkers to pitch their own tents and cook their own meals in the company of a friendly and curious herd of cows – several adorned with large bells around their necks. The ones with bells never seem to go to sleep at night, so be warned! There are also at least two haughty and very impressive BULLS sauntering through this scenario, but no hiker has actually been gored or trampled to death by wearing a red T-shirt (or even a Red Poppy) up until now as far as I know.

Animal life apart, if the weather at Subera is bad this will NOT be a fun night, so keep smiling. There is an ample supply of COLD fresh water for cooking, drinking and washing, but no toilet facilities exist. Please walk at least 200 metres from the base camp site before . . .

DAY THREE . . . *Saturday 9 July, 2011*

At 0800 on Saturday morning, the French contingent of hikers joins us for the last two days. There are usually about 60 of them which brings the total number of participants to 100-plus. The absolute limit is 120. After brief introductions all round and hot coffee provided by the French officials who had arrived the night before, we are now briefed by the professional mountaineers who will take charge of the party during these two most difficult days of the escape trail. In principle there will be one qualified mountain guide for every ten participants. A group of French police, *Gendarmes* from the local Mountain Rescue Team, will also be with us. All these professionals will be instantly recognisable by the armbands or special clothing they wear (usually yellow T-shirts and caps), so if any participant is in trouble physically and needs help, please seek out one of the pros.

The briefing will tell you that this is NOT a race, so RAF and military teams please leave any ideas you may have about inter-unit rivalry firmly locked up back at base. The pace we climb at is the pace of the slowest and there will be regular pauses for the hikers to re-group. One thing that the mountain guides insist on is trying to prevent an accordion effect, with a rambling line of hikers stretching further and further apart across the slopes. The idea is to keep the group firmly together. Naturally it doesn't always work, but at least the idea's good!

The hike starts at 0830 hours. In the first two hours we ascend from 1499 metres (4946 feet) at Subera to just over 2000 metres (6600 feet) to the place which the local French know simply as . . . *l'avion*, or aeroplane.

It was here at the base of the Pic de Lampau that a Halifax bomber from 644 Squadron Royal Air Force based at Tarrant Rushton in Dorset crashed on the 19th of July 1945 with the loss of all seven crew. The aircraft was on a cross-country training flight and more than 80 kilometres off-course when the accident happened at night and in bad weather. A fair amount of wreckage is still scattered around and you are asked to leave it untouched as a mark of respect. There is a memorial plaque at the crash-site and every year a British Royal Air Force representative lays a wreath, says a few words and asks for a minute's silence. High in the mountains and surrounded by pieces of twisted wreckage, this is truly a moving moment.

From the plane we climb ever more steeply upwards to the snow-line and the knife-edged ridge of rock that is the Col de Craberous at 2382 metres (7860 feet). The descent from this Col towards La Cabane des Espuges can only be described as dizzy, and because it is so steep, participants are fed down slowly ten at a time, aided by the guides. This process naturally slows the pace up and if you're forced to wait on the Col for some time before your turn comes, make sure you're wearing clothes warm enough to keep out the icy wind that often blows up there.

During the ascent and descent of this Col you'll often hear the shout or scream of *caill-oux*! (roughly pronounced *kai-yew*), which warns you of rolling stones or rocks dislodged by walkers above and now hurtling towards you at an alarming speed.

We descend to 2110 metres (6963 feet) and arrive at La Cabane des Espuges (a small mountain refuge) at approximately 1330 hours and stop an hour for lunch, which you have to provide yourself. There is a good supply of fresh water here, so fill your bottles. The afternoon will be long and hard.

We set off again at 1430 hours and for half an hour hike along a rutted, stony track overlooking three large mountain lakes, Milouga, Arauech and Cruzous. The height is now 2139 metres (7058 feet) and walkers re-group at this point to tackle the steep eastern slopes of Mont Valier which at 2838 metres (9365 feet) is the highest mountain in this section of the Pyrenees.

By 1700 hours, the walkers will have reached the Col de Pécouch at 2462 metres (8124 feet), which looks directly down on the Refuge des Estagnous where we'll eat and spend the night. It is another extremely steep (and in places dangerous) descent to the refuge, but once again the professional guides are there to help us. It's a difficult 45-minute scramble down, round and over enormous granite boulders.

The refuge at Estagnous (2242 metres, 7398 feet) was first built in 1912 but completely refurbished several years ago. It is now a magnificent building in the luxury class which can sleep 78 people and offer real toilets and even hot showers (you have to pay a modest fee for the hot water. Cold showers are free!) The food provided here for our evening meal is excellent, huge bowls of soup followed by conserve of duck, goose, then cheeses and pastries. Wine is also included in the overall price. The meals are divided into two sittings. Those in tents (the foreign contingent) eat first, followed by the French.

As mentioned, the refuge can sleep 78 people in dormitory-type accommodation. In principle all these places are occupied by the French while the foreign group (usually British, Dutch, Belgian and American) sleep outside in tents. Normally there are several two and three-man tents already pitched and available for our use, BUT . . . in previous years there has been so much confusion about how many tents are available and how many people can squeeze into them, that I am now advising all participants from abroad TO BE PREPARED TO PITCH AND USE THEIR OWN TENTS FOR THE NIGHT AT ESTAGNOUS. If by chance you ARE lucky enough to find room in a ready-pitched tent please consider it as a bonus and not a right!

Arrival at the refuge is usually around 1800 hours, a full ten-hour day from Subera. However, the night at Estagnous is a noisy and extremely merry one. As the worst part of the hike is over, several celebrations and even wine-drinking competitions have been known to take place. Be cautious . . . there is still day four to be faced and the freedom of the Spanish frontier to be reached!

DAY FOUR . . . *Sunday 10 July, 2011*

Continental breakfast is provided in the refuge from 0600 hours. The last day of the hike starts at 0800. There is a steep, slippery 45-minute descent to Lac Rond (the round lake), at 1929 metres (6365 feet), then a sharp, VICIOUS 30-minute climb up to Lac Long (the long lake) directly above at 2125 metres (7012 feet).

We now enter the snow-filled gully that leads directly to the Col de la Clauère and the Spanish frontier at 2522 metres (8322 feet). The professional guides take over again and kick steps in the frozen snow for the hikers to zig-zag their way upwards in single file, each person treading exactly in the footsteps of the person in front of him. The going is slow but reasonably comfortable.

We reach the frontier at approximately 1130 and immediately begin the steep descent into Spain. At the frontier the French police turn back and we are escorted downwards by the Spanish *bomberos* or local firemen who have climbed up to help us. Although this descent is steep, there are no rocks, just wide, snow-flattened grass slopes.

An hour into Spain we stop for lunch (self-provided) at the Lac de Clauère and then re-group for the final two hours' descent to the River Palleresa in the valley below, which we'll reach about 1530 hours. It is at this river that we are picked up by a series of four-by-four trucks and ferried in small groups to the village of Alos d'Isil, where a coach is waiting to take us the last 12 kilometres to our final destination, Esterri d'Aneu, for an official reception in the local community hall. There will be speeches by the mayor of Esterri and the mayor of Saint-Girons, plus votes of thanks from the Chemin Association President Colonel Guy Séris. All participants who have successfuly completed the four-day hike will be asked to sign the Royal Air Forces Escaping Society memorial book which was presented to the town of Saint-Girons by the society in 1997.

After the speeches a full, extensive buffet meal is laid on by the municipality of Esterri d'Aneu, and Chemin de la Liberté T-shirts and berets will also be on sale.

At approximately 2100 hours coaches will take all the hikers back to Saint-Girons. The journey takes about 3 hours, so don't expect to get to bed early. Those staying at Palétès will be taken directly there and dropped off at the level area below the centre itself.

Source Notes

Translations from French are my own and the place of publication is London unless otherwise stated.

Introduction

1 Bob Frost recalled his experiences on the run in a BBC interview in 2011. His journey is also described in Oliver Clutton-Brock, *RAF Evaders: The Comprehensive Story of Thousands of Escapers and Their Escape Line, Western Europe, 1940–45*, Grub Street, 2005.

3 Jean Cassou, *La Mémoire Courte*, Les Editions de Minuit, Paris, 1953.

5 The document *Tips for Evaders and Escapers* is reproduced in John Nichol and Tony Rennell, *Home Run: Escape from Nazi Europe*, Viking, 2007.

7 Hugh Dormer, *Hugh Dormer's Diaries*, Jonathan Cape, 1947.

14 'up to my testicles in snow': From an interview given to John Nichol and Tony Rennell, quoted in *Home Run*.

15 Hugh Thomas, *The Spanish Civil War*, Eyre and Spottiswoode, 1961.

1: Tales of Warriors

18 Peter Janes's diaries were edited by his son Keith, who published them in book form in 2004 (*Conscript Heroes*, Paul Mould Publishers, Great Britain). Keith Janes's introduction includes the remarkable story of the way they survived the war. The diaries are also available on the website referred to on page 20.

23 Brian Bond, *France and Belgium 1939–1940*, Davis-Poynter, 1975. These events are also described in Julian Jackson, *The Fall of France: The Nazi*

Invasion of 1940, Oxford University Press, 2003, and Robert Jackson, *The Fall of France: May–June 1940*, Arthur Barker, 1975.

23 'Two days later . . .': This episode is described by Martin Gilbert in Vol. 6 of his biography *Winston S. Churchill*, Heinemann, 1983. Churchill's words are from his book *Their Finest Hour*, currently available in Penguin Classics, 2005.

25 The Earl of Cardigan, *I Walked Alone*, Routledge & Kegan Paul, 1951.

27 A fragment of Lt Hopkins's diary and the record of his debriefing by MI9 have been preserved by his family and were shown to me by his niece, Mrs Geraldine Wimble.

29 A. J. Evans, *The Escaping Club*, Bodley Head, 1921.

31 The main sources for my account of MI9 were *MI9: Escape and Evasion 1939–45*, by M. R. D. Foot and J. M. Langley, Bodley Head, 1979; Airey Neave, *Saturday at MI9*, Pen and Sword Military, 2010; and John Nichol and Tony Rennell, *Home Run: Escape from Nazi Europe*, Viking, 2007. I interviewed Professor Foot in 2011.

33 Clayton Hutton's wartime career is recorded in his autobiography, *Official Secret*, Max Parrish, 1960.

36 Martin Francis, *The Flyer: British Culture and the Royal Air Force, 1939–1945*, Oxford University Press, 2008. For further reading on Bomber Command, see Patrick Bishop, *Bomber Boys*, Harper Press, 2007, and Max Hastings, *Bomber Command*, Dial Press/James Wade, New York, 1979.

38 'Bob Frost said . . .': BBC interview, 2011.

39 'It is perfectly true what people say . . .': Interview, 2011.

40 Aidan Crawley, *Escape from Germany*, HMSO, 1985. The stories of survival in the previous paragraph are from the same source.

'very firm on the frightful difficulties': Interview with M. R. D. Foot, 2011.

44 Stan Hope gave me this account of his experiences in an interview in 2011.

Cecil Beaton, *Winged Squadrons*, Hutchinson, 1942.

2: The Lines

45 M. R. D. Foot and J. M. Langley, *MI9: Escape and Evasion 1939–45*, Bodley Head, 1979.

47 'There are quite a lot of British people . . .': The letter is quoted in a book written by his son, Andrew Bradford, *Escape from St Valéry-en-Caux: The Adventures of Captain B. C. Bradford*, History Press, 2009.

There is a good account of Garrow's activities on Keith Janes's website www.conscript-heroes.com. They are also described in Oliver Clutton-Brock, *RAF Evaders: The Comprehensive Story of Thousands of Escapers and Their Escape Lines, Western Europe, 1940–45*, Grub Street, 2005; by John Nichol and Tony Rennell in *Home Run, Escape from Nazi Europe*, Viking, 2007; and by Airey Neave, *Saturday at MI9*, Pen and Sword Military, 2010.

49 'The Secret Police knew . . .': Dr Donald Caskie, *The Tartan Pimpernel*, Oldbourne, 1960.

Albert-Marie Guérisse's story is told in the sources cited for page 47 above and in Foot and Langley, *Escape and Evasion*. There is also an account of his wartime work in Helen Long, *Safe Houses are Dangerous*, William Kimber, 1985.

52 Rémy's book, *Réseau Comète, La Ligne de Démarcation*, Librairie Académique Perrin, Paris, 1966, is available only in French. Airey Neave's biography is *Little Cyclone*, Hodder and Stoughton, 1954.

56 'If she said do it . . .': Stan Hope interview, 2011.

57 'Escaping was very much a family business . . .' Janine de Greef was Bob Frost's escort on his journey south. She went into a care home at the time this book was being prepared for publication, and he described her as 'my last surviving helper' who 'deserves recognition'.

'like a drowned rat . . .': Bob Frost interview, 2011.

'Florentino has a face . . .': *Little Cyclone*, by Airey Neave.

58 'Florentino fell over several times . . .': Rémy, *Réseau Comète*.

'All we wanted was the neutrality of Spain': Quoted in Oliver Clutton-Brock, *RAF Evaders*. The quotations from Lord Halifax and Sir Samuel Hoare in this paragraph are from the same source.

60 Andrew Bradford, *Escape from St Valéry-en-Caux*.

62 Andrée Dumon described her experiences in a BBC interview in 2011.

3: Jeanne, Jews and the Camps

64 'Jeanne remembered . . .': My interview with Jeanne Rogalle was in 2011. There is also an account of her experiences in the history section of the website www.ariege.com

65 Serge Klarsfeld interview, 2011.

66 Michael Curtis, *Verdict on Vichy: Power and Prejudice in the Vichy France Regime*, Weidenfeld and Nicolson, 2002.

'The presence of a large number of foreign Jews . . .': Cable from Pierre Laval to Gason Henri Haye.

67 Jeanne Rogalle interview, 2011.

67 'At the beginning of September the *préfets* were asked to report back . . .': The reports are reproduced as an appendix in Serge Klarsfeld, *Vichy–Auschwitz: Le Rôle de Vichy dans la Solution Finale de la question Juive en France, 1942*, Fayard, Paris, 1984.

69 Jeanne Rogalle interview, 2011.

73 Nancy Johnstone, *Hotel in Flight*, Faber and Faber, 1939.

74 'I have seen women . . .': Quoted in Antonio Tellez Sola and Pilar Ponzán Vidal, *The Anarchist Pimpernel Francisco Ponzán Vidal (1936–1944): The Anarchists in the Spanish Civil War and the Allied Escape Networks of WWII*. The book is only available in translation as a Kindle edition, trans. Paul Sharkey, 2012.

75 'A forester in Argelès . . .': From Anne Grynberg, *Les Camps de la Honte: les internés juifs des camps français 1939–1944*, Editions La Découverte, Paris, 1991. There is a detailed history of the biggest of the camps, Gurs, in Claude Laharie's *Le Camp de Gurs 1939–45: Un aspect méconnu de l'histoire de Vichy*, J & D Editions, Pau, France, 1993.

77 'Koestler was a Hungarian-born Jew . . .': All my quotations of Arthur Koestler are from his *Scum of the Earth*, Jonathan Cape, 1941.

4: Ninette's Tale

85 'During the interwar years . . .': There is a good account of interwar immigration to France in Anne Grynberg, *Les Camps de la Honte: Les internés juifs des camps français 1939–1944*, Editions La Découverte, Paris, 1991.

86 The direct quotations from Lady Swaythling in this chapter are from an interview in 2011. For further information about the Dreyfus family, see Carmen Callil, *Bad Faith: A Forgotten History of Family and Fatherland*, Jonathan Cape, 2006.

All quotations from Viviane in this chapter are taken from Viviane Forrester, *Ce Soir, après la guerre*, J.-C. Lattes, Paris, 1992.

87 'French Jews are French . . .': Helbronner and Blum's words are quoted by Michael Curtis in *Verdict on Vichy: Power and Prejudice in the Vichy France Regime*, Weidenfeld and Nicolson, 2002.

88 'M. and Mme Dreyfus . . .': Viviane Forrester, *Ce Soir, après la guerre*.

89 'The official leaders of Judaism . . .': Adam Rayski, *The Choices of the Jews under Vichy*, University of Notre Dame, Indiana, 2005.

For further reading on Vichy anti-Semitic policies, see Adam Rayski, *The Choices of the Jews under Vichy*, and Michael Curtis in *Verdict on Vichy*.

91 'In March 1942 . . .': Carmen Callil, *Bad Faith*.

92 'Mme Dreyfus . . .': Viviane Forrester, *Ce Soir, après la guerre*.

5: Fanny/Joan's Tale 1

96 I interviewed Joan Salter in 2011. In describing her experiences I have also drawn on her essay in the Child Survivors Association collection *We Remember: Child Survivors of the Holocaust Speak*, Matador, 2011.

100 There are accounts of the Rafle du Vélodrome d'Hiver in Michael Curtis, *Verdict on Vichy: Power and Prejudice in the Vichy France Regime*, Weidenfeld and Nicolson, 2002; Serge Klarsfeld, *Vichy–Auschwitz: Le Rôle de Vichy dans la Solution Finale de la question Juive en France, 1942*, Fayard, Paris, 1984; and Julian Jackson, *France, the Dark Years, 1940–1944*, Oxford University Press, 2001.

6: Tales of Children

105 I interviewed Ruth Schutz in 2011 and have combined her memories with the account given in her sister Betty's essay in the Child Survivors Association collection *We Remember: Child Survivors of the Holocaust Speak*, Matador, 2011. All quotations from Betty Schutz (Bloom) are from this essay.

108 Inge Joseph's memoir forms the spine of a book put together by her nephew after her death: Inge Joseph Bleier and David Gumpert, *A Girl's Journey through Nazi Europe*, William E. Eerdmans Publishing Company, Grand Rapids, Michigan, and Cambridge, UK. All direct quotations from her in this chapter are taken from this book.

109 Sebastian Steiger's memories are recorded in his *Les Enfants du Château de La Hille*, Brunnen, Basle. The book was originally published in German; I have used the French edition, published in 1999.

Edith Goldapper's diary is quoted extensively in Sebastian Steiger's memoir above.

7: Belgians, Bravery and Betrayal

123 Roger Motz, *England and Belgium*, Lindsay Drummond, 1945.

124 Roger Motz, *Belgium Unvanquished*, Lindsay Drummond, 1942.

125 William Shirer's report is reproduced in *Belgium Unvanquished*.

126 José de la Barre's UP interview is reproduced as Appendix A of her memoir published under her married name, José Villiers, *Granny was a Spy*, Quartet Books, London and New York, 1988.

128 Cécile Jouan, *Comète, Histoire d'une ligne d'évasion*, Les Editions du Beffroi, Belgium, 1948.

M. R. D. Foot, *Resistance: An Analysis of European Resistance to Nazism, 1940–45*, HarperCollins, 1977.

128 Rémy, *Réseau Comète: La Ligne de Démarcation*, Librairie Académique Perrin, Paris, 1966.

129 'Nadine was betrayed by . . .' and the story that follows: BBC interview 2011.

132 Airey Neave, *Little Cyclone*, Hodder and Stoughton, 1954.

133 The Maréchals' story is told in Airey Neave, *Little Cyclone*, the same author's *Saturday at MI9*, Pen and Sword Military, 2010, and Rémy, *Réseau Comète*. Additional information about the family can be found in William Etherington, *A Quiet Woman's War*, Mousehold Press, Norwich, 2002.

135 'Stan recalled that . . .' and the story that follows: Interview, 2011.

139 Airey Neave, *Little Cyclone*. Masson's treachery is also described in Oliver Clutton-Brock, *RAF Evaders: The Comprehensive Story of Thousands of Escapers and Their Escape Line, Western Europe, 1940–45*, Grub Street, 2005.

140 Cécile Jouan, *Comète*.

'according to his grandson Bernard': Interview, 2011.

141 Rémy, *Réseau Comète*.

Sarah Helm, *A Life in Secrets: The Story of Vera Atkins and the Lost Agents of SOE*, Little, Brown, 2005.

142 'One of the most vivid accounts of camp life . . .': The quotations from Denise Dufournier that follow are taken from her *La Maison des Mortes: Ravensbrück*, Hachette, 1945.

143 Rémy, *Réseau Comète*.

144 'In the winter of 1944 the two Elsie Maréchals . . .': William Etherington, *A Quiet Woman's War*. The book is the source of young Elsie's description of her camp experiences.

146 Interview with Caroline McAdam Clark, 2012.

8: The Officer and the Legionnaire

148 Helen Long, *Safe Houses are Dangerous*, William Kimber, 1985.

Dr Donald Caskie, *The Tartan Pimpernel*, Oldbourne, 1960.

149 'Peter Janes referred to him as . . .': In the diaries edited by Keith Janes and published as *Conscript Heroes*, Paul Mould Publishers, Great Britain.

150 'Cole's ability to get through . . .': This account of the incident is taken from Helen Long, *Safe Houses are Dangerous*. The anecdote is a well-known one and Brendan Murphy has a slightly different version in *Turncoat: The True Case of Traitor Sergeant Harold Cole*, Futura, 1988.

Murphy, who interviewed Higginson, has Cole saying more bluntly, 'Look . . . he's shat in his briefcase.'

150 For further details of Cole's unmasking, see Keith Janes's website www.conscript-heroes.com and Oliver Clutton-Brock, *RAF Evaders: The Comprehensive Story of Thousands of Escapers and Their Escape Line, Western Europe, 1940–45*, Grub Street, 2005.

153 'If God is just, my dear Donald . . .': A facsimile of O'Leary's note to Donald Darling is reproduced in Helen Long, *Safe Houses are Dangerous*. Ian Garrow's comments about killing Cole are quoted in the same book.

154 The Abbé Carpentier's letter is quoted in Louis Nouveau, *Des Capitaines par Miliers*, Calman-Levy, Paris, 1958.

155 The story of Cole's final days is drawn from Brendan Murphy, *Turncoat*, Futura, 1989.

156 John Nichol and Tony Rennell, *Home Run: Escape from Nazi Europe*, Viking, 2007.

Airey Neave, *Saturday at MI9*, Pen and Sword Military, 2010.

157 O'Leary's encounter at Natzweiler is described in Sarah Helm, *A Life in Secrets: The Story of Vera Atkins and the Lost Agents of SOE*, Little, Brown, 2005.

9: Françoise and the Americans

159 'Françoise – to give her her *nom de guerre* . . .': These details are from Christian Mouly's article 'Une Héroïne Toulousaine, Marie-Louise Dissard, alias "Françoise"', published in *Résistance*, R4, No. 7, March 1979.

160 'In September 1942 a Vichy police report . . .': The report is quoted in Christian Mouly's article.

Fred Greenwell, *Evasion*, privately printed 1995, Houghton le Spring, Tyne and Wear, copy from Scott Goodall's archive.

161 'Another RAF man . . .': Frank Griffiths, *Winged Hours*, William Kimber, 1981.

'She showed similarly quick wits . . .': From the only known interview with Françoise, given to Fred Boulé in Toulouse in May 1946. A copy was provided to me by Keith Janes.

162 Earl Woodard, *The B-17 of La Goulafrière*, privately printed, 1998, copy from Scott Goodall's archive.

Nancy Wake, *The White Mouse*, Macmillan Australia, Melbourne, 1985.

164 Fred Greenwell, *Evasion*.

165 Donald Miller, *Eighth Air Force*, Aurum Press, 2007.

John Keegan, 'We Wanted Beady-Eyed Guys Just to Hold the Course', *Smithsonian Magazine*, 14, no. 5, 1993.

166 'Larry Grauerholz . . . told me . . .': Interview, 2011.

Fred Greenwell, *Evasion*.

167 M. R. D. Foot, *Resistance: An Analysis of European Resistance to Nazism, 1940–45*, Eyre Methuen, 1976.

168 Chuck Yeager with Leo Janos, *Yeager: An Autobiography*, Bantam Books, 1985.

171 Earl Woodard, *The B-17 of La Goulafrière*.

173 'Another evading airman, Robert Vandegriff, recalled . . .' in his memoir *More World War II Adventures Than I'd Planned On*, printed by the Defense Print Service, Aurora, Colorado, USA, 1997.

Grauerholz interview, 2011.

175 'He became interested in her story . . .': Clayton David, *They Helped Me Escape from Amsterdam to Gibraltar in 1944*, Sunflower University Press, Manhattan, Kansas, 1988.

10: Tales of Resistance

178 Pierre Péan, *Une Jeunesse Française: François Mitterrand, 1934–1947*, Fayard, Paris, 1994.

179 'Paul Broué, a little younger than the future president . . .': I interviewed Paul Broué in 2011. In telling his story I have used additional material from an extended interview he gave to Olivier Naduce, a local historian. It was privately printed and M. Broué provided my copy.

184 For further reading on de Gaulle, see Don Cook, *Charles de Gaulle*, Secker and Warburg, 1984, and Brian Crozier, *De Gaulle*, Charles Scribner's Sons, New York, 1973.

The text of de Gaulle's address is widely available online, in French and English translation.

185 Jean Texcier, *Ecrit dans la Nuit*, La Nouvelle Edition, Paris, 1945.

187 Julian Jackson, *France: The Dark Years, 1940–1944*, Oxford University Press, 2001.

188 Julian Jackson, *France: The Dark Years*.

M. R. D. Foot and J. M. Langley, *MI9: Escape and Evasion 1939–45*, Bodley Head, 1979.

189 'His *Combat* newspaper . . . declared . . .': Julian Jackson, *France: The Dark Years*.

189 For further reading about Jean Moulin, see Alan Clinton, *Jean Moulin 1899–1943*, Palgrave, Basingstoke and New York, 2002, Patrick Marnham, in *The Death of Jean Moulin: Biography of a Ghost*, John Murray, 2000, makes the controversial claim that Moulin was betrayed by communist members of the Resistance.

193 H. R. Kedward, *In Search of the Maquis: Rural Resistance in Southern France, 1942–1944*, Oxford University Press, 1993.

194 Fabrice Grenard, *Maquis Noirs et Faux Maquis*, Vendémiaire Editions, Paris, 2011.

196 H. R. Kedward, *In Search of the Maquis*.

197 'Henry Frenay . . . said . . .': Quoted in Fabrice Grenard, *Maquis Noirs et Faux Maquis*.

198 Scott Goodall, *The Freedom Trail: Following one of the hardest wartime escape routes across the central Pyrenees into Northern Spain*, Inchmere Design, Great Britain, 2005.

199 Emilienne Eychenne, *Montagnards de la Liberté: Les Evasions par l'Ariège et la Haute-Garonne, 1939–1945*, Editions Milan, Toulouse, 1984.

Interview with Paul Broué, 2011.

11: Guides, Smugglers and Spaniards

202 Emilienne Eychenne, *Montagnards de la Liberté: Les Evasions par l'Ariège et la Haute-Garonne, 1939–1945*, Editions Milan, Toulouse, 1984.

203 Scott Goodall, *The Freedom Trail: Following one of the hardest wartime escape routes across the central Pyrenees into Northern Spain*, Inchmere Design, Great Britain, 2005.

Francis Aguila, *Passeurs d'Hommes et Femmes de l'Ombre*, Le Pas de l'Oiseau, Toulouse, 2011.

205 H. R. Kedward, *In Search of the Maquis: Rural Resistance in Southern France, 1942–1944*, Oxford University Press, 1993.

206 José Villiers, *Granny Was a Spy*, Quartet Books, London and New York, 1988.

207 Interview with Lady Villiers, 2011.

208 Emilienne Eychenne, *Montagnards de la Liberté*.

209 Claude Benet, *Passeurs, Fugitifs, et Espions: L'Andorre dans la 2e guerre mondiale*, Le Pas de l'Oiseau, Toulouse, 2009.

210 Interview with Françoise Rouan reproduced as an appendix in H. R. Kedward, *In Search of the Maquis*.

211 See Antonio Tellez Sola and Pilar Ponzán Vidal, *The Anarchist Pimpernel Francisco Ponzán Vidal (1936–1944): The Anarchists in the Spanish Civil*

War and the Allied Escape Networks of WWII, trans. Paul Sharkey, Kindle edition, 2012.

212 'O'Leary was caught while they were in the mountains . . .': See Paddy Ashdown, *A Brilliant Little Operation: The Cockleshell Heroes and the Most Courageous Raid of World War 2*, Aurum Press, 2012.

213 Claude Benet, *Passeurs, Fugitifs, et Espions*.

214 'Nancy Wake wrote of them . . .': Nancy Wake, *The White Mouse*, Macmillan Australia, Melbourne, 1985.

215 'The *maquisard* will respect private property . . .': Quoted in Fabrice Grenard, *Maquis Noirs et Faux Maquis*, Vendémiaire Editions, Paris, 2011.

12: Death in the Mountains

217 Scott Goodall, *The Freedom Trail: Following one of the hardest wartime escape routes across the central Pyrenees into Northern Spain*, Inchmere Design, Great Britain, 2005.

218 Claude Benet, *Passeurs, Fugitifs, et Espions: L'Andorre dans la 2e guerre mondiale*, Le Pas de l'Oiseau, Toulouse, 2009. The quotation from Francesc Viadiu is from the same source.

220 George Millar, *Horned Pigeon*, William Heinemann, 1946.

222 'The *passeur* in question . . .': This story is well told by Emilienne Eychenne, *Montagnards de la Liberté: Les Evasions par l'Ariège et la Haute-Garonne, 1939–1945*, Editions Milan, Toulouse, 1984.

226 Emilienne Eychenne, *Montagnards de la Liberté*.

227 Francis Aguila, *Passeurs d'Hommes et Femmes de l'Ombre*, Le Pas de l'Oiseau, Toulouse, 2011.

For further reading on Jean Bénazet, see Claude Benet, *Passeurs, Fugitifs, et Espions*; Emilienne Eychenne, *Montagnards de la Liberté*; and Antonio Tellez Sola and Pilar Ponzán Vidal, *The Anarchist Pimpernel Francisco Ponzán Vidal (1936–1944): The Anarchists in the Spanish Civil War and the Allied Escape Networks of WWII*, trans. Paul Sharkey, Kindle edition, 2012.

228 'Bénazet . . . as he put it later . . .': From an interview quoted in Emilienne Eychenne, *Montagnards de la Liberté*.

230 Emilienne Eychenne, *Montagnards de la Liberté*.

The story of the Milice is touched upon in most general histories of wartime France but I have found no standard work which focuses on the subject. René Rémond's *Touvier et l'Eglise, Rapport par la Commission historique instituée par le cardinal Decourtray*, Fayard, Paris, 1992, includes some helpful background.

232 Andrew Roberts, *The Storm of War: A New History of the Second World War*, Allen Lane, 2009.

233 For Darnand's rise to power, see Carmen Callil, *Bad Faith: A Forgotten History of Family and Fatherland*, Jonathan Cape, 2006.

13: Endings

237 Carmen Callil, *Bad Faith: A Forgotten History of Family and Fatherland*, Jonathan Cape, 2006.

Henry Rousso, *The Vichy Syndrome: History and Memory in France since 1944*, Harvard University Press, Cambridge, Mass., and London, 1991.

238 Claude Delpla, *Il y a 50 ans . . . 21 et 22 Août 1944, Bataille de Rimont et de Castelnau-Durban . . . L'Ariège etait libérée*, printed by Barat, 09200 St Girons, France, 1994. This pamphlet was printed to mark the fiftieth anniversary of the Battle of Rimont and is now almost impossible to obtain (the copy I have used is from Scott Goodall's archive). However, a large part of Delpla's narrative can be found reproduced online at www.ac-toulouse.fr. and www.histariege.com

239 Francesco Nitti's story is told in Nitti, *8 Chevaux 70 Hommes*, Editions Chantal, Toulouse, 1944, and the book is the source of all quotations from him in this chapter.

243 Christian de Roquemaurel's memories are quoted on the website of the Amicales des Deportés du Train Fantôme, www.lesdesportesdutrain fantome.org, which carries eyewitness accounts of each stop on the train's journey.

246 For Paul Laffont's assassination, see Claude Delpla, *Il y a 50 ans . . . 21 et 22 Août 1944*.

249 'Joseph Darnand's reply is much quoted . . .': See Carmen Callil, *Bad Faith: A Forgotten History of Family and Fatherland*.

250 'Marie Bartette . . . described . . .': www.lesdesportesdutrainfantome.org

253 Claude Delpla, *Il y a 50 ans . . . 21 et 22 Août 1944*.

256 'There is a small marble cross . . .': I am grateful to Scott Goodall for this information.

257 ' "Commandant Robert" . . . described': Video of press conference, date unknown, given to me by Geoff Cowling, chairman of the Escape Lines Memorial Society.

14: Fanny/Joan's Tale 2

261 This chapter is based on my interview with Joan Salter and her essay in the Child Survivors Association collection *We Remember: Child Survivors of the Holocaust Speak*, Matador, 2011. See notes on Chapter Five.

265 'A report of an interview . . .': Quoted in the Child Survivors Association collection *We Remember: Child Survivors of the Holocaust Speak*.

15: Remembering

269 'In 1937 the poet Edmund Blunden wrote . . .': Introduction to Fabian Ware, *The Immortal Heritage: An Account of the Work and Policy of the Imperial War Graves Commission during Twenty Years 1917–1937*, Cambridge University Press, 1937.

271 Jean Cassou, *La Mémoire Courte*, Les Editions de Minuit, Paris, 1953.

'I have drawn heavily on the memoir left . . .': Inge Joseph Bleier and David Gumpert, *A Girl's Journey through Nazi Europe*, William E. Eerdmans Publishing Company, Grand Rapids, Michigan, and Cambridge, UK.

272 'a new edition . . .': Denise Dufournier, *La Maison des Mortes: Ravensbrück*, Julliard, Paris, 1991.

273 Interviews with Caroline and Alexandra McAdam Clark, 2012.

275 Henry Rousso, *The Vichy Syndrome: History and Memory in France since 1944*, Harvard University Press, Cambridge, Mass., and London, 1991, and Eric Conan and Henry Rousso, *Vichy: An Ever-Present Past*, Dartmouth College, Hanover, and London, 1998.

276 'As the American historian Robert Paxton has put it . . .': Introduction to Eric Conan and Henry Rousso, *Vichy: An Ever-Present Past*.

277 Henry Rousso, *The Vichy Syndrome*.

278 The text of André Malraux's address can be found online in French at www.charles-de-gaulle.org

279 Henry Rousso, *The Vichy Syndrome*.

280 'When Lyons fell to Free French . . .': See René Rémond, *Touvier et l'Eglise, Rapport par la Commission historique instituée par le cardinal Decourtray*, Fayard, Paris, 1992.

282 Georges Pompidou's press statement is reproduced in René Rémond, *Touvier et l'Eglise*.

284 'Goudard told us . . .': Interview for *Newsnight*, BBC TV, 1989.

286 'The judges described the Vichy regime . . .': Quoted in Eric Conan and Henry Rousso, *Vichy: An Ever-Present Past*.

288 'An earlier investigation into the case . . .': Eric Conan and Henry Rousso, *Vichy: An Ever-Present Past*.

289 René Rémond, *Touvier et l'Eglise*. The cardinal's press statement is reproduced here.

291 Olivier Wieviorka, *Nous Entrerons dans la Carrière: De la Resistance à l'Exercice du Pouvoir*, Seuil, Paris, 1944.

292 Pierre Péan, *Une Jeunesse Française: François Mitterrand 1934–1947*, Fayard, Paris, 1994.

293 President Chirac's speech is quoted in full in Eric Conan and Henry Rousso, *Vichy: An Ever-Present Past.*

294 'She said in an interview ...': Reproduced on the website www.ariege.com

295 Interview with Claude Henle, 2011.

Postscript

298 '*Caedite eos* ...': The remark was attributed to Arnaud-Amaury by Caesarius of Heisterbach, a thirteenth-century Cistercian. For further reading on the Cathars, see Professor R. I. Moore, *The War on Heresy: Faith and Power in Medieval Europe*, Profile Books, 2012.

Text and Picture Acknowledgements

Text Acknowledgements

The publisher has made serious efforts to trace the copyright owners of all works quoted in the text. The publisher is willing to acknowledge any rightful copyright owner on substantive proof of ownership and would be grateful for any information as to their identity.

15: extract from *The Spanish Civil War* by Hugh Thomas. Copyright © Hugh Thomas, 1961, 1965, 1977, 1986, 2001, used by permission of The Wylie Agency (UK) Limited.

18–22, 47, 50–1, 149: extracts from *Conscript Heroes* by Keith Janes © Paul Mould Publishers, 2004.

28: extract from Lieutenant J. W. Hopkins' diary reprinted by kind permission of Mrs Geraldine Wimble.

30–1: extracts from *The Escaping Club* by A. J. Evans © John Lane, The Bodley Head, 1921.

32, 37–8, 46–7, 188: extracts from *MI9: Escape and Evasion 1939–1945* by M. R. D. Foot reprinted by permission of Peters Fraser and Dunlop (*www.petersfraserdunlop.com*) on behalf of the Estate of M. R. D. Foot.

36: extracts from *The Flyer: British Culture and the Royal Air Force, 1939–1945* by Martin Francis, printed by permission of Oxford University Press.

44: extract from *Winged Squadrons* by Cecil Beaton, published by Hutchinson. Reprinted by permission of The Random House Group Limited, the estate of Cecil Beaton and Rupert Crew Limited.

49, 148–9: extracts from *The Tartan Pimpernel* by Dr Donald Caskie © Birlinn, 2006.

58–9, 140, 150: extracts from *RAF Evaders: The Comprehensive Story of*

Thousands of Escapers and their Escape Line, Western Europe, 1940–45 by Oliver Clutton-Brock © Grub Street, 2005.

66, 87: extracts from *Verdict on Vichy: Power and Prejudice in The Vichy France Regime* by Michael Curtis © Orion Books, 2002.

66–8: extracts from *Vichy-Auschwitz: Le rôle de Vichy dans la solution finale de la question Juive (1943–1944)* by Serge Klarsfeld © Librairie Arthéme Fayard, 1985.

75: extract from *Les Camps de la Honte: Les internes juifs des camps française 1939–1944* by Anne Grynberg © Editions La Découverte, 1991.

77–82: extracts from *Scum of the Earth* by Arthur Koestler reprinted by permission of Peters Fraser and Dunlop (www.petersfraserdunlop.com) on behalf of the Estate of Arthur Koestler.

91–4, 237, 249: extracts from *Bad Faith, A Forgotten History of Family and Fatherland* by Carmen Callil © Jonathan Cape, 2006.

105–6, 108–11, 115, 271–72: extracts from *A Girl's Journey Through Nazi Europe* by Inge Bleier and David Gumpert © William B. Eerdmans Publishing, 2004.

109, 117: extracts from an essay in the collection *We Remember: Child Survivors of the Holocaust Speak* by Betty Schutz (2011) printed by kind permission of Betty Bloom.

109–14: extracts from *Les Enfants du Château de la Hille* by Sebastian Steiger © Brunnen Verlag Basel, 1999.

128, 167–9: extracts from *Resistance: An Analysis of European Resistance to Nazism, 1940–45* by M. R. D. Foot reprinted by permission of Peters Fraser and Dunlop (www.petersfraserdunlop.com) on behalf of the Estate of M. R. D. Foot.

144–5: extracts from *A Quiet Woman's War* by William Etherington © Mousehold Press, 2002.

154: extract from *Des Capitaines par Milliers* by Louis-Henri Nouveau © Editions Calmann-Lévy, 1958.

156–7: extracts from *Saturday at MI9* by Airey Neave © Pen and Sword Books Ltd, 2010.

165–6: extracts from *Eighth Airforce* by Donald Miller © Aurum Press, 2007.

168–70: extracts from *Yeager: An Autobiography* by Chuck Yeager with Leo Janos © Century, 1985.

193, 196, 205, 210: extracts from *In Search of the Maquis: Rural Resistance in Southern France, 1942–1944* by H. R. Kedward, printed by permission of Oxford University Press.

194–5, 197, 215: extracts from *Maquis Noirs et Faux Maquis* by Fabrice Grenard © Editions Vendémiaire, 2011.

198, 217–18: extracts from *The Freedom Trail* by Scott Goodall © Inchmere Design, 2005.

212: extract from *A Brilliant Little Operation: The Cockleshell Heroes and the Most Courageous Raid of World War 2* by Paddy Ashdown © Aurum Press, 2012.

220–1: extracts from *Horned Pigeon* by George Millar © William Heinemann, 1946.

237, 277–79: extracts reprinted by permission of the publisher from *The Vichy Syndrome: History and Memory in France Since 1944* by Henry Rousso, translated by Arthur Goldhammer, pp. 7, 22, 90, Cambridge, Mass.: Harvard University Press, Copyright © 1991 by the President and Fellows of Harvard College.

269–70: extract from *The Immortal Heritage: An Account of the Work and Policy of The Imperial War Graves Commission during Twenty Years, 1917–1937* by Edmund Blunden © Cambridge University Press, 1937.

276–8, 286, 288, 293–4: extracts from *Vichy: An Ever-Present Past* by Eric Conan and Henry Rousso © University Press of New England, Lebanon, NH. Reprinted with permission.

281–2, 289–90: extracts from *Paul Touvier et l'Eglise: Rapport de la commission historique instituée par le cardinal Decourtray* by René Raymond © Librairie Arthéme Fayard, 1992.

291–2: extracts from *Nous Entrerons dans la Carrière: De la Résistance à l'Exercice du Pouvoir* by Olivier Wieviorka © Éditions du Seuil, 1984.

Picture Acknowledgements

Every effort has been made to trace the copyright holders of photos reproduced in the book. Copyright holders not credited are invited to get in touch with the publishers.

Illustrations in the Text

17: *Keith Janes personal collection.*

63: *courtesy Jeanne Rogalle.*

84: *courtesy the Dowager Lady Swaythling.*

96: *courtesy Joan Salter.*

103: *United States Holocaust Memorial Museum, courtesy of Sebastian Steiger.*

158: *photo Jean Dieuzaide.*

178: *AFP/Getty Images.*

202: *George Duffee DFC, private collection.*

217: *courtesy the Bénazet family.*

235: *photo Jean Dieuzaide.*

261: *courtesy Joan Salter.*

296: *Gamma-Rapho via Getty Images.*

Picture Section

Reading clockwise from top left:

'Escape' flying boots, 1943 (prototype 1942): *Imperial War Museum/UNI 12092.*

Spanish refugees in the Pyrenees, 4 April 1938: *Getty Images;* coaches outside the Vél d'Hiver, Paris, 16 July 1942: *Getty Images;* Jewish deportees, Drancy transit camp, 1942: *AFP/Getty Images;* entrance and huts, concentration camp, Le Vernet: *both l'Amicale des Anciens Internés Politiques et Résistants du camp de concentration du Vernet d'Ariège;* Spanish refugees in the camp at Le Perthus, 8 February 1938: *Getty Images.*

Background: *the author and Brice Esquerre, one of the guides;* 'Tante Go': *from the film* El último paso, *2010;* Ian Garrow: *courtesy **www.christopher long.co.uk**;* Pat O'Leary snapped by a Marseille street photographer: *courtesy **www.christopherlong.co.uk**;* Jean-François Nothomb: *from the film* El último paso, *2010.*

Grand marchpast of the 'Garde Française', Paris, Champs-Elysées: *Bundesarchiv, Bild 146-2010-0045;* 'Vous avez la clef des camps', poster, 1943: *akg-images;* French workers go to Germany, 1942: *akg-images/Paul Almasy;* René Bousquet at his trial, 21 June 1949: *Gamma-Keystone via Getty Images;* the *maquisards* enter Toulouse, 19 August 1944: *photo Jean Dieuzaide;* the Milice round up prisoners, July 1944: *Bundesarchiv, Bild 146-1989-107-24.*

All photos of the Chemin de la Liberté: *the author and Brice Esquerre, one of the guides.*

Index

agents de passage, 204, 210, 227
Agouau, Jean-Pierre, 65, 69
Agouau family, 65, 70–1
Aguila, Francis, 203, 227
AKAK group, 209, 210
Albigensian Crusade, 297–8
Alio, Jean-Baptiste, 255
American Friends Service Committee
    (AFSC), 262, 263
Andalousia group, 210
Andorra, 205, 206, 207, 208, 209
Angoulême, 98, 242–4
Argèles camp, 74–5
Arhex, Jean-Baptiste, 176–7
Armée de la Libération (AL), 127
Armée de l'Armistice, 229
Armée Française Nationale, 183
Armée Secrète, 191, 196, 246
Armistice, Franco–German (1940), 24–5,
    124, 199, 226, 231, 262
Asquith, Herbert, 122–3
Aulus-les-Bains, 63–5, 69–71, 90, 111, 180,
    193
Auschwitz, 88, 94, 95, 100, 113, 116
Ayeling, Arthur Francis, 127
Aylé, Robert and Germaine, 138–9

Bagot Jewitt, Charles, 299
Barbie, Klaus, 192
Barbier, Marie-Elisabeth, 142
Barrau, Louis, 218, 227, 305
Barrau family, 217–18
la Barre, José de (Lady Villiers), 125–6, 127,
    205–8
Bartette, Marie, 250
BBC: 'Allo 'Allo!, 275, 280; Chemin
    programmes, 5–6, 97; de Gaulle's appel,
    184–5, 278; Paris Bureau, 280, 283;
    wartime broadcasts, 11, 111, 124–5,
    193, 197, 285
Beaton, Cecil, 44
Belgium, 122–7

Bénazet, Jean ('Piston'), 74, 227–9, 233
Benet, Claude, 208, 209, 213, 218
Benjamin, Walter, 81–2
Berthet, Monique, 281
Beryl group, 210
Blair, Tony, 14
Bleier, Julie, 271–2
Blewitt, Mary Kayitesi, 270
Blum, Léon, 87
Blunden, Edmund, 269–70
Bodlet, Alfred, 19
Bomber Command, 35–7, 40
Bond, Brian, 23
Bordeaux, 98, 136, 212, 242, 244, 246–9
Bourgogne group, 209
Bousquet, René, 66, 100, 233, 290–2
Bradford, Berenger, 47, 48, 60
Brandy group, 209
Bret Morton group, 209
Broué, Mme (mother of Paul), 181
Broué, Paul, 179–83, 193, 195, 199–200, 204,
    299
Brunner, Alois, 93–4
Brussels: Cantine Suédoise, 133, 138; Comet
    Line, 51–3, 55–6, 62, 128, 132–4, 138–40;
    fall (1940), 106; Home General
    Bernheim, 105; St Gilles prison, 130,
    141; Stan Hope's story, 42–4, 134–5, 137;
    Zimetbaum family, 98–9
Buckmaster group, 209

Cabrero-Monclus, Lazare ('El Magno'),
    222–4
Cagoulards, 231
Callil, Carmen, 94, 237
Cannes, 90–1, 92–3
Cardigan, Earl of, 22–3, 25–9, 42, 46, 60–1, 82
Carpentier, Abbé Pierre, 154
Caskie, Donald, 48–9, 148–9
Cassou, Jean, 3–4, 187, 239, 271
Cathars, 15, 297–8
Catholic Church, 232, 280–2, 283, 289, 292

Cavell, Edith, 52, 128
Charette group, 210
Château de la Hille, 107–9, 116–18, 262, 271–2, 296
Chemin de la Liberté: commemorative trek, 4, 11–13, 119–22, 173–4, 183, 217, 259–60, 299–301; *Musée*, 179, 299–300; route, 4–5, 103, 198, 203, 303–13
Chirac, Jacques, 293–4
Churchill, Winston: Belgian alliance, 124; de Gaulle relationship, 23, 184–5; destruction of French fleet, 28–9; Franco–British union proposal, 23–4, 27; North Africa landings, 69; on Mandel, 277; Spanish policy, 58–9
Clayton Hutton, Christopher (Clutty), 33–7
Clutton-Brock, Oliver, 140, 150
Cockleshell Heroes, 212, 300
Col de la Core, 121, 205, 307
Col de la Crouzette, 241, 246, 248
Cole, Harold Paul, 147–55, 157, 159
collaboration: Milice, 95, 231–2; Mitterrand's position, 291, 292; Pétain's role, 24; postwar views of, 278, 280; reprisals against collaborators, 246, 258, 276, 277; Vichy regime, 76, 83, 181, 194
Collins, Maurice, 14
Combat (newspaper), 188, 189
Combat (group), 188, 197, 209
Comet Line: arrests, 134, 140–1; care of Allied aircrews, 1, 3, 44, 58, 127; casualties, 140–3; delivery to Spain, 61, 224; guides, 208; infiltration, 121, 133–4, 138–9; leadership, 2, 62, 138, 300; motivation of volunteers, 128, 145; name, 129; origins, 51–2; rebuilding, 121, 140
Conan, Eric, 276
concentration camps, French: conditions, 79–81; foreign undesirables, 76–7; Jews, 83; Spanish refugees, 72–6; term, 71; Le Vernet, 71–2
Conseil National de la Résistance (CNR), 191
Conseils à l'Occupé, 185–7
Corinne (child survivor), 117
Cot, Pierre, 190
Crawley, Aidan, 40
Creswell, Sir Michael ('Monday'), 60
Crockatt, Norman, 32–3, 35
Croix de Feu, 81, 188
Cromar, Jim, 54
Curtis, Michael, 66

Dachau, 80, 132, 201, 259
Daladier, Edouard, 76–7
Darling, Donald ('Sunday'), 59, 153
Darnand, Joseph, 230–3, 249
Darquier de Pellepoix, Louis, 91–2, 93
d'Astier de la Vigerie, Emmanuel, 12, 187
David, Clayton, 174–7
Davreux, Mme, 145
de Blicquy, Henri, 52
de Bourmont, Victor, 287
de Gaulle, Charles: BBC *appel*, 184–5, 278, 280, 294; Churchill relationship, 23, 184–5; Moulin relationship, 174, 191, 278–9, 282; myth, 278–9; purge of collaborators, 276
de Greef, Elvire ('Tante Go'), 53, 56–7, 135, 137
de Greef, Fernand, 53
de Greef, Freddy, 57
de Greef, Janine, 57
de Jongh, Andrée (Dédée, 'Postman'): appearance, 2, 55; arrest, 134–5, 300; British contact, 54–6; career, 52–4, 137–8; code name, 56; Comet Line, 2–3, 61, 132; DDD network, 54–5; guides, 53, 54–5, 57–8; imprisonment, 136–7; motivation, 128; routes to Spain, 121, 224; story, 2–3
de Jongh, Frédéric ('Paul'): arrest, 138, 142; background, 52; code name, 56; Comet Line, 56, 62, 132, 134–5, 142; death, 139–40
de Roquemaurel, Christian, 243
de Saivre, Roger, 200–1
Decourtray, Cardinal, 288–9
Dedieu, Clovis, 248–9
Delpla, Claude, 238, 246, 253, 255, 256
Deppe, Arnold, 52–3, 54
Deram, Madeleine, 150
La Dernière Colonne, 187, 188
Desoubrie, Jean-Jacques, *see* Masson
Deuxième Bureau, 78, 189
Didier, Christian, 290
Dissard, Marie-Louise ('Françoise'), 156, 158–64, 166–7, 209, 224, 236
Doriot, Jacques, 245
Dormer, Hugh, 7–8, 300
Dougnac, Albert, 182
Drancy holding centre, 101, 113
Dreyfus, Edgar, 88–9, 92, 93–5
Dreyfus, Ninette (Dowager Lady Swaythling), 86–8, 90–1, 95
Dreyfus, Viviane, 86, 88, 91, 92, 93–5

Index

Dreyfus family, 86, 88–9, 90, 91–4, 299
Dreyfus Affair, 87
Dubois, Maurice, 107, 112
Duffee, George, 39
Dufournier, Denise, 142–6, 273–5, 280, 300–1
Dumon, Andrée ('Nadine'), 62, 129–32, 137
Dumon, Eugène, 130
Dunkirk evacuation (1940), 18, 35
Duprez, François, 151–3
Duquaire, Monsignor Charles, 281
Dutch-Paris group, 209, 304

Eloise (*passeur*), 219
'escape boxes', 34–5, 36–7
escape lines, 45–6
Escape Lines Memorial Society, 4, 11, 132, 204
escapers and evaders, rights, 61
Evans, A. J., 29–31, 32
EWA (EVA) group, 209
Eychenne, Emilienne, 198, 199, 202–3, 208–10, 226, 230

F2 Polonais group, 209
Farell, Dr and Mrs, 264–7
Farras, Jean, 254
Feldgendarmerie (Field Police), 226
First World War: Belgian alliance, 133; British military intelligence, 31–2; Edith Cavell, 128; escapes, 33; executions for cowardice, 299; German occupation of Belgium, 52, 122–3; German surrender, 25; memorials, 84–5, 270, 277; Palestine position, 263; survival chances, 36; Western Front, 269–70
Foix, 68, 203, 226, 233, 249, 252, 256–7
Foot, M. R. D.: interview, 29–30; on 'escape boxes', 37; on escapers, 36; on maps, 37; on MI9 lectures, 40–1; on Resistance, 128, 188; on USAAF air raids, 167–8; on women, 45–6
Fort Montluc prison, 284, 288
Fort St Jean, Marseilles, 46–7
Francis, Martin, 36
Franco, General: Barcelona capture, 15; Koestler's position, 77, 78; Pétain relationship, 237; refugees from, 75, 179; regime, 212, 213; relationship with Germany, 58, 59–60, 164; victory (1939), 73, 211
Françoise, *see* Dissard (Marie-Louise)
Frank, Elka, 105, 107
Free French forces, 4, 181, 210, 277, 280

Free Zone, 28–9, 50, 224, 229, 263
Frenay, Henri, 189, 190, 197
Frost, Bob: escape strategy, 41–2, 44; journey to Spain, 1–4, 57–8, 61–2; shot down 38–9, 171

Gable (escaper), 220–2
Gallia group, 210
Garrow, Ian: arrest, 152, 153; career, 47–8; Cole relationship, 148, 149–51, 152–3; escape, 156; escape network, 49; Pat Line, 50, 148, 164, 211
Gestapo, 226, 287, 288
Gibraltar, 58, 59–60, 61–2
Gilberte (farmer's daughter), 21
Goicoechea, Florentino, 57–8, 61, 135, 208, 227
Goldapper, Edith, 109, 112, 113–14
Gonzales (guide), 207–8
Goodall, Scott, 170–1, 173–4, 198, 203, 217–18
Goudard, Louis, 283–5, 287
Gouet, Monsignor Julien, 281
Grauerholz, Larry, 166, 173
Greenwell, Fred, 160–1, 164, 167
Greindl, Baron Jean ('Nemo'), 132–4, 138
le Grelle, Jacques ('Jérôme'), 121, 140
Grenard, Fabrice, 194, 195
Grenoble, 114–15
Grenzschutz (Border Guards), 225
Griffiths, Squadron Leader Frank, 161
Groupe du Musée de l'Homme, 187, 189
Le Groupe Martin, 209
Groupes Mobiles de Réserves (GMR), 230
Grumbach, Jacques, 222–4
Guérilleros Espagnols, 214
Guérisse, Albert-Marie, *see* O'Leary
guides: arrested, 227; betrayal by, 116; Broué's journey, 182–3; Comet line, 53, 54–5, 57, 58, 61, 135; difficulties, 220–4, 228; Jewish groups, 69–70, 95, 101–2; payment, 49, 54, 56, 183, 208, 210; smugglers, 206–9; Swiss border, 115, 116–17; *see also* passeurs
Guillaume (escaper), 205–8
Gumpert, David, 271, 272
Gurs camp, 116

Halifax, Lord, 59
Hardy, Daphne, 77
Harms, Lieutenant, 254
Hasler, Major Blondie, 212
Helbronner, Jacques, 87, 88

Helm, Sarah, 141
'helpers', 204–5
Henle, Claude, 295
Henriot, Philippe, 245, 277, 284, 287
Herveau, Pauline, 155
Heydrich, General Reinhard, 66
Higginson, Flight Lieutenant 'Taffy', 150–1
Hitler, Adolf, 35, 59–60, 83, 230, 232, 247
Hoare, Sir Samuel, 58–9, 60
Holvoet, Bernard, 120–2, 140
Hope, Stan, 42–4, 61, 134–7, 171
Hopkins, Lt J. W. 'Hoppy', 27–8, 42
Hornby, Adam, 301
Hotaling, Jack, 171–2
Houdini, Harry, 33
Hoyland, Graham, 6, 10

Jackson, Julian, 187, 188, 191, 214
Janes, Keith, 17–20, 47, 50, 198
Janes, Peter: crossing into Spain, 51; diary, 19–21, 300; escape from POW column, 18–19, 46, 61; experiences on the run, 21–2, 27; smuggled south, 50–1, 149, 164
Jeannine Vocabule group, 209
Jews: assimilated French families, 86–9, 90–3; child refugees, 105, 262–8; deportation, 98–9, 193; escape across Pyrenees, 94–5, 96–7, 101–2, 199; escape from Paris, 101; immigrants to France, 85–6, 97–8; internment, 64–5, 101, 239; round-ups, 65–8, 69, 93–4, 100–1, 180; Vichy policy, 65–8, 83, 86, 89–93, 99–100, 189
Johnstone, Nancy, 73
Joint Distribution Committee (JDC), 263
Joseph, Inge (Bleier): at Château de la Hille, 108–11, 113; death, 271, 272; escape plan, 115–16; in Brussels, 105; journey south, 106; memoir, 271–2; survival, 116
Jouan, Cécile, 128, 139, 140–1

Kedward, H. R., 193, 196, 205
Keegan, John, 165
Kindertransport programme, 104
Klarsfeld, Serge, 65, 290
Knochen, Helmut, 226
Koestler, Arthur, 77–82, 99

labour for Germany, 76, 192–5, see also STO
Labro, Léon-Charles, 246, 247, 258
Laffont, Paul, 244–6, 247, 258, 284
Lart, Bruno, 174

Laval, Pierre: Jewish policies, 66, 93, 101; Milice formation, 230, 249; on Nazi regime, 225; Relève programme, 192; STO policy, 229
Lecussan, Joseph, 232
Lefebure, Edgard, 127
Lefebvre, Archbishop Marcel, 283
Legion of Turkestan ('the Mongols'), 253–5, 258, 296
Leneveu, Roger, 156–7
Libération, 188
Liénart, Cardinal, 195
Lindell, Mary, 209, 212
Long, Helen, 148–9, 151
Louis-Dreyfus, Louis, 86, 89, 92
Louis Napoleon, Prince (Captain Blanchard), 200
Lyons: British servicemen in, 29, 46; Cole's arrest and trial, 155; liberation, 280; Resistance arrests, 174, 191–2; Touvier case, 280–1, 283, 284, 287, 288
Lyrer, M. (teacher), 113, 114

Madrid, 61–2, 140
Malraux, André, 278–80, 282, 294
Mandel, Georges, 277, 284
maps, 31, 37
maquis: attacks on railways, 250; Battle of Rimont, 256–7; directive on conduct, 215; executions of collaborators, 246; German operations against, 240, 253, 279; image, 195; landscape, 127; maquis noirs, 215–16; origins, 196–8; recruits, 210, 213–14; relationship with escape groups, 204; supplied by Britain, 168, 197; term, 196
Maquis de la Crouzette, 241, 245–7, 249, 252, 253, 256
Maréchal, Elsie, 133–4, 144–5
Maréchal, Elsie (daughter), 144–5
Maréchal, Georges, 133–4
Maréchal, Robert, 133–4
Maréval (betrayer), 175
Marguet, M. (farmer), 172
Marie-Claire group, 209, 212, 304
Marly, Anna, 12
Marrus, Michael, 198
Marseillaise, 195, 200, 251, 284, 305
Marseilles, 46–9, 148
Masson, Jean (Jean-Jacques Desoubrie), 138–9
Maurice (in Brussels), 43–4, 134–5
Mauthausen camp, 2, 131–2, 137, 213, 233, 259
McAdam Clark, Alexandra, 274, 275, 300–1

Index

McAdam Clark, Caroline, 146, 273, 275
memorials and monuments: Cenotaph, 270, 298; Chemin de la Liberté, 11, 205, 306, 307, 310; First World War, 84–5, 270, 277; Mandel, 277; National Memorial Arboretum, 204, 299; Rimont, 236, 277; Le Vernet, 72; Yad Vashem, 112
Mers-el-Kébir, French fleet (1940), 28–9
MI9 (formerly MI IA): Bourgogne group, 209; Cole case, 149, 151, 153, 155; Comet Line repair, 121, 140; contact with underground groups, 45, 51, 59, 212; escape aids, 34–7; escape training, 37–8, 40–1; establishment, 31–2; funding for Pyrenees escapes, 49, 51, 56; objectives, 32; Pat Line, 51, 158; personnel, 32–3; Spanish role, 60
Michelli, Henri, 132
Michiels, Victor, 134
Milice: battle with Spaniards, 214; chaplain, 280–1; cruelty, 238, 248–9, 277; formation, 230–1; in Pau, 95; in Toulouse, 163; maquis relations, 240, 245, 247; personnel, 230–2; role, 232–3, 239; Touvier case, 283, 284
Millar, George, 220–2
Miller, Donald, 165
Miranda de Ebro camp, 61, 183
Mitterrand, François, 178–9, 188, 290–3
MJS (Zionist movement), 115, 117
MNB (Mouvement National Belge), 127
Morelle, Charles, 132
Moser, Kurt, 113, 116
Motz, Roger, 123, 124, 125, 127
Moulin, Jean ('Max'): arrest, 174; career, 189–90; de Gaulle relationship, 191; death, 191–2; London visit, 189, 191; Panthéon ceremony, 278–80, 282, 294; Resistance achievements, 191–2, 196, 197, 278–9
MUR (Mouvements Unis de la Résistance), 191, 196–8, 209, 245

Nacht und Nebel (Night and Fog), 130, 137
Naduce, Olivier, 233
Naef, Rosli, 111–13, 115
NANA group, 210
Neave, Airey: biography of de Jongh, 52, 53–5; description of Florentino, 57; description of 'Nemo', 132; Masson story, 139; MI9 recruitment, 32–3; Pat O'Leary story, 156–7; Pyrenean escape, 213, 300

newspapers, Resistance, 187–8
Nice, 93–4
Nichols, John, 156
Nitti, Francesco, 239, 241–4, 247, 248, 249–52, 258–9
Noé concentration camp, 182, 183
Nothomb, Jean-François ('Franco'), 140
Nouveau couple (in Marseilles), 49

Occupied Zone, 25, 49, 53, 89–90, 99–100, 224
O'Leary, Pat (Albert-Marie Guérisse): arrest, 156–7, 158, 163; background, 49–50; Cole case, 149, 151–3; imprisonment, 157; opinion of Vidal, 212; Pat Line, 50, 152, 155–6, 164, 209, 211
Operation Torch, 69
Organisation Juive de Combat (OJC), 209

Papon, Maurice, 294
parachutes, 38–40
Paris: BBC Paris Bureau, 280, 283; Comet Line, 132, 138–40, 142; German occupation (1940), 23, 185–6; Gestapo, 66, 136–7; Jews, 66, 86, 90, 97–101; Koestler's arrest, 77–8; liberation, 249, 252, 259; Panthéon, 278; Pat Line, 154–7; refugees, 46; Resistance, 191; SIPO, 226
Paris–Brussels group, 209
Pas de Calais 19, 20, 28, 50
passeurs, 11, 204–10, 217–24, 227
Pat O'Leary Line ('Pat Line'): Cole story, 148, 151–5; escape routes, 209, 304; Françoise's role, 158, 160; MI9 links, 51; name, 50; O'Leary's arrest, 156–7, 158; Spanish links, 211–12
Patterson, Pat, 169–70
Pau, 94–5
Paxton, Robert, 276, 278
Péan, Pierre, 178, 292
Pegum, Phil, 5
Pétain, Marshal: formation of Vichy government, 24–5, 83, 184, 230, 244, 276; Jewish policies, 89, 90, 93; Jewish support for, 88–9; Mitterrand relationship, 178, 291, 292; relationship with Franco, 237; relationship with Germans, 59, 93, 192; Resistance attitudes to, 189; STO policy, 198; view of Milice, 249
Pierlot, Hubert, 127
Pompidou, Georges, 282

Ponzán Vidal, Francisco, 210–13, 222, 224, 227–8
POUM group, 209
PPF (Parti Populaire Français), 245
prisoners of war (POWs), 18, 22–3, 30–1, 46–7
Pyrenees: American airmen crossing, 169–71, 198; crossing routes, 4–5, 13, 208, 209; escape lines and networks, 204, 209–11; French escapers, 198–200, 299; frontier, 15–16; numbers crossing, 198–200; *réfractaires* crossing, 195; region, 14–15; restaurants, 6; role of crossing, 299–300

RAF (Royal Air Force), 35–7, 40, 42, 125, 127–8, 165–6
Ramos, Conchita, 259
Ravensbrück concentration camp: conditions, 141–6; prisoners, 2, 131, 137, 144–6, 233, 273–5, 300; war crimes trials, 274
Red Cross, 107, 112, 115–16, 133
réfractaires, 194–7, 229–30, 248
Refuge des Estagnous, 8–9, 11, 182, 310–11
refugees: Belgian, 123–4; Spanish, 15–16, 73–6, 180, 213–15, 228
Relève system, 192–3
remembrance and remembering, 269–75, 298–301
Renault, Gilbert ('Rémy'), 52, 128, 141, 143, 282
Rennell, Tony, 156
Renseignements Généraux, 194
Résistance, 187
Resistance: arrests of leaders, 174; assassination of Henriot, 245; attacks on railways, 181; Battle of Rimont, 246, 256, 276; Belgian, 127; care of Allied airmen, 42, 127–8, 132, 138; care of Jews, 101; Cole story, 149, 155; de Gaulle's role, 184–5, 278–9; early, 185–9; emotions inspired by, 271; executions, 276; influence of German demands for labour, 192–6; Leneveu story, 156–7; liberation of Toulouse, 212; *maquis*, 168, 195–8, 204, 215, 240; membership, 188–9, 204; Milice attacks, 233, 240; movements, 188–9; newspapers, 187–8; recruits, 117, 188–9, 239; reputation, 276–80; songs, 11, 12; symbols, 41; United Movement (MUR), 191; uprising in southern France, 252; way of life, 3–4

Retirada, 16, 179, 228
Rexists, 123
Reynaud, Paul, 23–4
Ribero (guide), 207–8
Richards, Miss, 53–4
Rillieux-la-Pape, executions, 284, 286–8
Rimont, 235–6, 240, 244–5, 254–7, 296
Robert, 'Commandant', 257
Roberts, Andrew, 232
Rodocanachie, George, 49, 152–3
Rogalle, Jean-Baptiste, 65, 70
Rogalle, Jeanne (Agouau), 63–5, 67, 69–71, 294–5, 296
Rogalle family, 65, 70–1
Roo, Abbé, 205–6
Roosevelt, Eleanor, 264
Roosevelt, Franklin, 69
Roquejoffre, Michel, 294–5
Rouan, François, 210
Rousso, Henry, 237, 275–6, 277–8, 279–80, 286
Royal British Legion, 4, 9, 270
Rugby School, 33–4

Sabot group, 209
safe houses: baby in, 117; Bayonne, 135; Brussels, 133; Comet Line, 141; Foix area, 203; keepers, 46; Paris, 138, 142; Toulouse, 160
St Girons: bridge, 120, 203; Chemin de la Liberté, 4, 103, 120; German operations, 240; German restrictions, 224–5; liberation attempt, 252–4; museum, 179
St Valéry-en-Caux, Allied surrender (1940), 18, 28, 47
Salat, river, 179, 200, 203, 304
Salter, Joan, *see* Zimetbaum (Fanny)
Sauckel, Fritz, 192, 193
Scherhag, Lieutenant, 255
Scherlinck, Mme, 133
Schopplein, Major, 254, 255–8
Schuster, Vivienne, 97
Schutz, Bertha, 104–5
Schutz, Betty (Bloom), 104–7, 109, 110, 297
Schutz, Bronia, 105
Schutz, Ruth, 104–7, 110, 113–15, 117–18
SD (Sicherheitsdienst), 226
Seix, 9, 179–80, 230, 306
Serpa Pinto (ship), 262, 264, 267, 295
Shirer, William, 125
SIPO (Sicherheitspolizei, Security Police), 226

Index

smugglers, 206–9
SOE (Special Operations Executive), 48, 141, 174
SOL (Service d'Ordre Légionnaire), 231, 232
Song of the Partisans (*Chant des Partisans*), 11, 12, 278, 305
Spanish Civil War, 15, 58, 74, 77, 179, 211, 239
Sparks, Bill, 212
SS, 232, 240
Stalin, Joseph, 69
Stanton, Roger, 11
Statut des Juifs, 89, 90, 189
Steiger, Sebastian, 109–11
STO (Service du Travail Obligatoire), 193–5, 199, 229
Strauss, Walter, 110, 111, 115–16, 271

Texcier, Jean, 185–6
Thatcher, Margaret, 213
Thomas, Hugh, 15–16
Thornton (escaper), 223
Tips for Evaders and Escapers, 5, 38
Toft, Lieutenant, 173
Toulouse: detainees, 241–2; Françoise escape line, 159–64, 167, 173, 174, 204, 236; Gestapo, 226; helpers, 202–3; liberation, 212, 229; Pat Line, 156, 212; Red Cross, 107, 112; Resistance, 3, 176
Touvier, Paul: arrests, 280, 281, 285, 290; case against, 285–8, 290–1; Goudard's evidence, 283–5; life in hiding, 280–1, 283; presidential pardon, 282–3, 285; protected by Catholic Church, 280–2, 283, 288–90
train fantôme, 244, 246, 249–50, 252, 258–60
Tutu, Desmond, 270

United States Committee for the Care of European Children, 262
United States Eighth Air Force, 164–8

Valier, Mont, 6, 8, 182, 310
Vandegriff, Robert, 173
Varilhes, 211, 227–8, 233, 259
Vautherin, Abbé, 280–1
Vél d'Hiver round-up (1942), 100, 290, 291, 293–4

Vernet (deputy commander of Le Vernet), 239–40, 241
Le Vernet concentration camp: conditions, 79–81; description, 71–2; evacuation, 241; German prisoners, 258; German takeover, 239–41; internment of foreigners, 76–7, 78–9, 239; internment of Jews, 71, 83, 111, 112–13, 239; internment of Spanish refugees, 76, 211, 214
Le Vernet museum, 72, 79, 104, 251
Viadiu, Francesc, 219
Viatel, Paule ('Claire'), 174–7
Vichy government: anti-British feeling, 28–9; concentration camps, 76–7; escape of officials, 199, 200–1; formation, 25, 83; German relations, 59, 93, 162, 181, 192, 226, 229, 232–3; internment of British servicemen, 46; Jewish policies, 64, 65–9, 83, 84, 86, 88–93, 100–1, 189, 263; memories of, 278, 290; Mitterrand's position, 178, 291, 292; Resistance attitudes, 189; security services, 49, 152, 160, 218, 229–32; STO system, 193–8, 229–30; territory, 25; Touvier ruling, 286; treatment of Spanish refugees, 213
Villot, Cardinal Jean, 281
Visigoth-Lorraine group, 209
VNV (Flemish National Party), 123

Wake, Nancy ('the White Mouse'), 48, 49, 163–4, 214–15, 300
Warenghem, Suzanne, 155
Wieviorka, Olivier, 291
Wills Tobacco Company, 34–5
Woodard, Flight Lieutenant Earl, 162, 171–4

YAYA group, 210
Yeager, Chuck, 168–70

Zimetbaum, Bronia, 97–102, 262, 264, 265–8
Zimetbaum, Fanny (Joan Farell, Joan Salter), 96–102, 104, 199, 261–8, 271, 290
Zimetbaum, Jakob, 97–9, 101–2, 265–8
Zimetbaum, Liliane, 97–102, 262, 264–5
Zimetbaum family, 97–9, 299, 300

ABOUT THE AUTHOR

Edward Stourton is the author of six books. He is writer and presenter of several high-profile current affairs programmes and documentaries for radio and television, and regularly presents BBC Radio Four programmes such as *The World at One*, *The World This Weekend*, *Sunday* and *Analysis*. He is a frequent contributor to the *Today* programme, where for ten years he was one of the main presenters.